Global Politics of Celebrity

In the age of networked publics and global viral publicity, celebrity is transnational. Its circulation illuminates global, national, and local dynamics of power and resistance. Celebrity shapes concepts of race, gender, class, and national identity on a global scale. Governments use transnational celebrity as evidence of their country's cultural power, transmuting cultural influence into economic and political power. Meanwhile, celebrities who cross borders become potent and contested icons of national identity. At the grassroots level, citizens in diverse geographic contexts are becoming increasingly fluent in the global language of celebrity and are mobilizing it in new ways for personal and political projects. Reaching beyond the Global North, this book showcases research on transnational celebrity as a technology of soft power and counter-hegemonic organizing and as a driver of discourses of race and migration. It also explores self-presentation and self-branding in the globalized attention economy. This book demonstrates the need for a renewed politicized treatment of the topic of celebrity in its transnational and globalizing reach. The chapters in this book were originally published in the journal *Popular Communication*.

Mehdi Semati is Professor in the Department of Communication at Northern Illinois University, DeKalb, USA. His writings on international communication and global media have appeared in various scholarly journals. He is the co-author of *Iran and the American Media: Press Coverage of the 'Iran Deal' in Context* (2021).

Kate Zambon is Assistant Professor in the Department of Communication at the University of New Hampshire, Durham, USA. Her research in global media studies focuses on the politics of nationalism, migration, and cultural difference in Germany and Europe through the analysis of international sporting events, news, and entertainment media.

Global Politics of Celebrity

Edited by
Mehdi Semati and Kate Zambon

LONDON AND NEW YORK

First published 2023
by Routledge
4 Park Square, Milton Park, Abingdon, Oxon, OX14 4RN

and by Routledge
605 Third Avenue, New York, NY 10158

Routledge is an imprint of the Taylor & Francis Group, an informa business

Introduction © 2023 Mehdi Semati and Kate Zambon
Chapters 1–10 © 2023 Taylor & Francis

All rights reserved. No part of this book may be reprinted or reproduced or utilised in any form or by any electronic, mechanical, or other means, now known or hereafter invented, including photocopying and recording, or in any information storage or retrieval system, without permission in writing from the publishers.

Trademark notice: Product or corporate names may be trademarks or registered trademarks, and are used only for identification and explanation without intent to infringe.

British Library Cataloguing-in-Publication Data
A catalogue record for this book is available from the British Library

ISBN13: 978-1-032-46832-7 (hbk)
ISBN13: 978-1-032-46833-4 (pbk)
ISBN13: 978-1-003-38351-2 (ebk)

DOI: 10.4324/9781003383512

Typeset in Minion Pro
by codeMantra

Publisher's Note
The publisher accepts responsibility for any inconsistencies that may have arisen during the conversion of this book from journal articles to book chapters, namely the inclusion of journal terminology.

Disclaimer
Every effort has been made to contact copyright holders for their permission to reprint material in this book. The publishers would be grateful to hear from any copyright holder who is not here acknowledged and will undertake to rectify any errors or omissions in future editions of this book.

Contents

Citation Information		vii
Notes on Contributors		ix
Introduction The Global Politics of Celebrity Mehdi Semati and Kate Zambon		1
1	The commodified celebrity-self: industrialized agency and the contemporary attention economy P. David Marshall	7
2	Offshoring & leaking: Cristiano Ronaldo's tax evasion, and celebrity in neoliberal times Ana Jorge, Mercè Oliva, and Luis LM Aguiar	21
3	Speaking for the youth, speaking for the planet: Greta Thunberg and the representational politics of eco-celebrity Patrick D. Murphy	36
4	Celebrity migrants and the racialized logic of integration in Germany Kate Zambon	50
5	Turkey's TV celebrities as cultural envoys: the role of celebrity diplomacy in nation branding and the pursuit of soft power Ece Algan and Yeşim Kaptan	65
6	Micro-celebrity practices in Muslim-majority states in Southeast Asia Siti Mazidah Mohamad	78
7	Symbolic bordering: the self-representation of migrants and refugees in digital news Lilie Chouliaraki	93
8	Refugee testimonies enacted: voice and solidarity in media art installations Karina Horsti	110

9 How can we tell the story of the Colombian War?: Bastardized narratives and citizen celebrities 125
Omar Rincón and Clemencia Rodríguez

10 Transcendental meditation's tipping point: the allure of celebrity on the American spiritual marketplace 138
Corrina Laughlin

Index 151

Citation Information

The following chapters were originally published in various volumes and issues of the journal *Popular Communication*. When citing this material, please use the original page numbering for each article, as follows:

Chapter 1
The commodified celebrity-self: industrialized agency and the contemporary attention economy
P. David Marshall
Popular Communication, volume 19, issue 3 (2021) pp. 164–177

Chapter 2
Offshoring & leaking: Cristiano Ronaldo's tax evasion, and celebrity in neoliberal times
Ana Jorge, Mercè Oliva, and Luis LM Aguiar
Popular Communication, volume 19, issue 3 (2021) pp. 178–192

Chapter 3
Speaking for the youth, speaking for the planet: Greta Thunberg and the representational politics of eco-celebrity
Patrick D. Murphy
Popular Communication, volume 19, issue 3 (2021) pp. 193–206

Chapter 4
Celebrity migrants and the racialized logic of integration in Germany
Kate Zambon
Popular Communication, volume 19, issue 3 (2021) pp. 207–221

Chapter 5
Turkey's TV celebrities as cultural envoys: the role of celebrity diplomacy in nation branding and the pursuit of soft power
Ece Algan and Yeşim Kaptan
Popular Communication, volume 19, issue 3 (2021) pp. 222–234

Chapter 6
Micro-celebrity practices in Muslim-majority states in Southeast Asia
Siti Mazidah Mohamad
Popular Communication, volume 19, issue 3 (2021) pp. 235–249

Chapter 7
Symbolic bordering: The self-representation of migrants and refugees in digital news
Lilie Chouliaraki
Popular Communication, volume 15, issue 2 (2017) pp. 78–94

Chapter 8
Refugee testimonies enacted: voice and solidarity in media art installations
Karina Horsti
Popular Communication, volume 17, issue 2 (2019) pp. 125–139

Chapter 9
How can we tell the story of the Colombian War?: Bastardized narratives and citizen celebrities
Omar Rincón and Clemencia Rodríguez
Popular Communication, volume 13, issue 2 (2015) pp. 170–182

Chapter 10
Transcendental meditation's tipping point: the allure of celebrity on the American spiritual marketplace
Corrina Laughlin
Popular Communication, volume 18, issue 2 (2020) pp. 108–120

For any permission-related enquiries please visit:
http://www.tandfonline.com/page/help/permissions

Notes on Contributors

Luis LM Aguiar, Department of History and Sociology, University of British Columbia, Okanagan, Canada.

Ece Algan, California State University, San Bernardino, USA.

Lilie Chouliaraki, London School of Economics and Political Science, London, UK.

Karina Horsti, Department of Social Sciences and Philosophy, University of Jyväskylä, Finland.

Ana Jorge, CICANT/ Department of Communication Sciences, Lusófona University, Lisbon, Portugal.

Yeşim Kaptan, Kent State University, USA.

Corrina Laughlin, The Department of Communication Studies, Loyola Marymount University, Los Angeles, USA.

P. David Marshall, School of Communication and Creative Arts, Deakin University, Melbourne, Australia.

Siti Mazidah Mohamad, Geographical and Environmental Studies, Faculty of Arts and Social Sciences, Universiti Brunei Darussalam, Gadong, Brunei Darussalam; Faculty of Arts and Social Sciences (FASS), Universiti Brunei Darussalam, Bandar Seri Begawan, Brunei

Patrick D. Murphy, Department of Media Studies and Production, Klein College of Media & Communication, Temple University, Philadelphia, USA.

Mercè Oliva, Department of Communication, Universitat Pompeu Fabra, Barcelona, Spain.

Omar Rincón, Universidad de los Andes, Bogota, Colombia.

Clemencia Rodríguez, Department of Communication, The University of Oklahoma, USA.

Mehdi Semati, Department of Communication, Northern Illinois University, Illinois, USA.

Kate Zambon, Department of Communication, University of New Hampshire, Durham, USA.

The Global Politics of Celebrity

The recent proliferation of research on celebrity across a range of disciplines and fields of inquiry demonstrates a scholarly consensus regarding its increasing importance. Academic conferences, a journal dedicated to *Celebrity Studies*, and a spate of books on the topic reflect this consensus in communication, media, and cultural studies. Celebrity provides a key to understanding the present conjuncture, the contemporary cultural moment, and the emerging forms of capitalist exploitation of labor of various kinds. To the extent that it is intertwined with the dominant cultural, political, and economic values of the day, celebrity is poised to reveal the contours of that conjuncture. Celebrity tells us about a culture's notions of privacy, publicness, and intimacy. Celebrity is said to "re-style," "personalize," and even democratize politics. It has long been involved in diplomacy, humanitarianism, and the exercise of "soft power." Celebrity is a form of cultural power and a means of rationalizing and obscuring the contradictions of global capitalism.

In the age of networked publics, celebrity is transnational, and its circulation is illustrative of networks of affect and passion, mobilization and demobilization. The resurgence of contemporary populism cannot exist outside the space of celebrity. Alongside celebrity politicians speaking "directly to the people," social media platforms elevate celebrity provocateurs who generate and monetize networks of passion, outrage, and hate. At the same time, these tools and platforms also enable new kinds of celebrities representing traditionally disempowered populations, including young people, women, and members of minoritized groups. Transnational and global celebrity is a crucial site where discourses on race, gender, class, and national identity are negotiated, dramatized, and naturalized.

However, transnational and global theories and contexts have been largely neglected in celebrity studies, which, with the notable exception of studies in development and humanitarianism, tend to focus on Anglophone publics within the Global North. Studying celebrity from a critical transnational perspective allows us to deploy the insights of this literature while building its theoretical reach, scope, and utility. The goal is not only to expand representation but also to generate stronger theory. Critical transnational approaches not only include neglected places and populations but also reflect the reality that American and other major culture industries are and have always been global. In this context, studying global celebrity provides the opportunity to expand the literature and the social theory it could generate, contributing to comparative studies in culture, media, and the notion of the popular. If "the popular" was once defined in relationship to its constitutive outside, "the culture of the power-bloc," studying global celebrity (e.g., global popular, national-popular), allows us to reengage the notion of the popular on a new theoretical terrain. This volume brings together scholars from across areas in communication, media, and cultural studies to address these issues as a conversation and an occasion to reassess celebrity, the literature, and the conceptual tools we have used to explain it.

Today's proliferating forms of celebrity and its ubiquity are rooted in structural conditions of networked "attention economy," as the operative logic and the advertising-based business model for social media companies large and small. Self-presentation and self-branding practices intrinsic to digital capitalism driven by paid, unpaid, and "aspirational labor," all operate within the same attention economy. Social media expand the value of traditional forms of celebrity for cutting through the clutter of information overload. Meanwhile, it has amalgamated the aspirations of fame with the techniques of commercial branding and helped establish them as everyday cultural practice.

P. David Marshall's work over the years has focused on the structural conditions of celebrity and its political economy. The rapid expansion of the attention economy has given rise to the commodification of the celebrity-self and self-presentation on an industrial scale. Aspirations of fame in the form of successful self-branding have permeated the popular as a cultural logic endemic to the gig economy. Marshall's focus on "industrialized agency" is an analysis that enables us to follow the permeation of the prevailing logic of celebrity in the everyday practices and in the popular via individual modes of comportment and self-presentation.

In tracing the trajectory of transcendental meditation's (TM) allure from an Orientalized spiritual practice to a deterritorialized technology of commodified creativity and self-actualization, Corrina Laughlin shows how celebrity enacts changing hegemonic cultural and economic ideals. The story of TM begins with Maharishi Mahesh Yogi, a yoga guru from India who undertook multiple world tours beginning in 1958 to make TM a global spiritual practice. From the outset, TM thrived as a globalized phenomenon through its endorsement by celebrities as a tool for unlocking creative potential. Mahesh leveraged Western Orientalist fascination with the imagined exotic authenticity of Eastern spiritual practices to attract British and American celebrity followers who credited TM for creative breakthroughs. Since Mahesh's death in 2008, celebrity has subsumed the erstwhile spiritual practice, stripping it of the messiness and complications of its origins in a religion with historical roots. TM has been reterritorialized in Hollywood, the nodal point at the center of the floating space of globalized celebrity. This approach is tailored to the American spiritual marketplace by appealing to seemingly universalist ideals. Divested of its spiritual roots, this iteration of TM draws on scientific discourse and neoliberal ethics of self-care and the actualized entrepreneurial self, using celebrity success as its proof of concept.

Siti Mazidah Mohammad explores these dynamics in the celebrity culture in the developing field of micro-celebrities in Muslim-majority states in South East Asia, where the relatively small culture industry lowers the status of aspiring influencers, raising the question of what level of attention generation is required to even qualify as a celebrity. This combines with local cultural politics that subject domestic creators to more stringent policing of behavior than regional and global influencers and celebrities. Exploring practices and processes of microcelebrity as localized adaptations of transcultural flows and in the context of contested celebrity status, Mohammad shows how such processes have been mobilized by youth affectively and strategically for the purposes of social and economic mobility.

While industrialized celebrity agency typically serves commercial logics, Patrick Murphy explores Greta Thunberg's mobilization of the agency of celebrity to generate a systemic critique. Thunberg subverts the consumerist logics of celebrity that extend even to celebrity environmental activism, which typically invites audiences to revel in the beauty of nature. Instead, Thunberg commands attention and focuses it on a critique that resists transformation into a commodity. Thunberg's activism also demonstrates the transnational exchange of techniques of digitally mediated resistance, borrowing from the activist survivors of the mass shooting in Parkland, Florida. Their self-awareness and skill in the guerilla tactics of "clapping back" has enabled a new generation to convert criticism by powerful adversaries into a strategic opportunity. Thunberg's subversive form of celebrity activism transforms the attention economy into attention for politics.

In the same spirit of subverting commercialized expectations of celebrity, Rincón and Rodríguez offer a theoretical framework of "the popular" from Latin America. From this, they build a manifesto for narrating the stories of citizens' lives in societies affected by war. Narrations of war tend to center the stories of the perpetrators, erasing the lives of victims and survivors. Where victims' stories appear, they are frequently mired in their suffering and death rather than reflecting the complexity and vibrancy of their lives. Rincón and Rodríguez argue that stories of those affected by war are crucial for social restoration after conflict. Paraphrasing Martín Barbero (2002), they affirm that to *count* as a person, you must have the ability to *recount* your story. This storytelling should come from a "bastardized culture of the popular." The bastardized popular rejects commodified ideals of authenticity that attach the value of the popular to the stultified and ossified imaginary of the Other as pure and untouched by modern commodified culture. Rincón and Rodríguez call for a vision of the popular that is not about content or intellectual property but rather about the experience of recognition and emotional connection. The bastardized popular seeks the pleasure and empowerment of seeing and being seen in ways that are culturally specific – genuine rather than authentic. From this framework emerges the "citizen celebrity," a form of fame that centers on "being somebody" in the media to attain recognition in one's own community.

In recounting stories of those affected by war, the citizen celebrity forms part of a popular resistance whereby "subjugated subject, the marginalized, and the working classes push their own narratives into the circuits from which they have been excluded" (Rincón and Rodríguez, p. 125 of this volume). This mode rejects Orientalized forms of viewing the Other as a mere means of understanding the (Western) self. These concerns apply equally to the experiences of armed conflict within a nation as to the stories of those who are forced by violence and persecution to flee across borders. Karina Horsti and Lilie Chouliaraki's studies both explore modes of representing and witnessing refugee narratives in the context of two Eurocentric institutions: museums and international news organizations.

Chouliaraki explores the power dynamics at work in the representation of refugee selfies by Western news organizations. At first blush, the phenomenon of the refugee selfie fits with this mode of popular citizen celebrity. The selfie is a transnational feature of online popular cultures, a means of staging and performing the self for one's chosen public. However, as Chouliaraki shows, while the migrant selfie became a focal point of the coverage of refugees in 2015, their photographs and stories were invariably displaced in the news media. Chouliaraki examines three different types of migrant-related selfies in Western news: those taken to celebrate the arrival on safe territory after a dangerous voyage, those taken with famous

Western authority figures as expressions of solidarity, and those taken by celebrities posing as though they were migrants.

While the first two forms involve displaced people as active agents in self-representation, their remediation by Western news organizations focuses either on the act of taking the selfie – implicitly inviting the public to interrogate and pass judgment on the act – or on the meaning of the solidaristic selfie for Western leaders in the context of their policy. In both cases, the self-representations of refugees are marginalized along with the reasons for their flight. The final form – the celebrity posing as migrant – fully erases the refugee as agent. The selfies with celebrity leaders involve a kind of reciprocity, as a portion of the attention and symbolic capital of the leader transfers to the immigrant partner, while the leader benefits from the moral dividends of authenticity and virtue for their participation. In contrast, the celebrity posing as migrant fully erases the displaced person as communicative agents in Western news. While drawing attention to the cause, this hijacks the suffering of others and converts it into a discussion about "our" (Western) values, practices, and morals.

Karina Horsti's study likewise explores the ethics of using celebrity to attract attention for refugee narratives in two museum installations designed to produce solidarity among presumed white middle-class publics with people forced to flee. Using national and global celebrities to voice refugee narratives raises ethical concerns about the power imbalances of powerful Westerners "giving voice" to those living in highly precarious situations. Echoing Rincón and Rodríguez, Horsti notes that displaying narratives of flight also raises questions about how to portray the effects of war and persecution without producing additional suffering among the impacted. One of the exhibitions used the comforting familiarity of a Finnish celebrity voice to narrate stories of displacement from the national past with the implicit goal of evoking solidarity with current-day transnational refugees through "multi-directional memory" (Rothberg, 2009). However, the exhibition depended on a sanitized and simplified imaginary of the Finnish past that obscures the reality of suspicion and resentment towards newcomers – past and present.

The other exhibition by a Berlin-based South African artist drew reflexive attention to the politics of listening and witnessing using Hollywood celebrities to amplify refugee narratives, while also asking why this celebrity mediation is necessary to generate attention and caring. Unlike the celebrity selfie with migrants examined by Chouliaraki, which erased the stories and contexts of refugee subjects, here the artist and celebrity actors are tools to draw attention to refugee voices. The refugees are active agents who speak to the artist and the actors who will be performing their words. The two-part exhibition features both the edited, enacted celebrity portrayals and the original interviews, where listeners can hear the voice and gesture of the refugee storytellers directly. The exhibition critiques its own practice as well as the politics of the institutions that commissioned it. Ultimately, whether the attention-garnering capacity of celebrity can support ethical forms of witnessing and listening may depend on the critical attention paid to the structural power dynamics within and surrounding the exhibition. More importantly, it depends on whether the exhibition can deconstruct the "symbolic bordering" Chouliaraki observed in representations of migrant selfies to position refugees as human agents in the presence of equals.

Theorists have long noted celebrity's function as "the embodiment of collective individualism" (Dyer, 1998, p. 91), a reflection of the neoliberal fantasies that predominate among the global exporters of celebrity. Less attention has been paid to theorizing celebrity as a "personalization of normative collectivity" (Luthar, 2010, p. 692) and as a tool for identitarian boundary-making (Wimmer, 2013). This phenomenon is particularly salient when celebrities cross borders and enter into transnational politics of culture and identity. The global transit of celebrity creates an interpretive space for contesting and consolidating national identity as the primary interpretive lens for politics.

In transnational cultural politics, popular culture and the celebrity it produces create "soft power" resources that are particularly valuable to states facing scrutiny on the world stage. Algan and Kaptan show how the Turkish government has latched on to the growing international success of Turkish dramas to generate goodwill and dissipate criticism of its particular brand of "authoritarian neoliberalism" (Yesil, 2016). Ankara is using celebrity ambassadors to create global markets for consumer products, tourism, and even advantageous foundations for diplomacy. This project is becoming increasingly complex as the representational demands of the conservative government come into tension with the commercial imperatives of creating successful transnational content. While some creators attempt to resist the governments' demands, popular actors largely appear willing to offer up their celebrity for the government's cross-promotional purposes in the name of patriotism. The Turkish case disrupts the long-standing neoliberal orthodoxy that free market flows naturally undermine authoritarianism and promote liberal democracy.

Governments are not the only actors using celebrity to bolster nationalist bulwarks. Celebrities also provide narrative material for the citizenry to build projections of national ideals and of the nation's transnational Others. In their analysis of responses to tax evasion by transnational soccer star Ronaldo, Jorge, Oliva, and Aguiar illustrate how national contexts inspire dramatic differences in the interpretation of celebrity malfeasance. For the media and the general public, celebrity transgressions provide sites of contention to reflect on broader cultural and economic norms. In Spain, disappointment with the inequity of Spanish institutions was joined by interpretations of Ronaldo's actions through a combination of anti-elitism and nativism, railing against Ronaldo as the "ungrateful immigrant." Meanwhile, in Portuguese responses, the media and particularly audience commentaries tended to downplay the immorality of tax evasion, with some even celebrating what they saw as smart financial management in the face of a wasteful state. While Ronaldo's celebrity brought visibility to the problem of tax avoidance by wealthy elites, the emotional and identity-driven nature of public relationships with celebrity (Redmond, 2018) pushed many toward boundary maintenance and repair.

Celebrity also plays a central role in another cornerstone of neoliberal cultural politics: colorblind anti-politics. While it is certainly true that many celebrities of color have mobilized their visibility and representational capital to challenge racial and economic inequality, the mere existence of celebrities of color is not necessarily evidence of progress (Jackson, 2014). Instead, the success of minoritized celebrities also serves myths of colorblind meritocracy and individual responsibility. Zambon traces this phenomenon beyond the Anglophone world, addressing a self-described "integration campaign" from the German media industry. The government-supported campaign mobilized transnational German politicians, athletes, and entertainers behind the message that immigrants and their descendants cannot expect a dignified life without mastery of the German language. The campaign promotes the popular myth of the German-born perpetual "migrant" who is unable or unwilling to speak German. Meanwhile, the campaign images use the bodies of visible minority celebrities to sanction the project as apolitical and non-racist. This vision of integration demands a commitment to a white supremacist status quo that treats economic and social inequality as marginal or individual. What is especially noteworthy in Zambon's contribution is the way she highlights the normative foundations of both citizenship and celebrity, as they are both wrapped up in the state's racial and racializing logics through discourses of integration and its purported failure.

On the whole, the chapters in this volume demonstrate the need for a renewed politicized treatment of the topic of celebrity in its transnational and globalizing reach. They call for engaging concepts and practices of celebrity not only for normative claims and imperatives but also for the analytics that reveal the manners in which celebrity and the agency it facilitates shape the popular and everyday life. It is clear that celebrity has touched all aspects of contemporary life and societies, in the political, cultural, economic and social registers. On that note, the studies in this book make it clear that, as Nick Couldry (2015) has argued, celebrity studies needs social theory, just as social theory needs celebrity studies. Together, these studies demonstrate the value of the analysis of global celebrity as a means of critically theorizing the popular.

References

Couldry, N. (2015). Why celebrity studies needs social theory (and vice versa). *Celebrity Studies*, 6(3), 385–388.
Dyer, R. (1998). *Stars*. London, UK: Bloomsbury Publishing.
Jackson, S. J. (2014). *Black celebrity, racial politics, and the press: Framing dissent*. London, UK: Routledge.
Luthar, B. (2010). People just like us: Political celebrity and creation of national normality. *Cultural Studies*, 24(5), 690–715. https://doi.org/10.1080/09502380903546950
Martín Barbero, J. (2002). Identities: Traditions and new communities. *Media Culture and Society*, 24(5), 621–641.
Redmond, S. (2018). *Celebrity*. London, UK: Routledge.
Rothberg, M. (2009). *Multidirectional memory: Remembering the Holocaust in the age of decolonization*. Stanford, CA: Stanford University Press.
Wimmer, A. (2013). *Ethnic boundary making: Institutions, power, networks*. Oxford, UK: Oxford University Press.
Yesil, B. (2016). *Media in new Turkey: The origins of an authoritarian neoliberal state*. Urbana: University of Illinois Press.

The commodified celebrity-self: industrialized agency and the contemporary attention economy

P. David Marshall

ABSTRACT
This article looks at the emerging comfortability with how selling the self has become normalized transnationally. Commodifying the self has been the natural province of celebrities: they use their visibility for their own ends, but also to draw attention to particular issues that are beyond their celebrity value. These activities represent a form of agency and a means of effecting change and a technique to draw collective attention and action to particular events, activities and causes. The kind of agency that celebrities bring to the public world is infused with "Industrialized" Agency. This form of Industrialized Agency (IA) has been naturalized as billions now engage in some form of persona construction for the attention economy through their elaborate uses of social media. This transformation identifies the emergence of a new cultural politics that is connected to the successes of this widespread deployment of IA.

Introduction

Celebrities are an interesting collective entity. For media and cultural historians who have looked at the phenomenon, the very idea of a celebrity is modern. According to Fred Inglis (2016), celebrities do not predate 1750 and thus are a particular phenomenon that has been dependent on capitalism and the development of sophisticated mass media. Leo Braudy's epic work, *The Frenzy of Renown*, that mapped fame from antiquity to the contemporary, assiduously avoids using the term celebrity with subjects predating the 18th century even though he identifies the word's ancient Greek origins in "*celebritas*." (Braudy, 1997, p. 17). Van Krieken (2012), through his research into the work of 17th century historians has attempted to link 17th century portraiture to celebrity, but it is more accurate to connect it to the desire for fame by wealthy individuals at that time than anything that could resemble the organization of a public culture in the last 200 hundred years. Even 19th century usages of celebrity recorded in the Oxford English Dictionary identify the difference between celebrity and real influence: "M. Arnold (in Macmillan's Magazine) 'They [sc. Spinoza's successors] had celebrity, Spinoza has fame.'"

This article is an updated and revised version of my publication in German: Marshall, P. D. (2017). Kommodifizierung von Celebrity. Industrialisierte Agency und ihr Wert in der gegenwärtigen Aufmerksamkeitsökonomie. *Zeitschrift für Medienwissenschaft (ZfM)*, 2017(1), 49–60. The author wishes to thank *ZfM* and the special issue editor Brigitte Weingart for their support in its development.

Although certainly not always positively, the very idea of celebrity is centrally concerned with value. Most pointedly, the extensive historical investigation of celebrity by Antoine Lilti (2017) situates the emergence of celebrity in the 18th century and its different constitution of public identity. What can be discerned about celebrity as a particular public individual identity in the 19th and 20th centuries in its interplay with political and popular culture are three key points:

- Celebrity identifies a different constitution of relationship to and engagement with a constituted "public sphere." For Habermas, a new distant representative public through bourgeois private power shaped the public sphere from the 19th to 20th century and made it replicate the "representative public" of the middle ages and its dominating leaders and leadership (Habermas, 2010).
- Given that the emergence of celebrity through the entertainment industries linked them fundamentally to this bourgeois public sphere, celebrities in this approach are visible manifestations of democratic capitalism's construction of an appearance – as opposed to a real – presentation of the public. Celebrities "embody" their audiences through presentation of the self (Marshall, 2014a).
- This appearance and reality construction of celebrity identity does not fully identify the way that celebrity moves through collectives via the entertainment industry in the 20th century in particular. Celebrity, over time, constructed a regular connection to the populace in any culture through engaged audiences and related fan cultures (Hills, 2002). Their "embodiment" of people made them fundamentally intermediaries in how power was placed. The best way to describe the particular, sometimes indirect, but always present formation of influence, is through kinds of emotional bonds that linked audiences to celebrity figures. Celebrities have developed an interesting and complex form of "affective power" (Marshall, 2014b, p. xxxiv).

This article is a closer study of the ***value*** and power of celebrity and the proliferation of that value across cultures and into our transformed contemporary – and online – culture. Contrary to most of the histories and popular readings of celebrity, it begins with at least a neutral position related to the value of celebrities in order to identify its very particular and perhaps, peculiar value. From a study of the kind of public individuality – persona – that celebrity expresses, I argue that celebrity articulates a specific type of agency that is valuable in contemporary culture. This value is often overlooked because of its origins, its prevalence, and its integration into the sensibilities of public comportment and the configuration of individual value throughout the online social media platforms of everyday life. To explain this further, I identify that our structure of attention has shifted; what Goldhaber (2006) and Franck (1999) identified as an "attention economy" has become linked to a celebrity-initiated/modeled "Industrialized Agency" (Marshall, Moore & Barbour 2020) that integrates several dimensions of agency theory to explain this current and mutated iteration. What follows works to identify the emergence and then its extension beyond celebrity culture into how individuals comport themselves online and via social media to attempt to exercise their own constellation of power, influence and collective connection. It is not easy to identify how this pervasive industrialized agency and mutated system of individualized value is changing our political cultures, but this article begins the investigation into how it has emerged from the structures of value that have been privileged in celebrity culture at least for the last century.

The work of individuality in the attention economy

George Franck analyzed the organization of contemporary media and culture via an "economy of attention," where individuals produced stock-like value in their capacity to influence, their ability to draw other influential people, and a determination of their future value in capital-like exchanges (1999). Franck extended this study to claim that "it is one of the most significant economic changes of [the 20th] century that the service of rendering attention has overtaken all other production factors in economic importance" and labels it "mental capitalism" (1999). The more recent analysis by Goldhaber of online culture[1] as fundamentally and distinctively an "attention economy" extends Franck's approach to a closer study of how people both navigated and shaped their online presences and identified a new intensified and personalized mental capitalism. What Goldhaber was the first to identify was that this new generation of attention economy was driven by the dispersal of content and sharing via the Internet and was no longer organized and structured by traditional mass media (2006). Goldhaber also makes the claim that this new attention economy was not clearly monetized in online culture's patterns of sharing and exchange and thus produced a quite different path. In this diffusion of content, a markedly different monetary value and a general decline in the influence of media such as television, film, radio and print, a shifted cultural and information economy was developing: an online attention economy. The openness of new media forms presented a challenge to the hierarchies of how content became popular and known. Despite this decline in media, a paradox emerged: celebrities, those specific individuals that had depended on the twentieth century media structures of the attention economy as Franck outlined, did not decline; from most perspectives, celebrity as a public persona constellation of attention have become more significant in the last 15 years even as the array of visibility through the platforms of social media has proliferated new layers and generations of celebrities.

It is not easy to answer why this is the case. Part of the structure of the attention economy is its openness as Goldhaber's approach underlines. Different movements of information flourish; but even more generally the sources of information are dispersed across a sharing group of users with billions now relying on social media to determine what they read, watch and the content upon which they comment. On the surface at least, it would appear that the formations of public visibility are in flux. For more than a century legacy media – television, radio, film, and print – –were instrumental in providing powerful filtering devices and helped determine which individuals were celebrities and public figures. There has been a clear the decline in legacy media over the last two decades (Filloux, 2014). In the American context specifically, Pew Research's 2016 report described the downward spiral in traditional media as negating "tectonic shifts" (Mitchell & Holcomb, 2016). In contrast, there has been phenomenal growth of online culture. Legacy media were part of producing a "representational media and cultural regime" (Marshall, 2014a, p. 160, 2010, 2016), a linked system of political and cultural personalities that, with visible legitimacy, represented each particular national culture and, in an interlinked system, provided a transnational network of public identity. With legacy media's decline, one might have expected the accompanying celebrity system to be similarly compromised.

Certain analyses of contemporary celebrity make claims about why this is not the case. Couldry (2016) identifies that celebrities in some practices have transcended their media origins and provide a different structure in the new online attention economy, a new way to attract audiences and viewers. He translates this use of celebrities as a shifted way to generate a replacement myth of a media center, reorganizing it through online activities and social media. As media such as newspapers or television are less adept at garnering audiences, celebrities migrate into online spaces as points of visible recognition – the element that legacy media continues to try to sustain even as these celebrities are no longer dependent on the legacy media to sustain their value. Reworking Bourdieu's field theory and integrating Driessens' research on "celebrity capital" (2013), Couldry labels celebrities as a form of "meta-capital" in their capacity to traverse fields and produce attention across multi-platforms of online and legacy media as well as different dimensions or "fields" of contemporary culture (Couldry, 2016, pp. 106–110).

This capacity of celebrities to move across fields and to be deployed strategically in these various platforms and domains of contemporary life and society points to their convertible value. Businesses and industries attempt to quantify that value and use it for specific purposes. *Forbes Magazine* for instance, attempts to provide a yearly table or ladder of the relative *economic* value of celebrities. Thus, for 2020, Kylie Jenner has generated the greatest amount of income with US$590 million; Lionel Messi, the football star, is 5th at 104 million, while the British singer-songwriter Ed Sheeran is ranked 23rd at 64 million dollars. These top 100 celebrities generate more than 6.2 billion in pretax income (Greenburg & LaFranco, 2020). However, on the surface, this current composition of 100 top celebrities are almost all entities that have achieved their renown through traditional pathways: they are sporting, broadcasting, music, and film-acting stars and personalities whose income success is generally attached to 20th century patterns of public visibility. These leading celebrities are sponsored by hundreds of major corporations which represent the major pathway with which they expand their working wealth beyond their salaries (Forbes, 2020).

As these lists identify, celebrity value can be understood as a conversion into something that might be defined as economic value. As opposed to a product or a service, however, celebrities are individuals and this conversion into monetization does not quite capture the distinctive quality of celebrity value. Despite this potential differential value of what celebrities constitute in our cultures, Goldhaber's claim of a non-monetized online attention economy of mass-sharing has not transformed this financial system of reward and compensation: tracing this mutated system of individualized value that has been intensively advanced via social media platforms is what will be explored in the remainder of this article.

To investigate this celebrity value formation further, it is worthwhile to backtrack slightly from an analysis of celebrity and digital culture by integrating a Marxist approach around celebrity and value because of its particular relation to the transformation of meaning into a system of capitalism. Commodification is the process by which an object, a practice and in this case, an individual is converted into a product for exchange. From a Marxist perspective and championed by the critical theory derived from Lukacs, capitalism also serves to reify human activity (Vandenberghe, 2013). Processes and culture are transformed into things and in that transformation into things they can easily be converted into the structure of capital value – the commodity. This process of commodification is a form of alienation, one of the most destructive elements of capitalism as it reifies those cultural processes that define human relations and activities and allows those things/processes to be converted into systems of exchange that are no longer connected to the people who helped make their original value and meaning. Celebrities and their economically oriented activities regularly embody this reification of the self.

Celebrities express in the most extreme form the commodification of the individual; but, as opposed to a representation of the removal of the human subject and their capacity to express, they are its opposite. In all sorts of domains, celebrities articulate activity and *agency* at a super-individual level. Because of their visibility, celebrities do more than enact agency: they exemplify the exact and valued way that agency operates in contemporary culture. This form of commodified agency that celebrities both embody and express may appear to be abnormal – and it is in terms of its oversize dimensions; but, generally, it is not. What has occurred in our culture is a normalization of the commodification of the individual over more than a century of consumer capitalism.

The increasing normalization of the commodification of the individual can be seen in a structure of emulation that occurs across hundreds of national and regional cultures around the globe. Celebrities by their very definition are both extra-textual – that is, their public personalities move from their primary activity into forms of promotion, support and attention-attracting that cross into other domains and fields – and intertextual – that is, their meaning and significance inhabit other cultural spaces and venues as their personalities are called upon or interpellated into how our culture interprets situations. These extra- and inter-textual dimensions of celebrity create an elaborate cultural economy that both Couldry (2016) and Driessens (2013) correctly identify as transversal in where it can migrate into a form of convertible capital – "metacapital" as they have defined it. Currid-Halkett provides a similar reading of this celebrity value and its capacity to move through a culture so that it is effectively mined and then housed into other activities and other commodities: she labels it the "celebrity residual" in her efforts to place it within an economic, contractual, and proprietorial structure and further explains that this is the quality of celebrity that is valued economically in other parts of the culture for specific ends of attracting attention (Currid-Halkett, 2010, pp. 23–45).

The first stage of this emulation can be seen most clearly when celebrities link themselves to certain products and brands – a form of extra-textual agency and celebrity activity. The usual name for this process of linking is "brand ambassador." As Gunter's reading of the "consumer capital of celebrity" identifies, celebrities work in two ways in product endorsement (2014, pp. 61–102). Straight endorsement is a fee for service – a kind of payment for performance of the celebrity's testimonial relationship to the brand. The second form of product linkage is a license model "whereby the commercial brand becomes an extension of the celebrity and celebrity's name is integrated into the name of the product." (Gunter, 2014, p. 63 citing Mistry, 2006, pp. 33–34)

One can see various levels of endorsements that occur in consumer culture. For instance, in the perfume industry, the brand becomes closely linked to the star and sometimes blurs the fee for service and contract. Thus, certain stars have their own brand and product name and have a clear license relationship with the manufacturers of their fragrance. Beyoncé, for instance, has a license relationship with her strongly self-identified perfume range called "Heat" since 2008. Kim Kardashian West has successfully generated her own range of perfumes – collectively called KKW Fragrance: through her variety of forms of online narrative bursts related to different perfume sub-brands, Kardashian West has been able to generate sales more than once of $US 10 million in a single day (Morton, 2019). Chanel's relationship with Keira Knightley and Nicole Kidman was and is a powerfully close connection that is defined by multi-year/multi-million dollar relationships and attempts to strongly link the identities of these star personas to the brand (Marshall & Morreale, 2018). Likewise, the brand can sometimes serve as an identity marker and brand style for the celebrity.

These examples from the perfume industry's relationship with celebrities are exemplary of an endorsement culture that is endemic to contemporary corporate culture. Celebrities are conduits for products and services. Jason Karlin's study of celebrity and idol use in Japanese culture identifies that their use increases brand recognition by 20%: they simply attract attention and, in his case, maintain a relationship with a fan culture: interestingly, these Japanese pop idols are just used for their profile and do not actively endorse the product in these ads (Karlin, 2012). According to Karlin's background research, the use of celebrities varies but it remains ubiquitous in the advertising industry throughout the world: from 5% of television commercials in Sweden and 25% in the United States and China to the world leaders of Japan at 70% and South Korea at 60% (Karlin, 2015).

Perhaps because of the ubiquity of celebrities across so many sectors, there are regular studies related to the effectiveness of their endorsement value (Schimmelpfennig & Hunt, 2020). The argument I am advancing here is that the role of the celebrity in its commodified presentation is normalized and naturalized as a way in which we frame and structure activity and agency in contemporary culture and although the debates about effectiveness are important to the industry, their general use has created an ecology of celebrity that makes their formation of identity an acceptable form of contemporary engagement and activity.

Augmenting this highly public display of commodified self is a parallel world of normalcy in everyday culture with endorsements. Much like the use of celebrity in endorsement culture, the public display every day by individuals of product logos is ubiquitous and normal. For instance, the Nike Swoosh can be seen as individuals exercise or play a panoply of sports. Cyclists everywhere have normalized the wearing of many corporate logos on their bikewear. Quantifying the practice of visible brand-wearing by the world's populace would be an interesting investigation of cultural meaning; what it would point to is, once again, how normal and natural it is to link one's public identity with an array of commodities: it is a transnational culture of the commodified public self that stretches from celebrity culture to all of us as individuals.

One of the key elements of both celebrity commodified activity and our parallel world of everyday commodified activity is that they are expressions of individuality for our movements through a public world. They are the signs of the contemporary moment and the structures of economic value converted into things that we then display.

Agency: the link to the commodified (celebrity) self

It is very easy to dismiss this commodified identity and to see it simply as a sad complicity of contemporary life with the domination of corporations. However, it is important to recognize how celebrity culture has privileged this identity in a manner that often goes well beyond corporate endorsements. There is not the space here to detail the variety of ways that celebrities have traversed across cultural and political fields; but it is clear that they have engaged in politics and humanitarian concerns[2] that researchers such as Mark Wheeler (2013), Dan Brockington (2009, 2014), and Fridell and Konings (2013) among others have advanced in their various works and edited collections.

The commodified and related mediatized public identity of the celebrity possesses power and can affect change. Because of these dimensions, whether looking at celebrities' capacity to transform the sales of goods and services or whether observing their forays into politics and cultural transformation, it is perhaps useful to understand these activities as a form of "agency" that over the last century has been regularized and normalized.

Agency is a slippery concept. It is often positioned in opposition to structure and systems (Archer, 1996). Agency implies something that expresses power, the capacity to act, and a capacity to act in a manner that is not clearly inscribed and positioned by others. Structure, on the other hand, defines how what we do is patterned and pre-conditioned as we as individuals fit into existing social settings, work models, and institutions. For Marx, the absence of agency – the capacity to control the means of production and produce history – in capitalist labor structures produces a form of alienation and leads to a new form of agency and historical change. (Marx, 1978) Although not normally linked to this notion, Bruno Latour isolates the concept of agency in order to understand the social: an agent, which can be human or non-human, points to a moment of instability that reveals how the social actually operates – how things/relations are held together or not. Agency is the basis for the investigation of Actor Network Theory and its study of the relationship of things, humans and actions (Latour, 2007). As agents emerge, Latour uses the idea of their role as mediators of the social and as intermediaries in shaping the actions of others. Latour's approach to agents as intermediaries emerges from a reading of how technology helps shape patterns of actions in the social world and Latour extends that analysis to include all sorts of other relations between objects and humans in his re-theorization of what constitutes the social (Latour, 2012).

Emerging from business and economic theory, Agency Theory is also a useful way to understand the particular cultural power and formation that has emerged with celebrity culture. The theory attempts to explore how one agent or individual is incentivized to act in a certain way for a certain interest as well as acknowledging their own interest (Bamberg & Spremann, 1989). For instance, in basic Agency Theory how does one get a sharecropper – that is, the actual farmer who is an agent for a business – to work effectively for a landowner who is the "principal"? Although Agency Theory in business and economics has explored in great detail these kinds of economic relations and incentives, in general the approach identifies how the agent in business is a proxy for an action that will generate revenue in some way (Bosse & Phillips, 2014). Thus, advertising, talent, and real estate agencies all fit within this model of proxy but connected to mutual self-interest between the principal and the agent. By extending Agency Theory into how these agents in real estate, advertising and talent actually work it can be seen that the agent is a facilitator in the movement into and out of the commodity form and actively works on the conversion of value. For example, the talent agent is a go-between and thus works to convert the cultural value, creative resource, and impact of the star into a quantifiable salary or exchange and commodity value for the various strands of the entertainment industry.

To get us further into understanding the concept of agency's utility in making sense of this commodified celebrity self, it is also useful to see that agents produce some instrumental effect. The way that the term agent is used in chemistry or biology elucidates this catalyst effect where the coming together of two chemical agents produces something qualitatively different and transformed.

Perhaps most importantly for our linking the concept to the commodified and celebrity self, agency also implies – though not exclusively in terms of its definition – a relationship to the *individual*. Some writers such as Mayr refer to "human agency" in contrast to social conditions (Mayr, 2011). The dance theorist Carrie Noland uses agency to describe how the artist produces a "gesture" and thereby embodies agency as an individualized form of expression (Noland, 2010).

Connected to this individuality, agency was employed originally in French and then outward into other languages as an individual operative or – in Bond-like intelligence agencies – as a spy. In reality, this kind of agent is someone who can move and exercise power outside the normal range of legality *as an individual*. The classic extension of this is in the Bond/Fleming film franchise: "licence to kill" – an instrumental agent quality of James Bond – is certainly not part of a typical human right, but a recognition that the individual becomes an expression of action that cannot be done by the state directly and can only be done via the individual.

The agent is the re-presentation of individuality of work and serves this movement of value and economic rationalization of value. This understanding of agency – that it is a sign of Latourian activity, but also a sign of cultural change – helps reveal the complex structure of how the commodified celebrity self both operates and ultimately privileges a particular form of agency that works increasingly throughout our cultures.

The fabric of industrialized agency: persona, online culture and its proliferation

The concept and activity of agency identified in the above analysis when connected to the celebrity is particular and peculiar. It has emerged from what can only be described as an industrial relationship with the entertainment industry and then migrated out from those very prominent locations to be a model of individual comportment in contemporary culture. To avoid any confusion with other types of agency, it is best to label this commodified production of the self as "Industrialized Agency" or IA in its regular conversion and reconversion of value in the entertainment system and, as we have identified in this article, well beyond into other industries as well as other political (Marshall & Henderson, 2016b) and cultural activities.

This Industrialized Agency is based on a strategic form of identity – a persona – that is designed to negotiate a relationship by the individual into the social world (Marshall, 2014; Marshall, Moore, & Barbour, 2020). As a celebrity identity, it is already highly mediatized (Hjarvard, 2013; Lundby, 2014) – a working fiction of the individual for their own activity and agency that is visible predominantly in some mediated way. Also, as we have detailed above, the value of this agency is regularly calculated by the industry itself. For example, there is a corporate service run by The Marketing Arm and known as the Davie Brown Index or DBI which was established in 2006 and superseded the Hollywood Q Index. It now represents at least one of the industry standards that calibrates the industrial and convertible value of any celebrity. As their service identifies, the DBI "quantifies and qualifies consumer perceptions of celebrities" and is "designed to provide superior brand-relevant insights" (DBI, 2016). The DBI claims to evaluate 5,000 celebrities in 15 markets across the world which in their structures "represents the views of more than 1.6 billion people – approximately 50% of the world's adult population." (DBI, 2016). In a March 2020 study of celebrity that it shares with corporations, DBI has investigated through its audience categories such as "awareness," "influence," and "aspiration" the impact of Prince Harry and Meghan Markle's recent exit from official royal duties (TMA, 2020a). In addition, DBI mapped the transformation of influence that TikTok has had in varying the pathways to influence by established celebrities as they compete with a whole new cluster of stars such as the TikTok originally based dancer Charli D'Amelio and her capacity to represent Procter&Gamble in a COVID-19 inspired competition built through the hashtag #distance-distance (TMA, 2020b)

As opposed to a separate world of Industrialized Agency just for the famous, this industrialized agency is pandemic and identifies a pathway for everyone to comport the self in public. The will-to-visibility is naturalized via our online communities. Like our celebrity counterparts, billions are mediatized in an array of social media platforms from Facebook, Instagram, Twitter, WeChat, TikTok, YouTube, Weibo, and Snapchat where building a network of friends and followers is naturalized and normalized in the same way as the entertainment industry builds its audiences of viewers, listeners and fans. According to Hootsuite, there are now 3% more mobile phone connections than the world's population (Kemp/Hootsuite, 2020a). Social media use is roughly 3.8 billion or almost 50% of the world's population and world-wide. On average, the world's population use and also share versions of ourselves across 8.3 social media platforms (Kemp/Hootsuite, 2020b). The genius of these platforms is their capacity to blend interpersonal, communicative and interactive features with this mediatization of the self to produce what I have called in previous research the "intercommunicative public persona" (Marshall, 2016, p. 71): via social media, we are simultaneously constructing a public persona, participating in conversations with others, and producing personalized data that is aggregated and fed back into the elaborate attention economy. Accompanying these social networks – where the data of our mediatized selves is both collected and aggregated – other services have emerged to index and track what can be called online network metrics that at least resemble what has already occurred with celebrities. Since 2008, a service called Klout attempted to make this Industrialized Agency of individuals online continuous from the most famous to the least active. Klout calibrated your status as an "influencer" – a ranking out of 100, where Justin Bieber vied with Barack Obama for highest ranked influencer in 2012 (Hearn & Schoenhoff, 2016). Although Klout never gained universal approval as to its metrics or its rankings, it did identify that we had moved into an era where visibility was generally culturally and economically valuable, an era where Industrialized Agency was accepted.

IA's naturalized integration into virtually every culture can be seen in the uses made of each of these platforms by hundreds of millions. For example, TikTok, the social media platform with corporate origins in China has expanded to over 800 million subscribers since 2018 (Hootsuite, 2020a). These statistics identify the pandemic movement of what we "like," share, and engage with for hours each day via predominantly McLuhan-like extensions of ourselves through our mobile phones.

Research related to this expanded pandemic of display of the self-online captures the now millions of TikTok "influencers." In many ways, these new celebrities with millions of views of their short and fun videos replicate the massive micro-celebrity structures that YouTube developed over the last 15 years. Stars such as PewDiePie have more than 104 million YouTube subscribers (Statista, 2019), but it is useful to see how this focus on the very top end misses the pandemic quality of this construction of a public self – an online persona. According to SocialBlade, 5000 YouTube channels that have between 2.89 million and 147 million subscribers each with generally millions of views (Statista, 2019). Extending that outward, according to Statista in 2019, 36.7% of the worldwide Instagram accounts had between 10,000 and 100,00 followers; moreover, 19.5% Instagram accounts had between 100,000 and 1 million followers. Perhaps, the accounts that have only between 1,000 and 10,000 followers (12.6%) may not have the IA to make a living from their activity, but it nonetheless identifies that this presentation of a public online persona has become naturalized and normalized for approximately 1.047 billion Instagram account holders (91%) that have more than 1,000 followers on the platform.

Other services such as LinkedIn with its 663 million members (Statista, 2019) have worked to professionalize our online selves so that we all can construct a working persona that at least strategically presents us in a positive and public light. Millions on LinkedIn, beyond looking for work and possibilities, are also sharing their own information and thoughts as well as continually trying to connect with colleagues to maintain the visibility of their own professional identity. Our collective professional IA over these sites and others has constructed a new world order that makes us all part of the spectrum of the elaborate attention economy: this IA labor from influencers, aspiring opinion sharers – what Abidin (2018) has analyzed as Internet celebrities – has allowed the online powerhouses such as Google, Facebook, LinkedIn's Microsoft and others to build a further reconstruction of power through this data-sharing that becomes contemporary culture's relatively new economic advertising engine. A pandemic of Industrial Agency ensures that we all produce what Zuboff has identified as the "behavioural surplus" of data (Zuboff 2019) that has produced algorithmic structures and models of mass programmatic, highly targeted advertising transnationally.

Conclusion: the ambience of a new politics

Industrialized Agency (IA) is a new form of public identity. At both the level of the celebrity and the level of social media user, IA is a form of power and influence in contemporary culture. It is linked to two dimensions which have produced IA's extensive transversal across fields of activity and into the consciousness of billions and originally been heralded by the extensive and visible work of celebrities. The first dimension is a growing comfortability with the implications and values of the mediatization of the self. As this article has identified, online culture – in all its variations within and across cultures/subcultures/collectives and via social media platforms in particular – has generalized the value of individual visibility from its original home via legacy media in celebrity culture and both normalized it as a practice for the wider populace and structured a changed and intensified visibility. Wedded to this mediatization process of the self has been a new comfortability with the commodification of the self, first with celebrities' generally collective embrace of their own identity as commodities, then with celebrities' natural public identity affinity with corporate brand culture, and finally with the normalization of these kinds of practices by billions of people across many cultures and perhaps best articulated through the proliferation of online micro-celebrities (Abidin, 2018; Marwick, 2016; Senft, 2013).

There are political, cultural and economic implications of this naturalization of Industrialized Agency and this article has only begun to identify them. It has to be understood that IA does feed into the new economic structures of a digital economy by ensuring that more of us and more elements of our lives are collected, calibrated and evaluated: as the DBI and Klout classify graphically, our public identities – our personas – are now reconstructed into the values and cultures by and for the related new economies. Our personal awareness of this process of public-identity-formation signifies our own individual level with which we have naturalized, embraced and potentially redeployed its agency. The redeployment of this public identity formation – our persona – nominates a new formation of politics, power and influence. With celebrities, we can see their activities into politics at a level that challenges traditional institutions of power. With commodified individuals and celebrities, we can see an expanding commodity activism emerging that shifts how we designate what are public and private activities – a "privlic" culture (Marshall, 2016a; Marshall et al., 2020). Although the concept of neo-liberalism has been used to describe this cultural transformation to an economic individualism, it inadequately maps the actual agency that has emerged. Exploring our transformed cultures needs an understanding of how we have naturalized this Industrialized Agency from its most elite and visible celebrity culture to its everyday use by billions. This article serves to begin this reading and critiquing of IA.

Notes

1. Online culture is used in this article to identify the use of digital media platforms and the web itself: employing "culture" to describe this helps identify that it is far from a uniform experience and varies across ethnicities, nations, collectives, genders, and other forms of identity construction. Nonetheless, online culture curates these formations of identity, both collective and individual.
2. Think here of the highly visible and politically driven activities of Bono, George Clooney, and Angelina Jolie (Totman, 2017) as merely the most prominent celebrities in these areas, but the numbers of active celebrities that have specific political and cultural missions or serve as ambassadors of nonprofit organizations is very large and across a variety of nations. Dan Brockington's remarkable work on celebrity advocacy builds how celebrities represent an interesting conduit to represent an image of popularity in an era that sustains representational democracy but really "post-democracy," when it no longer is working in its relation to the populace (Brockington, 2014, pp. 8–10). The deep analysis of celebrity activism by Mukherjee and Banet-Weiser (2012, pp. 97–113) and the connection to Hurricane Katrina by Brad Pitt and the "Make it Right" Campaign are also valuable further steps into this space.

Disclosure statement

No potential conflict of interest was reported by the author(s).

References

Abidin, C. (2018). *Internet celebrity: Understanding fame online.* Bingley, UK: Emerald Publishing.

Archer, M. S. (1996). *Culture and agency: The place of culture in social theory.* Cambridge, UK: Cambridge University Press.

Bamberg, G., & Spremann, K. (Eds.). (1989). *Agency theory, information and incentives.* Berlin, Germany: Springer-Verlag.

Bosse, D. A., & Phillips, R. A. (2014). Agency theory and bounded self-interest. *Academy of Management Review, 41*(2), 276–297. doi:10.5465/amr.2013.0420

Braudy, L. (1997). *The frenzy of renown : Fame & its history* (1st Vintage Books ed.). New York, NY: Vintage Books.

Brockington, D. (2009). *Celebrity and the environment: Fame, wealth and power in conservation.* London, UK: Palgrave Macmillan.

Brockington, D. (2014). *Celebrity advocacy and international development.* London, UK: Routledge.

Couldry, N. (2016). Celebrity, convergence, and the fate of media institutions. In P. D. Marshall & S. Redmond (Eds.), *A companion to celebrity* (pp. 98–113). Malden, MA: Wiley Blackwell.

Currid-Halkett, E. (2010). *Starstruck : The business of celebrity* (1st ed.). New York, NY: Faber and Faber.

DBI. (2016). *The celebrity Davie Brown index.* Retrieved from http://repucom.net/celebrity-dbi/

Driessens, O. (2013). Celebrity capital: Redefining celebrity using field theory. *Theory and Society, 42* (5), 543–560. doi:10.1007/s11186-013-9202-3

Filloux, F. (2014, September 1). Legacy media: The lost decade in six charts. *Monday Note.* Retrieved from https://mondaynote.com/legacy-media-the-lost-decade-in-six-charts-54de4746a1a2#.uh90ua9gq

Franck, G. (1999). ['Ökonomie der Aufmerksamkei, *Merkur,* (1993)]. *Telepolis.* Retrieved from https://www.heise.de/tp/features/The-Economy-of-Attention-3444929.html

Fridell, G., & Konings, M. (Eds.). (2013). *Age of icons: Exploring Philanthrocapitalism in the contemporary world.* Toronto: University of Toronto Press.

Greenburg, Z. O. M., & LaFranco, R. (2020). The world's highest paid celebrities. *Forbes.* Retrieved from https://www.forbes.com/celebrities/

Gunter, B. (2014). *Celebrity capital : Assessing the value of fame.* New York, NY: Bloomsbury.

Habermas, J. (2010). The public sphere: an encyclopedia article (1964). In M. G. Durham & D. M. Kellner (Eds.), Media and Cultural Studies: Keyworks Revised edition (pp. 73–78). Malden MA: Blackwell

Hearn, A., & Schoenhoff, S. (2016). From celebrity to influencer: Tracing the diffusion of celebrity value across the data stream. In P. D. Marshall & S. Redmond (Eds.), *ACompanion to celebrity studies.* (pp. 194-212) Boston, MA: Wiley.

Hills, M. (2002). *Fan cultures.* London, UK: Routledge.

Hjarvard, S. (2013). *The mediatization of culture and society.* New York, NY: Routledge.

Hootsuite. (2020a). *Digital 2020: Global digital overview.* Retrieved from https://p.widencdn.net/ywgwct/Digital2020GlobalYearbook_Report_en

Hootsuite. (2020b, January 20). *Digital 2020: LinkedIn audience overview* (p. 136). Retrieved from https://p.widencdn.net/ywgwct/Digital2020GlobalYearbook_Report_en

Inglis, F. (2016). The moral concept of celebrity: A very short history told as a sequence of brief lives. In P. D. Marshall & S. Redmond (Eds.), *A companion to celebrity* (pp. 21–38). Malden, MA: Wiley Blackwell.

Karlin, J. (2015, July 24). *Idols in the media mix*. Presented at the Mediated Worlds: Sociality, Publicness and Celebrity Summer Program, Tokyo, Japan: University of Tokyo.

Karlin, J. G. (2012). Through a looking glass darkly: Television advertising, idols, and the making of fan audiences. In J. G. Karlin & P. Galbraith (Eds.), *Idols and celebrity in Japanese media culture* (pp. 72–96). New York, NY: Palgrave.

Latour, B. (2007). *Reassembling the social: An introduction to actor-network-theory*. Clarendon Lectures in Management Studies. Oxford; New York: Oxford University Press.

Latour, B. (2012). *We have never been modern*. Cambridge, MA: Harvard University Press.

Lilti, A. (2017). *The invention of celebrity: 1750–1850*. Malden, MA: Polity.

Lundby, K. (Ed.). (2014). *Mediatization of communication*. Berlin, Germany: De Gruyter Mouton.

Marshall, P. D. (2010). The promotion and presentation of the self: Celebrity as marker of presentational media. *Celebrity Studies*, *1*(1), 35–48. doi:10.1080/19392390903519057

Marshall, P. D. (2014a). Persona studies: Mapping the proliferation of the public self. *Journalism*, *15* (2), 153–170. doi:10.1177/1464884913488720

Marshall, P. D. (2014b). *Celebrity and power: Fame in contemporary culture - 2nd Edition*. Minneapolis: University of Minnesota Press.

Marshall, P. D. (2016). *Celebrity persona pandemic*. Minneapolis: University of Minnesota Press.

Marshall, P. D. (2016a). When the private becomes public: Commodity activism, endorsement and making meaning in a privatized world. In P. D. Marshall, G. D'Cruz, S. McDonald, & K. Lee (Eds.), *Contemporary publics: Shifting boundaries in new media, technology and culture* (pp. 229–245). New York, NY: Palgrave Macmillan.

Marshall, P. D., & Henderson, N. (2016b). Political persona 2016 - an introduction. *Persona Studies*, *2* (2), 1–18. doi:10.21153/ps2016vol2no2art628

Marshall, P. D., Moore, C., & Barbour, K. (2020). *Persona studies: An introduction*. Hoboken, NJ: Wiley Blackwell.

Marshall, P. D., & Morreale, J. (2018). The institutionalization of branding and branding of the self. In Marshall, P. D. & Morreale, *Advertising and promotional culture: Case histories.* (pp. 173–189). London, UK: Palgrave Macmillan.

Marwick, A. (2016). You may know me from Youtube: (Micro-)celebrity in social media. In P. D. Marshall & S. Redmond (Eds.), *A companion to celebrity* (pp. 333–350). Boston, MA: Wiley Blackwell. Print.

Marx, K. (1978). The economic and philosophic manuscripts of 1844. In R. C. Tucker (Ed.), *The Marx-Engels reader* (2nd ed., pp. 66–125). New York, NY: Norton & Co.

Mayr, E. (2011). *Understanding human agency*. Oxford, UK: Oxford University Press.

Mistry, B. (2006). Star spotting. *Marketing*, *7*, 33–34.

Mitchell, A., & Holcomb, J. (2016, June 15). *State of the news media 2016*. Retrieved from http://www.journalism.org/2016/06/15/state-of-the-news-media-2016/

Morton, M. (2019). A celebrity perfumes still relevant? *Page Six*. Retrieved from https://pagesix.com/2019/01/17/are-celebrity-perfumes-still-relevant/

Mukherjee, R., & Banet-Weiser, S. (Eds.). (2012). *Commodity activism : Cultural resistance in neoliberal times*. New York, NY: NYU Press.

Noland, C. (2010). *Agency and embodiment: Performing gestures/producing culture*. Cambridge, MA: Harvard University Press.

Schimmelpfennig, C., & Hunt, J. B. (2020). Fifty years of celebrity endorser research: Support for a comprehensive celebrity endorsement strategy framework. *Psychology & Marketing*, *37*(3), 488–505. doi:10.1002/mar.21315

Senft, T. M. (2013). Microcelebrity and the branded self. In A. Bruns, J. Burgess, & J. Hartley (Eds.), *A companion to new media dynamics* (pp. 346–354). Chichester ; Malden, MA: John Wiley & Sons.

SocialBlade. (2020). *Top 5000 subscribed YouTube channels*. Retrieved from https://socialblade.com/youtube/top/5000/mostsubscribed

Statista. (2019). *Distribution of Instagram accounts worldwide as of June 2019, by number of followers.* Retrieved from https://www.statista.com/statistics/951875/instagram-accounts-by-audience-size-share/

TMA – The Marketing Arm. (2020a, March 2). *Celebrity DBI examines impact of royal exit.* Retrieved from https://share.themarketingarm.com/celebrity-dbi-examines-impact-of-royal-exit/

TMA – The Marketing Arm. (2020b, April 20). *On TikTok, stars are just like us (safer at home).* Retrieved from https://share.themarketingarm.com/on-tiktok-stars-are-just-like-us-safer-at-home/

Totman, S. (2017). The emergence of the super-celebrity activist: George Clooney and Angelina Jolie. In J. Raphael & C. Lam (Eds.), *Becoming brands: Celebrity, activism and politics* (pp. 21–31). Toronto, Canada: Waterhill Publishing.

Van Krieken, R. (2012). *Celebrity society.* Hoboken, NJ: Taylor and Francis.

Vandenberghe, F. (2013). Reification: History of the concept. *Logos: A Journal of Modern Society & Culture, 12*(3), 427–436.

Wheeler, M. (2013). *Celebrity politics : Image and identity in contemporary political communications.* Cambridge UK: Polity.

Zuboff, S. (2019). The age of surveillance capitalism: *The fight for a human future at the new frontier of power.* New York, NY: Public Affairs - Hachette Book Group.

Offshoring & leaking: Cristiano Ronaldo's tax evasion, and celebrity in neoliberal times

Ana Jorge, Mercè Oliva, and Luis LM Aguiar

ABSTRACT
This article examines how the news media framed the allegations made in 2016 against Cristiano Ronaldo for evading taxes through offshores, and how audiences discussed this online, in Portugal, where he is originally from, and Spain, where he played football at the time. These countries were amidst an "austerity culture" justifying welfare cuts, promoting entrepreneurialism as "success", and presenting neoliberal policies as "common sense". Our analysis reveals Ronaldo portrayed as a member of the economic elite criticized for the high earnings of football players and celebrity tax privileges; as an ungrateful immigrant who does not contribute enough to society; and as "one like us" maneuvering to evade taxes. The comparative analysis shows audiences had double standards based on their feelings toward the celebrity, and they interpreted this case positively or negatively in relation to the inefficiency of the fiscal and justice systems in Southern Europe.

Introduction

On December 3, 2016, the European Investigative Collaborations (EIC), a consortium of 12 media outlets, bridging several countries, published information showing several footballers' tax evasion practices. This information was leaked after an extensive review of documents pertaining to offshore tax shelters. According to Football Leaks, as the revelations were labeled by EIC, Cristiano Ronaldo (the globe's most famous athlete) owed €15 million to the Spanish Tax Office for offshoring €150 million from his image rights revenue. The Office mounted an investigation charging Ronaldo with tax evasion on June 17, 2017. After approximately 1 year of denials, refutations, and rebuttals, Ronaldo admitted guilt and paid a fine of €18.8 million with a two-year suspended jail sentence (Pinedo, 2018).

While Ronaldo amassed and hid his wealth, Spain, where he committed the crime, and Portugal, where he was born, endured severe economic decline in the wake of the 2008 global financial crisis. The latter was subsequently exacerbated by the implementation of harsh austerity policies to "fix" the deteriorating economic situation in the two countries and discipline their population by reigning in their "excessive" spending and unreasonable demands on the State.

This article examines the Portuguese and Spanish media's framing of the allegations against Ronaldo from December 2016 to the end of the prosecuting processes and trial in 2017. Additionally, it analyses audiences' reactions to this revelation by discussing how they interpret the portrayal of the offshoring practices by Ronaldo at a time of severe economic downturn in Portugal and Spain. Our analysis builds upon previous academic literature on offshoring practices, tax imaginaries, media leaks and celebrity scandals, as well as the connections between celebrity, neoliberalism, and post-recessionary values and imaginaries. Football Leaks, continuing the effect of Panama Papers, put a spotlight on offshoring practices carried on by corporations and wealthy individuals, including celebrities. This article contributes to the current literature on celebrity, scandal, tax shaming and austerity culture by carrying out a comparative analysis of Spanish and Portuguese media and audiences. On the one hand, it shows how by analyzing the media portrayal and audience discussion of a celebrity's tax evasion scandal we can better understand not only how offshoring and celebrity are publicly understood, but also how these discourses are linked to broader social debates about equality, austerity, charity, and taxation as means of wealth redistributions in the context of post-recession. On the other hand, it also advances the field of audiences of celebrity, where cross-country comparative analysis of audiences remains rare (Mendick, Allen, & Harvey, 2015; Van den Bulck & Claessens, 2014, 2013a, 2013b). Moreover, this article addresses a gap in the current scholarship about celebrity malfeasance, which traditionally have mostly focused on Anglo-American countries and celebrities, by focusing on a Southern Europe case study.

Offshoring: celebrity culture, neoliberalism and austerity

It is estimated that nearly 10% of the global GDP is in offshore accounts (Piketty, 2014, p. 466); the OECD in 2011 estimated that the corporate "savings glut" hidden away in offshore tax havens totaled US$1.7 trillion (Fernandez & Wigger, 2016).

Corporations are actively and aggressively pursuing tax havens to hide their wealth and avoid paying taxes, and the banking sector is "the most prolific user of tax havens" (Urry, 2014, p. 2). While these serendipitous activities are often enough to sustain the economies of entire island-nations like the Cayman Islands, it means "most companies pay no tax on their income, profit and capital gains so long as their principal business is conducted elsewhere" (p. 53); they are unaccountable to the State, in part, on the account of globalization and mobility and liquidity of money. There are three rule-breaking practices to offshoring: (1) tax evasion which entails disregarding rules and regulations to illegally avoid paying taxes; (2) tax avoidance which isn't illegal though it goes against the spirit of existing laws; and (3) the use of legislations in one country to undermine those in another and thus gain advantage (p. 9). Yet, according to Bramall (2018), these rules and regulations are insufficiently broad and inclusive to discipline high-income earners to pay their taxes rather than facilitate the hiding of money with impunity.

The practice of offshoring intensified from the 1980s onwards when neoliberalism deregulated financial markets and allowed the free flow of capital across borders with no or little accountability (Harvey, 2006). In addition, neoliberals argued that *laissez–faire* business practices through reduced State interference in commerce, would create jobs, develop economies, and grow wealth to benefit all (Harvey, 2006). However, Urry (2014, p. 46) shows offshoring made "it possible for the rich class to get even richer" while the general population endured poorer services because the wealthy pay little to no taxes. In other words, money stashed away in tax havens is not in State coffers, thereby reducing the ability of the State to inject money into the welfare system and make it more equitable by enhancing existing social programs and creating new ones. To add insult to injury, the general population also endures the tyranny of credit, rising personal debt, and the seemingly perpetual fiscal crisis of the State (Aguiar & Noiseux, 2018; Fernandez & Wigger, 2016, p. 422).

With the turn to the new millennium, tax evasion and the role of tax havens have been increasingly discussed in the public sphere (Urry, 2014). NGOs and other organizations and agencies have exposed many different forms and aspects of "tax dodging" in a "global movement" of "tax shaming" (Bramall, 2016, 2018), at a time of increasing public outcry against unprecedented elite wealth accumulation via rigged structural mechanisms and nefarious activities (Littler, 2013). Celebrities have had a central role in these practices of "naming and shaming," since "a dominant perception, expressed in diverse ways by a number of different influential commentators and social actors, [is] that tax shaming can play a significant role in the fight for tax justice" (Bramall, 2018, p. 3).

By their nature, and even if there is a tension between *achieved* and *ascribed* forms of celebrity (Rojek, 2001, pp. 17–18), celebrities are symbols of Western individualism and embody the myth of upward social mobility at the heart of capitalist values; they are traditionally portrayed as individuals who achieve privileged positions thanks to talent, hard work and luck (Dyer, 1979, p. 42; Littler, 2004). The rhetoric and performance of "giving back" to the disenfranchised in society, via charity, for instance, owes to a western conception of civil society, and contributes to instill in society this individualism further (Littler, 2008). Celebrity is thus not only "indicative of a society with profoundly unequal concentrations of [social and economic] power" (Cross & Littler, 2010, p. 396), but it is also said to legitimize and naturalize social and economic inequality (Littler, 2013) through stories of "the heroic individual who succeeds against the odds" (Mendick et al., 2015, p. 45).

After the financial crisis of 2008–09 and subsequent recession, austerity was implemented through discourses justifying welfare cuts, entrepreneurialism as means to individual "success," and neoliberal policies as "common sense" explanations for the way out of the crisis (Hall & O'Shea, 2013; Jensen, 2014). A new, anti-welfare common sense re-imagines welfare "as fostering toxic forms of 'welfare dependency' amongst citizens" (Jensen & Tyler, 2015, p. 472). But "tax justice discourses" arose contra-austerity (Bramall, 2016, p. 35). Today, tax evasion continues to be publicly condemned (Bramall, 2013) and, in the case of the UK, the avoidance of taxation by corporations and individuals is condemned as "immoral, irresponsible and wrong" (Bramall, 2016, p. 31).

Celebrity is at the center of these debates. Under the wider cultural and social moment of austerity, on the one hand, celebrities come to embody the values consistent with wider discourses and (gendered and raced) subjectivities, both embodying "good and bad citizens" (i.e., entrepreneurial and deserving vs. undeserving celebrities), such as the analysis of pop culture female celebrities (such as Beyoncé, Katie Price, or Kim Kardashian) has demonstrated (Allen, Mendick, Harvey, & Ahmad, 2015). On the other hand, "tax shaming" practices connect with narratives of fall and misfortune of celebrities, such as cases of bankruptcy or "broke celebrities" (Oliva & Pérez-Latorre, 2020), which inspire *Schadenfreude*, a form of pleasure for audiences that shows public unrest provoked by inequality, but expressed in personal attacks (and not a critique of the structures that make this inequality possible) (Cross & Littler, 2010, p. 410).

By analyzing Ronaldo's case, this article discusses how offshoring practices – which have proliferated under the neoliberal regime – are portrayed by the media and discussed in the public sphere, including how audiences respond to them, and the role celebrity culture plays in these depictions and public debates. In the next section, we develop the concept of media leaks and celebrity scandal, to better support our case study.

Leaking: celebrity, media and scandal

In this era of transnationalism and neoliberalism, the global capitalist class works to secure its position through, among other means, practices of concealment, secrecy and even deceit (Palan, Murphy, & Chavagneux, 2010; Urry, 2014). A Durkheimian perspective on deceit argues that deceitful acts threaten trust and order in the functioning social structure by undermining shared norms, values, and customs (Schilling & Mellor, 2015). Such a perspective presumes a fundamentally sound and stable social order with boundaries and structures of behavior encouraging the sanctity of values and their reproduction. However, this view overlooks why transgressors escape the socialization of norms and values in practicing deceit and malfeasance.

Recent views on leaks and revelations argue that their emergence works to reinforce the checks and balances in place in society and thus prevent future leaks (Bramall, 2018; Gamson & Sifry, 2013). The pattern here, however, is often to individualize and scapegoat the perpetrator of the leak and leave untouched deeper sources of discontent expressed in the form of the original leak. Girard (1986) argues that scapegoating is a ritualized cultural practice to unite the community (however small), by assigning blame to someone – anyone – so that the community reinforces its boundaries and returns to "normal" as quickly as possible without self-cannibalizing with deeper divisive issues and practices.

Fraser (1992) focuses on the intent behind divulging insider information and secrets through leaks. She reminds us of the importance of examining who gets to define (and when) the relevance and significance of leaks. This process varies according to the perception of the seriousness and exceptionality of the offense, e.g., corruption (Hajdu et al., 2018). It is important, then, in this context, to consider the threat to the legitimacy and centrality of mainstream news media in social life, by social media and other information-based platforms, including networked, citizen-based leaks (Hindman & Thomas, 2014). Moreover, the economic crisis is believed to have undermined media and journalists' independence, particularly in countries where their role has been traditionally more subservient to political and economic power, such as Spain and Portugal (Sampedro, López–Ferrández, & Carretero, 2018, pp. 258–259). In fact, Woodall (2018) explains collaboration across news organizations under EIC not just by the fact that the information was complex and of sizable dimension, but also as a means to lower the risk of not publishing it.

For a leak to constitute a scandal, other conditions need to be present – the first of which is a wide circulation and impact of the news story. The EIC coordinated the release of Football Leaks worldwide at a moment when traditional news sources of football institutions were coming to a Christmas break. Scandal is constituted by the transgressions of accepted behavior violating the social values, norms and consensus enfolding as "ritual" and "social drama" (Jacobsson & Löfmarck, 2008). In this process, transgressors are often punished (shamed, for instance) and used as examples in the restoration and reinforcement of existing norms and values. This was the case in the shaming ritual the news media imposed on Strauss-Kahn's crime of rape, although news discourse reporting was different in USA, where the crime occurred, and in France, the country of origin of the offender (Boudana, 2014). But the punishment for such transgressions and crimes is often haphazard, and sentence-lite. This is especially so when public pressure for accountability and shaming discourses quickly dissipates and disappears from the public sphere, replaced by other issues attracting the media's focus.

The media scandal also involves its narrativization, dramatization and storytelling (Lull & Hinerman, 1997). In the case of celebrity, scandals can occur through the discrepancy between the public image the person portrays and their hidden behavior, jeopardizing, in the process, the reputation capital the celebrity has accumulated. The celebrity image is the product of the interplay between the professional persona and the private life, but also "the 'real' person behind the construction, 'off-guard, unkempt, unready' (Holmes, 2005, p. 21)" (Van den Bulck & Claessens, 2013a, p. 47). Therefore, a central part of the mediatization of the revelation is trying to make clear whether the action of the celebrity happened with or without intention or consent. Sport celebrities, in particular, have special pressures toward the integrity of their moral behavior (Whannel, 2005), as they continue to be seen as figures whose merit is less possible to be fabricated than other fields of celebrity. Sports celebrities' credentials are also associated with increased authenticity (Andrews & Jackson, 2002). Regarding the reaction of the celebrity to the scandal, there are cultural expectations on the rehabilitation of a celebrity's reputation after a "perceived betrayal of public trust," which stresses emotional labor and performed authenticity (Nunn & Biressi, 2010). The celebrity *mea culpa* can then, ironically, lead to eliciting sympathy from the public for being upfront (Bramall, 2018; Rojek, 2001).

A constructivist view on scandal holds that, for a scandal to be sustained, the claims implicit in the leak "must be made consistent with the moral order on which those realms are based" (Fine, 2019, p. 19). Van den Bulck and Claessens (2013a) found that audience reactions to news of a celebrity sex scandal – similarly to what they found regarding the news of a celebrity suicide (2013b) – "either adopt[ed] the frame presented in the media article or develop[ed] a (counter-)frame (...), resulting from framing moderators, including personal experiences, interaction with peers and parasocial relationships" (2013a, p. 53). The authors argue celebrity scandal is a way for audiences to discuss norms, but which ultimately works to reproduce them. They also note the double standard audience members adopt when positioning themselves in relation to the transgressed norms depending on those personal factors. Tiger (2013) noted this in the media coverage, readers' letters, and online comments regarding Lance Armstrong and Whitney Houston drug cases, where differences emerged according to race and gender: Armstrong's abuse was framed as a means to enhance his athletic performances but was quickly overshadowed by stories about his humanitarianism and cancer scare; whilst Houston's was seen as a case of addiction. In cases of tax avoidance scandals, Bramall remarks that there is an incorrect assumption that they will "be met with public opprobrium, [as] disapproval and anger is contextualized as arising from the pain of austerity" (2018, p. 38), when in fact, people show "multiple forms of identification and disidentification" (p. 40) with the scandalous stories and celebrities, as we found with Ronaldo's tax evasion.

Materials and methods

When Football Leaks published its stories in early December 2016, Cristiano Ronaldo was having "the best year of his career" (Lovett, 2016): he captained Portugal's national team to winning the European Championship for the first time in that summer. The allegations were made public on the heels of the *Ballon d'Or* gala and Ronaldo winning this most prestigious individual athletic prize for a record fourth time. He was the most recognizable global celebrity with approximately 240 million followers on social media (Badenhausen, 2016), and his earnings were the highest for any athlete and the 4th highest on Forbes' list of the top 100 earning celebrities (Greenburg, 2016). His net worth in 2018 was approximately US $450 million, and his investments ranged from fragrance lines to hotels (Geeter, 2018). His global status only enforces the "rags to riches" story, common among football players. Ronaldo was born in Madeira Island, to a poor family whom he supports, and who are occasional celebrities in the media riding on Ronaldo's coattails (Jorge, 2015). The sports and mainstream media often depict Ronaldo as selfish, egotistical, arrogant, and self-centered possessing a vacuous personality, someone who protects his brand jealously (Bar-On, 2014).

In 2016, Ronaldo was playing in Real Madrid, Spain. Spain and Portugal had gone through financial collapse, in which "living beyond our means" discourses were extensively used by politicians as the explanation (Alonso et al., 2011), followed by welfare cuts, high rates of unemployment, more inequality. In Spain civic movements "Indignados" contested corporations' and the rich's dominant place in society. Against a common background of tax evasion cultures, in Spain there were a series of scandals with corruption and tax evasion by politicians and companies following up Panama Papers, news about celebrities that owe money to the Hacienda, the national tax office (Oliva & Pérez–Latorre, 2020) as well as a general tax amnesty impulse by the Spanish Government (2012) to try to regularize more than €25,000 million of "dark" money, in exchange for just paying a 10% tax. In Portugal, the process of fiscal modernization to fight the shadow economy has put emphasis on small companies and consumers; and the fiscal agenda was marked by the unprecedented case of investigation of a former Prime Minister (2005-11), José Sócrates, since 2014.

This paper analyses how Cristiano Ronaldo's tax evasion was portrayed by the Spanish and Portuguese media and how the audiences in these two countries discussed those narratives of malfeasance, after the period of austerity. To the point, it poses the following research questions: a) How were tax evasion and offshoring practices by a celebrity discussed? b) How were taxes and the welfare state conceptualized in the wake of the economic crisis and austerity policies?

To answer these questions, we used purposive sampling to select a combination of quality and popular news media, from press, television, and radio in both countries (Portugal: *Expresso, Público, Sol, Sábado, RTP, SIC, Renascença*; Spain: *El Mundo, La Vanguardia, El Mundo Deportivo, El Periódico, El Confidencial, Marca, Atresmedia*), including online comments in social media posts as well as in their websites' comment sections to discuss Ronaldo. The corpus included news and comments since the scandal broke (3/12/2016-3/01/2017) and until the prosecution (15/06/2018). We used inductive, qualitative analysis (Corbin & Strauss, 2008) to identify the main themes in the news stories and comments. Two of the authors independently collected the material and exchanged notes among the three authors until the main themes were identified.

Tax justice discourse

In the Spanish press, when the Football Leaks scandal first broke, Ronaldo's case was presented not as an isolated case, but as a "new example" of offshoring practices and tax avoidance by wealthy individuals and big corporations revealed by Panama Papers. In the first press articles, especially in *El Mundo* (a quality newspaper), the news about the scandal were accompanied with other articles that discussed – and tried to explain to a non-expert audience – terms such as tax avoidance, tax evasion or tax havens, and bring into the foreground debates about the existence of tax havens in the EU. At the same time, in Spain, Ronaldo emerged as the person who embodies these practices – with a much more prominent presence than other footballers and personalities involved in the Football Leaks scandal such as football coach José Mourinho, or Spanish footballer Xabi Alonso. The visibility of a case such as Ronaldo's was crucial to pave the ground for a movement of "naming and shaming" and sustain a tax justice discourse against the backdrop of austerity (Bramall, 2016, 2018) where tax avoidance and evasion was framed as immoral, greedy, and egotistic. As in other celebrity scandals, this is a way for audiences to discuss social norms (Tiger, 2013), in this case duty regarding taxation. In both opinion articles and audience comments, taxes were not only presented as a legitimate and necessary mechanism of redistribution of wealth in a context of economic crisis and welfare cuts, but also as the only fair thing to do in the industry of sports that lives off fans:

> The people who spend their savings in taking their kids to a match to enjoy watching Cristiano play are not those who live in the Virgin Islands. These football players owe it to the fans that have made them rich. Their "goals" to the taxpayers of the countries where they live are a disgrace (*El Mundo*, 5/12/2016 –SP)

The rationale underlying the commentary above is that citizens sustain celebrities through buying tickets, merchandising, or simply by paying attention to them; therefore, celebrities should pay their taxes to support the welfare state that benefits citizens. Readers are keenly aware that the money offshored is unavailable to governments to support social programs for its citizens.

The audience comments also denote the othering of Ronaldo as a foreign/immigrant and position him as ungrateful. This adds to the moral evaluation of the dodging practices, and connects with and fostering austerity imaginaries that blame and shame particular social groups (especially immigrants) for not contributing enough to society (Jensen, 2014; Jensen & Tyler, 2015):

> The Portuguese man should refill the pension's piggybank by paying the fine . . . (Comment, *La Vanguardia*, 2/12/2016 – SP)

> Even if it were legal, I think that evading the taxes of their big winnings is shameful (. . .). He is an egoist and greedy for not wanting to share anything, not even a dime, with the citizens of the country that have embraced him and made him immensely wealthy.(. . .) The orphans and pensioners of the Virgin Island and Switzerland will be very grateful to him (Comment, *El Mundo*, 13/12/2016 – SP)

In the Spanish press articles and comments, we found several mentions of pensions, poverty, orphans, and widows, pointing to a post-recession scenario in which the welfare state funds have been depleted and impacting most seriously vulnerable citizens. Here, welfare cutbacks are conceptualized as either a consequence of tax evasion and avoidance or a consequence of the economic crisis that, according to media portrayals, "affects everybody evenly" (Oliva & Pérez-Latorre, 2020) but not as a consequence of austerity policies. We also found, however, signs of criticism for the management of the State: "the Tax Office wants this money to do what it likes best: waste money" (comment, *El Mundo*, 26/12/2016) or "The parasitic Spanish Tax Office lives off exhausting Spaniards' money to pay with our money 17 regional governments that we don't need" (comment, *El Mundo*, 26/12/2017).

In Portugal, arguments about the immorality of tax evasion were less frequently expressed. For instance, independent commentator Miguel Sousa Tavares framed tax evasion as "stealing from those who pay taxes: the more they escape taxes, the more those who can't escape will pay" (*SIC*, 5/12/2016). He went on to argue that Portuguese people involved in the scandal – Ronaldo and Mourinho – should pay taxes and "undertake public social action" in the form of charitable donations. This reasoning calls for sympathy with those less well off, and morally defends some benefit brought to the home country by fellow citizens who have done well through football. One audience comment also said "it's because guys like him making millions that don't pay their taxes that we have to pay the huge taxes they ask of us", to add that "(I'm not saying that he evades taxes)" (*DNotícias*, 14/12/2016 – PT).

Some appreciating fans, and the Portuguese in particular, expressed disappointment considering Ronaldo's well-crafted representation. However, a more salient reception from the Portuguese audience was one of empathy. In fact, we found quasi-dismissive and congratulatory reactions for hiding taxes from the government, as a form of identification (Bramall, 2018). There was an evaluation that "every common Portuguese citizen" tries to evade taxes (Hajdu et al., 2018), and "all rich people do it" – or the "unknown" rich people should pay. Furthermore, it is seen as Spain's problem, not Portugal's, as paying those taxes would not benefit the group where the audience member lives. All these factors deflate the scandal, while implicitly expressing a suspicious position regarding the role of the State with the rise of neoliberalism and libertarian values:

> People are just jealous[,] everyone does it[,] if I could I'd do the same thing[,] this man is a role model. Stay strong Cristiano (Comment, *Sábado*, 04/12/2016 – PT)

> Every person/company with income does it ... does anyone doubt that? Go CR7 (Comment, *Sol*, 01/12/2016 – PT)

> He's right if he escapes taxes, thus instead of giving it to the state he does charity and the state should take it from the rich people who won't give water to a poor man. (Comment, *Sol*, 01/12/2016 – PT)

> I can understand that the Spanish will feed this news, but for us Portuguese it's enough. They should talk about Sócrates,(...) now that is real news. (Comment, *Rádio Renascença*, 09/12/2016 – PT)

Charity is another key topic that appeared in both the media and audience comments. On the one hand, the news about the tax evasion scandal appeared next to news about charity events and donations by Ronaldo. As he usually does around Christmas time, in 2016 Ronaldo doubled-up his humanitarian work with children, especially those who are sick. Working with *Save the Children*, "Cristiano Ronaldo makes a donation and sends a moving message to the Syrian children" (e.g. *El Mundo Deportivo*, 23/12/2016); and he won "the prize for best and most–charitable football player" (*El Periódico*, 18/12/20016). Charity is "a hallmark of the established star" and one of the key aspects that legitimize celebrities' wealth by "giving back" while being portrayed as compassionate and caring (Littler, 2008, pp. 238–239). At the same time, charity, as a way of wealth distribution based on individual decision-making and voluntary donations, solidifies the neoliberal regime by appearing to address inequality.

Ronaldo's acts of charity were read in relation to tax evasion and accordance with – or to accentuate – the judgment that columnists and readers already held for him. While charity seems a good alternative to paying taxes for some of the Portuguese audience members, as seen above, some Spanish columnists and readers resent these actions from Ronaldo, as charity not only seems more arbitrary and questionable, but also insincere and even done for publicity – as often pointed in celebrity philanthropy (Van den Bulck, 2018):

> The same star who claims help for Haitian children does not contribute as he really could to these noble causes, because he hid at least €75 million from the tax office in the British Virgin Islands between 2009 and 2014 (*El Mundo*, 05/12/2016 – SP)

> His greed has no limits. On top of that, this Christmas he will have the cheek to donate toys to poor children in some hospital!!! Pay as you should and where you should pay!!!! (comment, *El Mundo*, 7/12/2016 – SP)

Inequality and unfairness

In the talk about the scandal, meanings circulated relating to wider inequality in society, where celebrities, politicians, aristocracy, and other elites are cast against ordinary citizens. Thus, conceptions and perceptions of power in contemporary, mediatized societies were negotiated during the cycle of the scandal. As demonstrated above, shaming was predicated on the football players' (and coaches') high earnings. For Ronaldo, this was accentuated in the revelations of the contracts whose taxes he had hidden through tax dodging, appearing in both Spanish and Portuguese EIC media:

> Contracts' clauses: Ronaldo earns €163 for signing a card (*El Confidencial*, 7/12/2016 – SP)

Moreover, this was articulated with mentions to eccentricity and conspicuous consumption, especially around luxury cars. After Christmas, news reports revealed he bought "a €150,000 Mercedes for Christmas" (*Marca*, 28/12/2016 – SP) or "a flashy car for Christmas" (*El Mundo Deportivo*, 28/12/2016 – SP). Right after the scandal broke, Portuguese influential commentator Miguel Sousa Tavares stated that "You can't understand how, making the money they make – Cristiano has a garage with luxurious cars –, these people can escape taxes" (*SIC*, 05/12/2016 – PT).

This discussion was articulated with how the State treats – through the political, judiciary and economic systems – citizens differently, i.e., unfairly. This is a key question to investigate in the context of discussions about solidarity and fairness, shame or cleverness of practitioners, or shown as the product of a lax state that "permits" these activities to take place with minimal policing or punishment. Especially evident in the Spanish media and audiences, as the story progressed in the judicial process, but likewise with some audience in Portugal, a division was created between "us" and "them." The latter referred to "football players," especially with international origin, or "the rich." Stars are treated with impunity by the State, while ordinary citizens must fulfill their obligations regardless of circumstances or accept penalties.

> It's not just the poor people who should pay, rich people too, and Ronaldo with the kind of money he has, would he need to escape taxes? The law is for everyone, I think!! (Comment, *RTP/Facebook*, 08/12/2016 – PT)

> What is not fair is that the average citizen must pay all their taxes, under threat of being sanctioned if they don't, and the people who earn a lot of money can evade without consequences. It can be Ronaldo, Imanol Arias,[1] the Popular Party … It is inexcusable and the Tax Office must act with severity. We are all the Tax Office and we all must be equal before the law and fulfil our obligations and duties. (Comment, *El Mundo*, 26/12/2017 – SP)

Further evidence of the perception of unequal treatment is how audiences see the State dealing with different celebrities, even football players. In the newspapers published in Barcelona, audiences metaphorically conceptualize the distinction between the "average citizen" and the "elites" through the opposition between Messi and Cristiano. Ronaldo's relationship with football fans has never been easy or affectionate, contrary to his great rival Messi who seems to be universally loved, even after being too caught in a tax scandal and sentenced in 2017. At the same time, the comments reveal the audiences' use of the scandal to negotiate and preserve previous relationship with their preferred celebrity, while resenting that Ronaldo's case was not treated in the exact same way.

> Messi evades €4 million, the Tax Office and the public prosecutor's office refuse to conclude a deal, and he is condemned to 21 months in jail and pays a fine of €50M in fines. Cristiano evades €15M(…) and now the Tax Office wants to reach an agreement, withholds the report and just asks for €30M. Please, somebody explain this to me (Comment, *La Vanguardia*, 02/12/2016 – SP)

Portuguese audiences see the investigation of Ronaldo after the leak as a campaign by the Spanish judiciary system unfairly targeting him. The comment below not only refers to his statute as an immigrant in Spain but also racializes him:

> … You're Portuguese[,] you're 'screwed' … those 'guys' won't let you go (you're the 'black man' of Europe) (Comment, *Rádio Renascença*, 9/12/2016)

After having his agent, Jorge Mendes, initially deny the allegations by stating that they were invented and fabricated, and providing documents contradicting the indictment in Football Leaks (*RTP*, 04/12/2016), Cristiano Ronaldo responded: "If you've got nothing to hide, you've got nothing to fear" (*RTP*, 08/12/2020). A few days later, this escalated to a statement of further victimization and persecution: he declared he felt like an "innocent person imprisoned," "as there are many" wrongly incarcerated in the system (e.g. *Sol*, 13/12/2020). He also expressed personal disappointment in being targeted by such allegations, which is hardly surprising since he often expresses feelings of persecution by people envious of his good fortune and achievements. Through this position, Ronaldo also emphasized a populistic discourse that not only says the State is corrupt or at least arbitrary to prosecute some individuals over others, but also that the judicial system fails citizens in not offering them fairness in treatment and judgment.

Discussion

Ronaldo's tax evasion practices, made public by EIC's Football Leaks, are an exemplary case to understand media portrayals and public views on offshoring practices and taxes in

Southern Europe. This study focused on a case of celebrity malfeasance and showed the missed the opportunities of a celebrity scandal to promote public discussion and debate on social norms and political will regarding taxation, inequality, wealth redistribution, and social justice.

In the discussions about Ronaldo's tax evasion scandal, in both Spanish and Portuguese articles and comments, a traditional definition of taxes, as a mechanism of redistribution of wealth, was fostered and legitimized. Taxes were mostly viewed as necessary and, in the case of celebrity, as a way of celebrities "giving back" the support they receive from audiences and fans, instead of charity. This was the case of our corpus, particularly in the Spanish case. In this imagined model, celebrity and taxes are conceptualized as "tied together," which would keep a system of unequal wealth distribution fundamentally unchanged – but not aggravate it. This owes to "a 'residual' conception of taxation that emphasizes its function as a mechanism of redistributive justice, and, relatedly, a conception of the 'welfare state' which tends not to take account of the intensified marketization of health, education and welfare provision in austerity" (Bramall, 2016, p. 31). So, in this case, we could not find results that pointed to the existence of an "anti-welfare common sense" (Jensen, 2014). Under this view, charity works as a way for celebrities to legitimize their wealth and counteract the unrest stirred up by their high earnings and luxurious consumption (Van den Bulck, 2018), as well as to restore their image – but not as a valid way to sustain welfare.

A concurrent view, mostly present in comments rather than the media, accepted tax avoidance or evasion as a cultural norm, especially from Portuguese audiences (Van den Bulck & Claessens, 2013a); or even argued in favor of such practice out of a perception of the welfare state as "immoderate," as not allocating resources properly and efficiently, especially from Spanish audience members. Under this view, charity is favored over welfare – and this constitutes another way to foster the delegitimization of the welfare state under neoliberalism (which favors individualized solutions). This view is also acceptive of Ronaldo's conspicuous consumption symbolized by his car collection.

As Boudana found (2014), the news discourse reporting in the country where the malfeasance occurred, and that in the country of origin of the perpetrator, were different. This will set the forms of "identification" and "disidentification" (Bramall, 2018) with Ronaldo expressed by the audience through their comments. Spanish articles expressed a profound unrest and disillusionment with Spanish institutions and a perception of Spain as an unequal society and continued a previous discussion on the role of football in particular in the moral economy of taxation. Comments from Spain were more often ardently negative toward Ronaldo, othering him as immigrant, as ungrateful for what he received from playing football in the country for some years. The Portuguese media reporting resulted in a more individualistic and moralistic frame, where Ronaldo and his supporters received more space for a restoration, with a pose of transparency through document proofs and the "nothing to hide" statement. Audiences expressed more sympathy, whether in the form of him "being smart like us," a victim, or a hero untouched by a minor act (Bramall, 2018). This does not translate that audiences follow the predominant media frame promoted – as media work was also put into question– but that audience reactions to scandal vary according to the previous relationship with the celebrity (Tiger, 2013; Van den Bulck & Claessens, 2013a, 2013b) and that, in a cross-national comparison, the cultural pertaining of the celebrity strongly weighs in the audiences' evaluation. The close, yet rival, relationship between neighbor countries Portugal and Spain should help to explain this tension.

Our study contributes to the scholarship on celebrity and taxation imaginaries as seen through audiences' discussions in a comparative manner, while also empirically investigating Bramall's (2018) thesis that "tax shaming" strategies are ineffective and "powerless" to make change on tax reform. In the Ronaldo's case of tax dodging, we have seen how some comments show an emotional connection to the football player. Moreover, several journalists and audience members talk *as* taxpayers. As Bramall argues, "the taxpayer identity is not a progressive one" and its meaning and significance "is produced in opposition to both the undeserving, welfare-claiming, non-contributive poor and a 'free-riding super rich' elite" (2018, pp. 11, 14). In the Spanish case, Ronaldo embodies this tension, since he is portrayed as *both* a member of the economic elite, and as an immigrant that has stolen from Spaniards. In both cases, stories about Ronaldo's tax evasion connects with several anxieties and tensions of the Southern European societies regarding fiscal inefficiency, inequality, and corruption, showing a profound disillusionment with institutions, but, at the same time, a profound longing for equality.

Note

1. A well-known Spanish actor that appeared in the Panama Papers scandal and who is in 2020 under trial for tax evasion.

Disclosure statement

No potential conflict of interest was reported by the author(s).

ORCID

Ana Jorge http://orcid.org/0000-0002-4069-6212

References

Aguiar, L. L. M., & Noiseux, Y. (2018). Roll-against neoliberalism and labour organizing in the post-2008 crisis. In K. Ward, A. Jonas, B. Miller, & D. Wilson (Eds.), *The Routledge handbook on spaces of urban politics* (pp. 232–244). New York: Routledge.

Allen, K., Mendick, H., Harvey, L., & Ahmad, A. (2015). Welfare queens, thrifty housewives, and do-it-all mums. *Feminist Media Studies*, 15(6), 907–925. doi:10.1080/14680777.2015.1062992

Alonso, L. E., Fernández Rodríguez, C. J., & Ibáñez Rojo, R. (2011). Del consumismo a la culpabilidad: En torno a los efectos disciplinarios de la crisis económica. *Política y Sociedad*, 48(2), 353–379. doi:10.5209/rev_POSO.2011.v48.n2.8

Andrews, D. L., & Jackson, S. J. (Eds.). (2002). *Sport stars: The cultural politics of sporting celebrity*. London: Routledge.

Badenhausen, K. (2016, February 23). Cristiano Ronaldo is first athlete with 200 million social media followers. *Forbes*. Retrieved from https://www.forbes.com/sites/kurtbadenhausen/2016/02/23/cristiano-ronaldo-is-the-first-athlete-with-200-million-social-media-followers/

Bar-On, T. (2014). *The world through Soccer: The cultural impact of a global sport*. Lanham: Rowman & Littlefield.

Boudana, S. (2014). Shaming rituals in the age of global media: How DSK's perp walk generated estrangement. *European Journal of Communication*, 29(1), 50–67. doi:10.1177/0267323113509361

Bramall, R. (2013). *The cultural politics of austerity: Past and present in austere times*. Basingstoke: Palgrave Macmillan.

Bramall, R. (2016). Tax justice in Austerity: Logics, residues and attachments. *New Formations*, 87(87), 29–46. doi:10.3898/NEWF.87.2.2016

Bramall, R. (2018). A 'powerful weapon'? Tax, avoidance, and the politics of celebrity shaming. *Celebrity Studies*, 9(1), 34–52. doi:10.1080/19392397.2017.1325762

Corbin, J., & Strauss, A. L. (2008). *Basics of qualitative research*. Thousand Oaks, CA: SAGE.

Cross, S., & Littler, J. (2010). Celebrity and Schadenfreude: The cultural economy of fame in freefall. *Cultural Studies*, 24(3), 395–417. doi:10.1080/09502381003750344

Dyer, R. (1979). *Stars*. London: BFI.

Fernandez, R., & Wigger, A. (2016). Lehman brothers in the Dutch offshore financial centre: The role of shadow banking in increasing leverage and facilitating debt. *Economy and Society*, 45(3–4), 407–430. doi:10.1080/03085147.2016.1264167

Fine, G. A. (2019). Moral cultures, reputation work, and the politics of scandal. *Annual Review of Sociology*, 45(1), 247–264. doi:10.1146/annurev-soc-073018-022649

Fraser, N. (1992). Sex, lies, and the public sphere: Some reflections on the confirmation of Clarence Thomas. *Critical Inquiry*, 18(3), 595–612. doi:10.1086/448646

Gamson, W. A., & Sifry, M. L. (2013). The# occupy movement: An introduction. *The Sociological Quarterly*, 54(2), 159–163. doi:10.1111/tsq.12026

Geeter, D. (2018, June 15). The business of being Cristiano Ronaldo. *CNBC*. Retrieved from https://www.cnbc.com/2018/06/15/cristiano-ronaldo-world-cup-football-soccer-michael-jordan-real-madrid.html

Girard, R. (1986). *The Scapegoat*. Baltimore: Johns Hopkins University Press.

Greenburg, Z. O. (2016, July 11). Celeb 100: The world's highest-paid celebrities of 2016. *Forbes*. Retrieved from https://www.forbes.com/sites/zackomalleygreenburg/2016/07/11/celeb-100-the-worlds-highest-paid-celebrities-of-2016/.

Hajdu, M., Pápay, B., Szántó, Z., & Tóth, I. J. (2018). Content analysis of corruption coverage: Cross-national differences and commonalities. *European Journal of Communication*,33(1), 7–21. https://doi.org/10.1177/0267323117750673

Hall, S., & O'Shea, A. (2013). Common-sense neoliberalism. *Soundings, 55*(55), 9–25. doi:10.3898/136266213809450194

Harvey, D. (2006). *Spaces of global capitalism: Towards a theory of uneven geographical development.* London and New York: Verso.

Hindman, E. B., & Thomas, R. J. (2014). When old and new media collide: The case of WikiLeaks. *New Media & Society, 16*(4), 541–558. doi:10.1177/1461444813489504

Holmes, S. (2005). 'Off-guard, unkempt, unready'?: Deconstructing contemporary celebrity in heat Magazine. *Continuum: Journal of Media & Cultural Studies, 19*(1), 21–38. https://doi.org/10.1080/1030431052000336270

Jacobsson, K., & Löfmarck, E. (2008). A sociology of scandal and moral transgression: The Swedish 'nannygate' scandal. *Acta Sociologica, 51*(3), 203–216. doi:10.1177/0001699308094166

Jensen, T. (2014). Welfare commonsense, poverty porn and doxosophy. *Sociological Research Online, 19*(3), 277–283. doi:10.5153/sro.3441

Jensen, T., & Tyler, I. (2015). 'Benefits broods': The cultural and political crafting of anti-welfare commonsense. *Critical Social Policy, 35*(4), 470–491. doi:10.1177/0261018315600835

Jorge, A. (2015). 'Cristiano Ronaldo is cheap chic, twilight actors are special': Young audiences of celebrities, class and locality. *Celebrity Studies, 6*(1), 39–53. doi:10.1080/19392397.2015.995467

Littler, J. (2004). Making fame ordinary: Intimacy, reflexivity, and 'keeping it real'. *Mediactive, 2*, 8–25.

Littler, J. (2008). "I feel your pain": Cosmopolitan charity and the public fashioning of the celebrity soul. *Social Semiotics, 18*(2), 237–251. doi:10.1080/10350330802002416

Littler, J. (2013). Meritocracy as plutocracy: The marketising of 'equality' under neoliberalism. *New Formations, 80–81*(80), 52–72. doi:10.3898/NewF.80/81.03.2013

Lovett, S. (2016, December 12). Ballon d'Or: Cristiano Ronaldo wins fourth award after historic year with real Madrid and Portugal. *Independent.* Retrieved from https://www.independent.co.uk/sport/football/international/ballon-dor-winner-cristiano-ronaldo-how-many-times-won-record-a7470741.html

Lull, J., & Hinerman, S. (1997). *Media scandals: Morality and desire in the popular culture marketplace.* New York: Columbia University Press.

Mendick, H., Allen, K., & Harvey, L. (2015). 'We can get everything we want if we try hard': Young people, celebrity, hard work. *British Journal of Educational Studies, 63*(2), 161–178. doi:10.1080/00071005.2014.1002382

Nunn, H., & Biressi, A. (2010). 'A trust betrayed': Celebrity and the work of emotion. *Celebrity Studies, 1*(1), 49–64. doi:10.1080/19392390903519065

Oliva, M., & Pérez-Latorre, Ó. (2020). 'Celebrities also suffer from the economic crisis': Broke celebrities and neoliberal narratives from Spain's great recession. *Celebrity Studies, 11*(2), 237–256. doi:10.1080/19392397.2018.1557533

Palan, R., Murphy, R., & Chavagneux, C. (2010). *Tax havens: How globalization really works.* Ithaca, NY: Cornell University Press.

Piketty, T. (2014). *Capital in the 21st century.* Cambridge, MA and London: Harvard University Press.

Pinedo, E. (2018, June 15). Soccer: Real Madrid's Ronaldo reaches deal with Spanish tax authorities–Source. *Reuters.* Retrieved from https://in.reuters.com/article/soccer-taxation-ronaldo/soccer-real-madrids-ronaldo-reaches-deal-with-spanish-tax-authorities-source-idINKBN1JB1LL

Rojek, C. (2001). *Celebrity.* London: Reaktion Books.

Sampedro, V., López-Ferrández, F. J., & Carretero, Á. (2018). Leaks-based journalism and media scandals: From official sources to the networked fourth estate? *European Journal of Communication, 33*(3), 255–270. doi:10.1177/0267323118763907

Schilling, C., & Mellor, P. A. (2015). For a sociology of deceit: Double identities, interested actions and situational logics of opportunities. *Sociology, 49*(4), 607–623. doi:10.1177/0038038514546661

Tiger, R. (2013). Celebrity drug scandals, media double standards. *Contexts, 12*(4), 36–41. doi:10.1177/1536504213511214

Urry, J. (2014). *Offshoring.* Cambridge: Polity Press.

Van den Bulck, H. (2018). *Celebrity philanthropy and activism: Mediated interventions in the global public sphere.* Abingdon, UK: Routledge.

Van den Bulck, H., & Claessens, N. (2013a). Guess who Tiger is having sex with now? Celebrity sex and the framing of the moral high ground. *Celebrity Studies*, *4*(1), 46-57. doi:10.1080/19392397.2012.750110

Van den Bulck, H., & Claessens, N. (2013b). Celebrity suicide and the search for the moral high ground: Comparing frames in media and audience discussions of the death of a flemish celebrity. *Critical Studies in Media Communication*, *30*(1), 69-84. doi:10.1080/15295036.2011.645496

Van den Bulck, H., & Claessens, N. (2014). Of local and global fame: A comparative analysis of news items and audience reactions on celebrity news websites people, heat, and HLN. *Journalism*, *15*(2), 218-236. doi:10.1177/1464884913488725

Whannel, G. (2005). *Media sport stars: Masculinities and moralities*. London and New York: Routledge.

Woodall, A. (2018). Media capture in the era of megaleaks. *Journalism*, *19*(8), 1182-1195. doi:10.1177/1464884917725166

Speaking for the youth, speaking for the planet: Greta Thunberg and the representational politics of eco-celebrity

Patrick D. Murphy

ABSTRACT
Greta Thunberg is the world's best-known environmental activist. She has been covered by the international press, featured on television talk shows, presented in music videos, and been the object of social media memes – a visibility that has made her a global celebrity. But unlike other public figures whose stardom is attached to, rather than driven by environmental activism, Thunberg's eco-celebrity is anchored to her role in starting a *global* climate movement. Her activism is youth-centric and her eco-politics highly confrontational. Focusing on English language media from around the world, this essay explores how Thunberg's rise to global eco-celebrity has been media-centric while still being remarkably resistant to co-optation within the broader terrain of climate change politics. Emphasis is placed on how Thunberg has used her celebrity status to take aim at the material realities and social practices that have caused the climate crisis, and push for radical and immediate change.

Greta Thunberg is perhaps the world's best-known environmental activist. Not only was she named *Time Magazine*'s 2019 "Person of the Year," but she has been covered by the international press, featured on talk shows, presented in music videos, and been the object of social media memes. This visibility that has made her an international celebrity, a status has been shaped and framed via the recognition she's received from other public figures and interest groups, earning praise from presidents, royalty and Hollywood stars, hanging out with fellow environmental activist Vandana Shiva, and marching with First Nations Indigenous peoples. She's even been on the receiving end of scornful tweets by former US President Donald Trump. But unlike other public figures whose stardom was attached to, rather than driven by environmental activism (e.g., Leonardo DiCaprio, Gisele Bündchen, Sting), Thunberg's rise as an eco-celebrity is tied directly to her role in starting *Skolstrejk för Klimatet* (School Strike for Climate) – a global, youth-based climate movement that generated the largest environmental demonstrations in human history.

In this essay, I argue that Thunberg is the "ideal performer" (Chouliaraki, 2013) for a youth-centered climate movement in that her meteoric rise to global eco-celebrity has been media-centric while still being remarkably resistant to co-optation within the broader terrain of climate change politics. Indeed, in many ways she represents a new kind of celebrity conservationist who breaks from the individualistic and promotional hypocrisies typical of most eco-celebrities even as she is enmeshed in the same system of representational politics that create them. The 18-year-old Swede's activism is unabashedly youth-centric, and she speaks for the Earth in climate science-driven terms. Her eco-politics are squarely focused on taking aim at the material realities and social practices that have caused the climate crisis, and the strikes are a mechanism to push for radical and immediate change. She rejects the prevailing economic order and directly confronts those who represent it, explicitly holding the older generation responsible for its failure to move the world toward low carbon societies despite having recognized the scope and depth of global warming.

Focusing on the "discursive intertextual chains" (Fairclough, 1995) circulated by English language news and current affairs media from around the world, I explore how Thunberg has achieved global celebrity status despite being what *Time* magazine described as "an ordinary teenage girl." Emphasis is placed on how her celebrity is a product of the dialectical and constitutive nature of these dynamic mediascapes; that is, how media coverage across a range of platforms has transformed and been embedded in subsequent texts, elevating her as an eco-celebrity pushing for radical environmental reform even as many prominent voices and powerful media institutions have tried to diminish her status. Within this interpretive framework, attention is also given to Thunberg's tactical and strategic use of media, and how – deliberately or not – these have rendered her as a "non–nation state actor" (Boykoff & Goodman, 2009) giving her a prominent place in the public conversation about climate change. This includes how, through coverage of her international speeches and travel, statements by and relationships with other public figures, and her promotion of the voices of other climate change activists, Thunberg's combination of confrontational rhetoric, committed activism, lifestyles choices and public persona (e.g., the "ordinary school girl" of humble origins with Asperger's syndrome), connects her to some of the more foundational tropes and premises of environmentalism (apocalypticism, ecological jeremiad, importance of science).

Celebrities, environmentalism and media representation

In the seminal book, *Celebrity and the environment*, Brockington (2009) asserts that on a global scale one of the main reasons that we have seen the rise of environmental celebrities is because their emergence is tied to the growth of conservationism around world at the same time as the exponential expansion of corporate capitalism. Within this context, commercial media serve as discourse rendering institutions, promoting "the pursuit if wasteful cultural practices and ecologically unsustainable lifestyles" even as they present audiences with "environmentally progressive themes" (Murphy, 2017). These discursive arrangements can foster a sense that reacting to climate change is a question of individualized responses – e.g., adopting a "consumer citizen" approach to environmental citizenship (Boykoff, Goodman, & Curtis, 2010, pp. 138-139). In essence, the public is encouraged to save the whales even as it is invited to eat all of the fish. As highly visible actors within these consumer-centered mediascapes, celebrity environmentalists are often merely commodified extensions of commercial conservation strategies. As Meister (2015) puts it, celebrities "do not try to save the world, but rather remake it by participating in global production, circulation and consumption" (p. 284). This has led to charges of hypocrisy, which is at its core, "an accusation of inconsistency of celebrity endorsed environmentalism and the structural nature of neoliberal economic systems" (p. 285).

To appreciate this inconsistent and compromised role, Craig (2019) contends that celebrity must be understood as a convergence of representational and promotional power of the media, and is expressed in two ways. First, celebrities derive representational power through textual (images and stories) and social (relationship to others, e.g., audiences and publics) articulations. These articulations "embody and give public expression to values, styles, and pleasures" (p. 779). Second, as products of media and promotional industries, celebrities are commodities, as well as "agents in the production of a commercial culture that is increasingly oriented around promotion" (p. 779). In fact, most activist celebrities now deliberately invest in this commodification, "branding" their activism through integrated, multiplatform media models that can involve a combination of campaigns, media events, films or TV programs they produce, press coverage they seek, websites they create, and social media they use (Huggan, 2013; Rojek, 2012). This investment is designed to connect and even interact with, the public. Celebrities thus perform functions of advocacy while seeking legitimacy, allowing them to "capture the embodiment of a concern about a certain issue" (Craig, 2019, p. 780).

Be the cause environmental or other, this connection to "concern" is tied to the rise of celebrity humanitarianism, which Chouliaraki (2013) observes is a relatively recent development involving shifting celebrity from a "powerless elite" to an official communication strategy of government and non-governmental organizations and major private initiatives. According to Chouliaraki, celebrity humanitarianism's elevated place within the global public sphere has unfolded through three interrelated dynamics: 1) The decline of public trust in bureaucratic institutions, 2) The expansion of the fields of social marketing and show business into politics, and 3) The shifting policy priorities in humanitarian institutions toward corporate models of communication (p.78). From this (new) position of power, celebrities are imbued with the expertise to articulate moral discourses that "massively touch our hearts and minds" (p. 79). Nevertheless, it is through this elevated status of elite power – e.g., "the ideal performer" – that celebrity also "brings into focus the inherent theatricality of humanitarianism as an arrangement of separation between those who watch at a distance and those who act" (Chouliaraki, 2013, p. 80). In many cases, this involves the celebrity acting as a "bridge between a (Western) audience and a faraway tragedy" (de Waal, 2008 p. 44), implicating an underlying connection to Eurocentric imaginaries (Shohat & Stam, 1994).

With regard to environmentalism, this position of performative power is important to understand. First, because celebrities have become significant "non-nation state figures in the discursive, material and media politics surrounding climate change" they are much more than just "distractions" and possess real power (Boykoff & Goodman, 2009, p. 396). Second, as a form of representational politics, celebrity endorsement of environmental causes demonstrates "the power of representations of nature and the authority of representation over experience" (Brockington, 2008, p. 553). That is, celebrities are granted the power to speak for nature, or at least a vision of a fragile ecosystem or environmental cause that they take up as their own. This allows them to be associated with goals that are not necessarily rooted in people's everyday realities but rather their environmental imagination.

There is, of course, a long list of popular culture celebrities from around the world that scholars can consider when analyzing eco-celebrity (e.g., Leonardo DiCaprio, Gisele

Bündchen, Cate Blanchett, Amitabh Bachchan, Jackie Chan). What of these "celanthropists"–the celebrity who voluntary participates in humanitarian fundraising, publicity awareness and charity building (Rojek, 2012, p. 67) – have in common is that all have leveraged the social capital of their celebrity to increase the visibility and importance of an environmental issue and/or serve as the voice of an environmental advocacy group. Yet this representational privilege has also left them vulnerable to criticism, particularly along the lines of their "inauthenticity" (e.g., not being an expert) or the "constructedness" of their environmental politics (Turner, 2016). As Turner (2016) asserts, the celanthropists is almost always a compromised figure, as their motives are suspect and cause seen as self-serving even if philanthropic, so their commitment to or understanding of a cause treated with skepticism (p. 812). In this respect celebrity power has its limits as it is defined in part by the fact that celanthropists are sometimes seen as "unwelcomed interventionists" (p. 813).

What makes Greta Thunberg different from "A-list" celanthropists is that she did not leverage a preexisting status as celebrity to confront a particular environmental problem or align herself with a particular group. Rather, her ascent to celebrity has been the direct result of her environmental activism. She is what scholars have labeled a "celebrity conservationist" (Brockington, 2008, 2009; Huggan, 2013) and can be understood more in the tradition of Jacque-Yves Cousteau or David Attenborough than DiCaprio or Bündchen. But she is also fundamentally different from these examples in several important ways. First, contrary to the celebrity conservationists' practice of giving "their audiences the satisfaction of watching them actually being there in real wild places and interacting with real wildlife" (Brockington, 2008, p. 562), Thunberg's appeal is derived from her Friday climate strikes in front of city hall, confrontational speeches at international summits, sober television studio interviews, or online grappling with critics. Second, rather than limiting her celebrity power, Thunberg's capacity to attract derision, especially from powerful figures, has actually fueled her celebrity status. Through these two distinctions she has developed an environmental politics of performance *for* the natural world, rather than *in* the natural world.

The celebrity who wasn't

One of the defining aspects of Greta Thunberg's rise to eco-celebrity is how it has been anchored in media narratives of how she is ordinary yet transformative. The BBC News wrote, "Greta Thunberg is a Swedish teenager who skipped school and inspired an international movement to flight climate change." In a *The Rolling Stone* feature story, Thunberg is framed by "How one Swedish teenager armed with a homemade sign ignited a crusade and became the leader of a movement" (Rodrick, 2020). In *Wired* magazine she is described as a "messiah with a side braid" (Ellis, 2019). *Forbes* offered, "(b)efore she became a household name, the teenager started a school strike that has now lasted more than 2 years. She wasn't part of any lobbying group and wasn't a mouthpiece for any professional organization at the time. She was just a kid with an idea" (Brandon, 2020). And in *Time*, Thunberg is presented as "an ordinary teenage girl who, in summoning the courage to speak truth to power, became the icon of a generation" (Alter, Haynes, & Worland, 2019). These renderings of her rise to celebrity conservationist juxtapose the simple schoolgirl origins with the exceptionalism of her ascent. Thunberg's journey is thus a central feature of her representational power, giving her activism "authentic" resonance by grounding it in humble origins.

Most mainstream media accounts trace that journey back to an environmental awakening triggered through an experience at school. The condensed version of her story, as presented rather cryptically by Britain's *The Sunday Times* reads like a film trailer:

> A girl who would be born in Sweden in 2003; who would first hear about climate change when she was eight; who would find this revelation so horrifying that she would descend into a yearlong depression; who would be diagnosed with Asperger's syndrome; who would renounce air travel and overconsumption and animal products; who would leave school to strike outside the Swedish parliament to demand more political action; and who has now, just one year later, become one of the most powerful environmental activists in the world. (Hartford, 2019)

In a very short period of time, Greta's *Skolstrejk för klimatet* went from a party of one (Thunberg) to school strikes around Europe, then to tens of thousands around the world. By September 2019 her strikes had grown exponentially, generating what has been estimated to be the largest environmental demonstrations in human history (Barclay & Resnick, 2019). Unlike most environmental activists, Greta did not adhere to the notion that we are all responsible for the climate crisis. Rather, she blames the older generation for its inaction and complicity, and the strikes were designed to call out this inaction while motivating other youth to confront the existential threat of climate change.

Reportedly, the idea to strike was inspired by the Parkland students, who walked out of school in protest of Florida gun laws that enabled a massacre at their school (Watts, 2019). Parkland students also presented Thunberg with an example for using social media to draw attention to a cause (Ellis, 2019). As developed further below, she has built on this blueprint and expanded participation in her climate strike movement "Fridays for Future" through a combination of continuing activism, accessibility to the press, focus on and repetition of core facts and ideas, skillful use of media to hold the powerful accountable, making the right friends (and enemies), ecocentric lifestyle choices, and sharing the spotlight with others.

Thunberg and the global media

A survey of Thunberg's place within today's global media landscape is a study in not only representation politics and practices, but of the interlaced and mutually constitutive logics of journalism, commercial entertainment, and social media. In addition to being selected as *Time's* 2019 Person of the Year, she has been covered by the international press (e.g., CNN, Fox News, Al Jazeera, NPR, *The Times of India*, *The South African*, *The Jakarta Post*, *The Japan Times*, *The Portugal News*, *The Guardian*), invited to highly rated talk shows (e.g., *Ellen*, *The Daily Show with Trevor Noah*), featured on everything from *Democracy Now!* to *Access Hollywood*, and even landed on the covers of the *Wired* and British *GQ*. She's also inspired a Paris fashion week, co-wrote a song about climate change with the band The 1975, and starred as a crystal ball reading psychic in Pearl Jam's music video about climate change, *Retrograde*. Most recently, the BBC announced the creation of a new TV series about climate change activism featuring Thunberg.

Within this international mediascape, much has been made of Greta's global travel and modes of transportation. Her trips by train and subway use have received ample coverage, but it was her zero emissions journey via the high-tech yacht *La Vagabonde* across the

Atlantic and back again that received the most attention (e.g., Germanos, 2019; *The Portugal News*, 2019). She also famously borrowed a Tesla from Arnold Schwarzenegger to drive to across the US (Bryant, 2019). On *The Daily Show*, Thunberg spoke about her decision to adopt eco-conscious travel: "I have, since a few years, stopped flying because of the enormous impact that aviation has on the climate. And to make a stand. I am one of the very few people in the world who can actually do such a trip, so I thought, why not?" (*The Daily Show*, 2019). Other eco-warrior celebrities have received scrutiny for their travels, such as Al Gore and Leonardo DiCaprio, both of whom were criticized for the hypocrisy of using air travel to attend climate summits where progressive policies to curb carbon outputs were discussed. Anticipating this kind of surveillance, Thunberg has very consciously modeled low emissions travel, a decision that been credited with creating the "Greta Effect" – a no-fly movement that has inspired individuals and even businesses to establish carbon offset practices (The Greta Thunberg Effect, 2019).

Thunberg's sensitivity to issues of voice and context has become one of the defining aspects of her profile, and in 2020 led to a wave of articles about "the other" youth environmental activists. In what could be called "the other Greta Effect," CNN, ABC News, BBC News Mundo, *The Guardian*, and *National Geographic* have all featured stories about different young environmental activists from around the globe, many of whom have been working for change long before Greta. This sudden interest was triggered after Uganda environmental activism Vanessa Nakate, the only black person and only African in a photo shoot, was cropped out of an AP Press photo which showed only the four white activists, including Thunberg (Branchereau, 2020). Not long afterward Thunberg held a press conference at the Greenpeace Sweden office featuring fellow eco-activists from Kenya, Uganda and South Africa to address the invisibility of African climate activists. To extend her efforts to cultivate a more diverse, global approach to climate crisis coverage by the press, Thunberg also developed a web series, Talks for Future (#TalksForFuture!) to recognize the work of youth climate activists from the Global South and indigenous communities. Streamed live on Fridays via Instagram and Facebook, and archived on YouTube, these "international webinars" have already tackled issues ranging from indigenous environmental rights and climate change's impact on rising seas – topics that get fleeting attention by the mainstream press.

All of this coverage has taken place in a period of just over 2 years.

Greta's "superpower" and the climate crisis

In addition to the exponential force of these intertextual chains and activities, one of the most important reasons that Greta has excelled in the media spotlight is that she has an exceptional capacity to remain focused. Indeed, a characteristic of Thunberg's public persona commented on by journalists is her extraordinary ability to stay on point when others attempt flattery or to personalize her crusade. *Rolling Stone* writer Stephen Rodrick observed that, when a prominent magazine editor asked her about how "she dealt with all the haters," Greta responded by saying "I would like to say something that I think people need to know more than how I deal with haters," and then launched into "details from the Intergovernmental Panel on Climate Change's latest report" (Rodrick, 2020)

Greta has Asperger's syndrome, which she self-describes as a "superpower" that allows her to "think differently." According to *Time*, "she doesn't operate on the same emotional register as many of the people she meets. She dislikes crowds; ignores small talk; and speaks in direct, uncomplicated sentences. She cannot be flattered or distracted. She is not impressed by other people's celebrity, nor does she seem to have interest in her own growing fame" (Alter, Haynes, & Worland, 2020). *The Guardian* columnist Jonathan Watts (2019) asserts that Thunberg has "weaponized" this superpower for meetings with political leaders and billionaire entrepreneurs, which is given form via her capacity to put things into immediate, apocalyptic terms. In her speech at the UN Climate Action Summit in New York City, she said, "People are suffering. People are dying. Entire ecosystems are collapsing. We are in the beginning of a mass extinction, and all you can talk about is money and fairy tales of eternal economic growth. How dare you!" She echoed this sentiment during *The Daily Show* interview, albeit in a gentler yet no less urgent way: "But (people) don't understand how severe this crisis actually is . . . . We are right now in the beginning of a sixth mass extinction, and people don't know these things."

Thunberg's evocation of tropes of "extinction," "collapse," and "climate crisis" (over "climate change") in her public addresses and interviews are an effective means through which to evoke the cultural resonance of environmental apocalypticism. Apocalypticism is grounded in "sensibilities of loss, fear, and imaginings of doom" (Lewis, 2012, p. 13), and has long been a defining metaphor in mainstream environmentalism, persisting today in a broad range of commercial entertainment and popular culture around the world (Branston, 2016; Garrard, 2004). Greta's deployment of this rhetorical tool kit is a means to push back on frames that lack sufficient urgency or implicitly support the existing economic and political status quo – something that she clearly sees as untenable.

Complementary to her use of apocalyptic tropes, and one of her primary strategies for having her message heard about the climate crisis is repetition. "Where others speak the language of hope, Thunberg repeats the unassailable science: Oceans will rise. Cities will flood. Millions of people will suffer" (Alter, Haynes, & Worland, 2019). She has repeated on many occasions that the climate change crisis is not treated as a crisis, and she is especially impatient with narratives that present it as solvable via convenient adjustments tied to current models of growth and sustainability. For instance, in a recent interview on *The Late Show with Steve Colbert,* Colbert asked her about why she and other activists had decided to publish an open letter to EU leaders, who had consistently failed to address climate change in their future economic plans. She responded,

> To tell them . . . you need to stop pretending that we can solve this within today's system, and you need to start treating the climate crisis like a crisis, because if we don't treat it like a crisis, we won't be able to solve it . . . And to say to them that we are no longer going to play your game on your terms, because this is crisis, and this is a matter of life and death for so many people (Brandon, 2020).

In addition to her rhetorical skills, Thunberg has become very adept at using different media platforms to magnify her message and manage her image. She's used Facebook, Instagram, and Twitter to post photos of herself at Standing Rock Reservation (North Dakota), with other teen climate activists, with rescue dogs, etc. She's also trolled critics, advocated for veganism, and encouraged followers to sign environmental petitions and support social justice causes.

Not surprisingly she is also often the object of material echoed through social media. *Wired* wrote, "she makes faces that beg to be memed" (Ellis, 2019). Case in point is the now famous "stare down" video of her looking at the climate change denier Donald Trump while he passes her at the United Nations in New York on the morning on the morning of Sept. 23, 2019. The video, which immediately went viral, was describe by *The New York Times Magazine* as, "a complete narrative, a story told so deftly – with such faithfulness to Aristotelian dramatic principles and so sure a command of cinematic clichés – that it's hard to believe that it wasn't cooked up in Hollywood" (Rosen, 2019).

Clips from the video have become a social media meme, with many observers projecting an underlying battle of morality, juxtaposing the small but mighty defender of the planet against the lumbering monstrosity of the status quo who is committed to the limitless pillaging of the earth. The meme also produced slogans like "Make America Greta Again" (Prance, 2019), which subsequently became the title of a *Wired* documentary about Greta. Other Greta memes include, "How dare you!" "I want you to panic," and "Our house is on fire" – lines from her public addresses at the UN, World Economic Forum and elsewhere, the last of these which was produced as a commercial by Fridays for Future featuring a family ignoring their home going up in flames as they blindly attend to their daily routine (Fridays for Future, 2020). One Thunberg meme even casts her as a time traveler who's trying to save the planet (Common Dreams, 2019), a story that was picked up by the TV gossip program *Access Hollywood*.

In addition to this digital presence, Thunberg has also used legacy media to continue her activism into the pandemic, and even expose hypocrisy. During a Swedish radio broadcast in June 2020 she complained about how high-ranking figures have tried to earn points with an eco-curious public by seeking photo opts with her at public events.

> Presidents, prime ministers, kings and princesses came and wanted to talk to me. They saw me and suddenly saw the chance that they could take a photo with me for their Instagram account . . . . It seemed as if they had forgotten for a moment to be ashamed that their generation had let future generations down. (*The Guardian*, June 27, 2020)

Through this apparent refusal to fall prey to her own celebrity and lose focus, she has also been largely effective in using mainstream media opportunities and social media tools to stay with key talking points and direct attention to the climate crisis. This combination of media savvy and narrative focus is important because it has allowed her cultivate a message that is consistently in line with "Change the system, not the climate" calls that reverberate in most youth-based climate activism, targeting business as usual economic growth and related social policies (O'Brien, Selboe, & Hayward, 2018). As such, Thunberg departs from the kind of promotional exercises that typically define celebrity endorsements as a matter of impression management (e.g., a celebrity's narrow association with a safe issue that has corporate backing) (Brockington, 2009). Yet neither is the "epideictic role" (the articulation of society's moral and ethical beliefs) (Meister, 2015, p. 286) that she plays anchored to her proximity to the nature world. Rather, it is defined through her moral outrage at society's environmental inaction, particularly in generational terms.

Celebrity endorsements and critics

Thunberg's capacity to steer the narrative about her activism does not mean that she is not also implicated in impression management. In fact, she is deeply invested in it, and based on her social media activities, quite deliberate about how she goes about cultivating her image.

Her celebrity endorsers include a diverse international mix, from Leonardo DiCaprio to Malala Yousafzai to the Pope. Significantly, Greta has also been endorsed and even defended by other famous eco-activists and ecologically minded politicians, as well as embraced by environmental movements such as Extinction Rebellion in the UK and proponents of The Green New Deal in the US. These associations underscore that a key aspect of the representational power of her celebrity is her association with other celebrities (Craig, 2019), as these associations have helped amplify her message, broaden her public, and in many ways, serve as a barometer of her impact.

One of the more interesting dynamics in these celebrity endorsement exercises is how Greta has caused action and reflection by even some of the world's most established environmental activists. Channeling Thunberg's success in mobilizing teens to participate in her *Skolstrejk för klimatet*, climate change author and activist Bill McKibben challenged a crowd comprised of adults to take similar action: "It was our parents' and grandparents' generation who faced the crisis of fascism in Europe. We are in an existential emergency of the same kind, so staying away from work for a day and organizing is not too much to ask" (Green, 2019). Arguably the greatest praise came from climate guru Al Gore, who in an interview for the *Rolling Stone* feature story about Thunberg, reflected,

> The phrase 'A little child shall lead them' has come to mind more than once. She said to the assembled world leaders, 'You say you understand the science, but I don't believe you. Because if you did and then you continue to act as you do, that would mean you're evil. And I don't believe that.' Wow. There have been other times in human history when the moment a morally-based social movement reached the tipping point was the moment when the younger generation made it their own. Here we are. (Rodrick, 2020)

Gore's framing of Thunberg in biblical terms elevates her to jeremiadic status, underscoring her resonance even among the high priests of environmentalism. More broadly, that celebrity activists and activist celebrities alike admire, support and even emulate Greta provides her with immense cultural currency in the public sphere, further legitimizing and magnifying her status along the lines of celebrity representational politics described earlier (e.g., values, styles, pleasures) (Craig, 2019; see also Chouliaraki, 2013; Huggan, 2013). Thunberg has embraced these endorsements and used the exposure to keep the media focused on the climate crisis. Yet her interactions with the celebrity activists and activist celebrities have also caused some to reassert their own eco-activism.

Possibly even more indicative of her growing celebrity influence has been her capacity to collect numerous high-powered critics in a very short period of time. These include, more broadly, the conservative press, and more specifically, former US President Donald Trump, Russian President Vladimir Putin, Brazil President Jair Bolsonaro, and a host of other politicians and pundits. Among these her motives have been suspect and, as Turner (2016) has observed that is often the case with celebrities, her activities framed as unwelcomed interventions or unrepresentative impositions.

The negative response to Thunberg has been particularly fierce in countries where climate change is still debated as a matter of one's beliefs. In the UK, *The Spectator's* Iain Martin wrote, "On what basis can someone claim to speak for future generations? Was there a vote? How? Radical Green religion looks post-democratic" (Warren, 2019). In Australia, Thunberg was called a "deeply disturbed messiah of the global warming movement" and the "priest of a cult" by *Herald Sun* columnist Andrew Bolt, who added, "I have never seen a girl so young and with so many mental disorders treated by so many adults as a guru" (Bolt, 2019). According to global media scholars Maxwell and Miller (2019), other Rupert Murdoch media have followed suit, even seeding the conspiracy theory that Greta "may be 'a schoolgirl puppet controlled by more sinister forces'." In the US, Fox news pundits have referred to Thunberg as a "mentally ill Swedish child" and compared her to children in the Stephen King horror film "Children of the Corn," which centered on Christian fundamentalist children who ritually murder all the adults in their small town (Baragona, 2019).

Donald Trump has displayed an especially odd level of discomfort with the attention that Thunberg has received. In response to Thunberg's impassioned address at the UN, Trump sarcastically trolled: "Seems like a very happy young girl looking forward to a bright and wonderful future. So nice to see!" (@realDonaldTrump, Sept. 23, 2019). Later, he was reportedly incensed that *Time* selected her as the 2019 "Person on the Year" (an award that he won 2016), and tweeted, "So ridiculous. Greta must work on her Anger Management problem, then go to a good old fashioned movie with a friend! Chill Greta, Chill!" (Wamsley, 2019).

Drawing lessons the Parkland student examples, Thunberg has become exceptionally skilled at "clapping back" at her critics. She mockingly responded to Trump, updating her Twitter bio to read: "A teenager working on her anger management problem. Currently chilling and watching a good old fashioned movie with a friend." Only days before she reacted to Brazilian President Jair Bolsanaro, who called her a "brat," by revising her Twitter bio to read "Pirralha" – the translation of "brat" into Portuguese (Reilly, 2019). Bolsanaro was upset because Thunberg had posted a video about Indigenous leaders being assassinated for defending the Amazon. Another example involved U.S. Treasury Secretary Steve Mnuchin, who smugly told the teenage climate activists to study economics before talking about sustainable policies. Greta tweeted back with, "it doesn't take a college degree in economics to realise that our remaining 1,5° carbon budget and ongoing fossil fuel subsidies and investments don't add up." She also hit back at the *Sun Herald*'s Holt with the tweet, "I am indeed 'deeply disturbed' about the fact that these hate and conspiracy campaigns are allowed to go on and on and on just because we children communicate and act on the science. Where are the adults?" (Collett, 2019).

In addition to these examples of sparring with these more powerful voices, she even took the trouble to react to a *Daily Mail* interview with rock star Meat Loaf, who asserted that Greta has been "brainwashed into thinking that there is climate change and there isn't" (Aviles, 2020). In response, Thunberg soberly refocused the interview, tweeting "It's not about Meatloaf, It's not about what some people call me. It's not about left or right. It's all about scientific facts ... Unless we start to focus everything on this, our targets will soon be out of reach." To illustrate her point, she attached a Carbon Brief graph showing the target emission drop needed by 2027.

There have been, of course, a slew of other critics. Anticipating the need to take more control over the narrative, Thunberg posted a long statement she crafted on her Facebook account on Feb. 2, 2019. What follows is a condensed version featuring key parts:

> Many people love to spread rumors saying that I have people 'behind me' or that I'm being 'paid' or 'used' ... But there is no one 'behind' me except for myself .... I am not part of any organization. ... I am absolutely independent and I only represent myself. And yes, I write my

own speeches. But since I know that what I say is going to reach many, many people I often ask for input . . . . And I do what I do completely for free . . . I am just a messenger, . . . I am just saying what scientists have repeatedly said for decades. (Thunberg, 2019)

As these interactions show, Thunberg demonstrates an advanced capacity to tactically redirect criticism back at her critics – ironically a skill that often makes her sound like the adult in these exchanges. More significantly still is how she is able to turn even the worst criticism into strategic opportunities to focus once again on the bigger fight: the climate crisis. The most powerful example of this was her reaction to a highly disturbing cartoon depicting her sexual assault, which was printed on bumper stickers circulated among Canadian oil workers. Thunberg countered with a simple but deliberate response via Twitter: "They are starting to get more and more desperate . . . This shows that we're winning" (Sjoberg, 2020).

Conclusions

Environmental celebrity scholars Goodman and Littler (2013) suggest that, "with its individualized mode of power, its concentration of wealth, its imbrication in systemic profit-making, celebrity might be the exact opposite of what biodiversity and the environmental crisis needs: participation, co-operation, regulation against exploitation and systemic political change?" (p. 269). But as Thunberg's activities as an eco-celebrity show, it is clear that she *is* interested in policy, *is* interested in emission targets, *does* espouse collaboration, *does* challenge power, and overall, *is* dedicated to radical, systemic change in order to tackle the existential threat of the climate crisis. She is, therefore, a radically different kind of eco-celebrity.

Yet Thunberg's connection to the natural world she is defending is less about narrow causes than it is a sort of controlled fury over its global degradation. Hers is a politics of youth-centered, righteous rage ("I want you to panic") born on the imperative to act on the vulnerability of that which cannot speak– planet Earth. She reprimands the current generation on behalf of those who are inheriting the mess, speaking for the planet in scientific, action-oriented, uncompromising terms, which is precisely the quality that invites her followers to interpret her as authentic and credible and her critics to see her as hysterical or dangerous.

In many respects Thunberg is thus the "ideal performer" (Chouliaraki, 2013) for a contemporary youth-centered climate movement as she has played an important role as "non-nation state" actor (Boykoff & Goodman, 2009) within the cultural politics of climate change. While centered on her confrontational public addresses and climate strike-related activities, her eco-celebrity status has been shaped through exceptionally powerful and dynamic intertextual chains involving news coverage, entertainment fare, social media memes, and careful image management centered on message control and moral responsibility (e.g., choosing sustainable travel options; giving voice to others). Moreover, her performance as celebrity is neither hollow nor hypocritical and resists media co-optation, as it has a humble origin that sparked a movement, draws from and aligns with other activism, is filled with conviction, and animated by a "superpower" that entrenches the focus of climate change in science, urgency, and action. Because of this profile she eschews commodification, speaking for the world's youth as she speaks for the planet.

Disclosure statement

No potential conflict of interest was reported by the author(s).

References

Alter, C., Haynes, S., & Worland, J. (2019, December 23-30). 2019 person of the year, *Time*. Retrieved from https://time.com/person-of-the-year-2019-greta-thunberg/

Aviles, G. (2020, January 6). Greta Thunberg responds to Meat Loaf comment that she's been 'brainwashed'. *NBC News*. Retrieved from https://www.nbcnews.com/pop-culture/pop-culture-news/greta-thunberg-responds-meat-loaf-comment-she-s-been-brainwashed-n1111436

Baragona, J. (2019, September 23). Laura Ingraham compares Greta Thunberg to 'Children of the Corn'. *Daily Beast*. Retrieved from https://www.thedailybeast.com/laura-ingraham-compares-greta-thunberg-to-children-of-the-corn-on-fox-news

Barclay, E., & Resnick, B. (2019, September 20). How big was the global climate strike? 4 million people, activists estimate. *Vox*. Retrieved from https://web.archive.org/web/20190921012020/https://www.vox.com/energy-and-environment/2019/9/20/20876143/climate-strike-2019-september-20-crowd-estimate

Bolt, A. (2019, August 1). The disturbing secret to the cult of Greta Thunberg. *Herald Sun*. Retrieved from https://www.heraldsun.com.au/blogs/andrew-bolt/the-disturbing-secret-to-the-cult-of-greta-thunberg/news-story/55822063e3589e02707fbb5a9a75d4cc

Boykoff, M. T., Goodman, M. K., & Curtis, I. (2010). Cultural politics of climate change. In M. Boykoff (Ed.), *The politics of climate change* (pp. 136–154). London and New York: Routledge.

Boykoff, M. T., & Goodman, M. K. (2009). Conspicuous redemption? Reflections on the promises and perils of the 'Celebritization' of climate change. *Geoforum*, *40*(3), 395–406. doi:10.1016/j.geoforum.2008.04.006

Branchereau, G. (2020, February 3), Greta Thunberg puts Africa's climate activists in media spotlight. *The Jakarta Post*. Retrieved from https://www.thejakartapost.com/life/2020/02/03/greta-thunberg-puts-africas-climate-activists-in-media-spotlight.html

Brandon, J. (2020, July 22). Greta Thunberg was on Stephen Colbert last night and made this profound comment. *Forbes*. Retrieved from https://www.forbes.com/sites/johnbbrandon/2020/07/22/greta-thunberg-was-on-stephen-colbert-last-night-and-made-this-profound-comment/#1ac700883687

Branston, G. (2016). Apocalyptic imaginings. *Environmental Communication*, *10*(6), 807–810. doi:10.1080/17524032.2016.1209320

Brockington, D. (2008). Powerful environmentalisms. *Media, Culture and Society*, *30*(4), 551–568. doi:10.1177/0163443708091182

Brockington, D. (2009). *Celebrity and the environment*. London and New York: Zed Books.

Bryant, K. (2019). Arnold Schwarzenegger helped Greta Thunberg acquire a Tesla. *Vanity Fair*. Retrieved from https://www.vanityfair.com/style/2019/10/greta-thunberg-arnold-schwarzenegger-tesla

Chouliaraki, L. (2013). *The ironic spectator*. Cambridge, UK: Polity Press.

Collett, M. (2019, August 1). Greta Thunberg, the teen behind climate strikes, hits back at Andrew Bolt column. *News*. Retrieved from https://www.abc.net.au/news/2019-08-02/thunberg-hits-back-after-being-called-deeply-disturbed/11376724

Common Dreams. (2019, November 21). Is Greta Thunberg a time traveler 'here to save us' from climate emergency'? *Common Dreams.* Retrieved from https://www.commondreams.org/news/2019/11/21/greta-thunberg-time-traveler-here-save-us-climate-emergency-120-year-old-photo

Craig, G. (2019). Sustainable everyday life and celebrity environmental advocacy in Hugh's war on waste. *Environmental Communication, 13*(6), 775–789. doi:10.1080/17524032.2018.1459770

Da, Waal, A. (2008). The humanitarian carnival. *World Affairs Journal, 171*(2), 23–55.

Ellis, E. G. (2019, September 28). Greta Thunberg's digital rise calls back to a pre-digital era *Wired.* Retrieved from https://www.wired.com/story/greta-thunberg-social-media/

Fairclough, N. (1995). *Media discourses.* London: Hodder Education.

Fridays for Future. (2020, April 21). *Our house is on fire.* Retrieved from https://www.youtube.com/watch?v=eT32UFzA7E8&feature=youtu.be

Garrard, G. (2004). *Ecocriticism.* London and New York: Routledge.

Germanos, A. (2019, July 29). To deliver 'fundamental message' for 'survival of future generations,' Greta Thunberg to sail Atlantic for Americas. *Common Dreams.* Retrieved from https://www.commondreams.org/news/2019/07/29/deliver-fundamental-message-survival-future-generations-greta-thunberg-sail-atlantic

Goodman, M., & Littler, J. (2013). Celebrity ecologies. *Celebrity Studies, 4*(3), 269–275. doi:10.1080/19392397.2013.831623

Green, M. (2019, June 14). 'Tame the nightmare': U.S. writer McKibben pushes climate strike. *Reuters.* Retrieved from https://www.reuters.com/article/us-climate-change-strike/tame-the-nightmare-us-writer-mckibben-pushes-climate-strike-idUSKCN1TF0S1

Greta Thunberg - Inspiring Others to Take a Stand Against Climate Change. (2019, September 14). *The Daily Show.* Retrieved from https://www.youtube.com/watch?v=rhQVustYV24

'Greta Thunberg effect' driving growth in carbon offsetting. (2019, November 8). *The Guardian.* Retrieved from https://www.theguardian.com/environment/2019/nov/08/greta-thunberg-effect-driving-growth-in-carbon-offsetting

Greta Thunberg hits out at leaders who use her fame to 'look good'. (2020, June 27). *The Guardian.* Retrieved from https://www.theguardian.com/environment/2020/jun/27/greta-thunberg-hits-out-at-leaders-who-use-her-fame-to-look-good

Greta Thunberg to sail into Lisbon on Tuesday. (2019, December 12). *The Portugal News.* Retrieved from https://www.theportugalnews.com/news/greta-thunberg-to-sail-into-lisbon-on-tuesday/52199

Hartford, A. (2019, October 13). What's our duty to future generations? Greta Thunberg demands an answer. *Sunday Times.* Retrieved from https://www.timeslive.co.za/sunday-times/lifestyle/2019-10-13-whats-our-duty-to-future-generations-greta-thunberg-demands-an-answer/

Huggan, G. (2013). *Nature's saviours.* London and New York: Routledge.

Lewis, J. (2012). *Global media apocalypse.* London and New York: Palgrave.

Maxwell, R., & Miller, T. (2019, September 9). Why are so many adults so frightened of Greta Thunberg? *Psychology Today.* Retrieved from https://www.psychologytoday.com/us/blog/greening-the-media/201909/why-are-so-many-adults-so-frightened-greta-thunberg

Meister, M. (2015). Celebrity culture and environment. In A. Hansen & R. Cox (Eds.), *The Routledge handbook of environmental communication* (pp. 281–289). London and New York: Routledge.

Murphy, P. (2017). *The media commons: Globalization and environmental discourses.* Champaign, Illinois: University of Illinois Press.

O'Brien, K., Selboe, E., & Hayward, B. (2018). Exploring youth activism on climate change. *Ecology and Society, 23*(3), 42–54. doi:10.5751/ES-10287-230342

Prance, S. (2019, September 24). Greta Thunberg's "death stare" at Donald Trump has now become a meme. *PopBuzz.* Retrieved from https://www.popbuzz.com/internet/viral/greta-thunberg-meme-donald-trump-stare-gif/

Reilly, N. (2019, December 12). Greta Thunberg changes Twitter bio to mock Donald Trump tweet: "Currently chilling". *NME.* Retrieved from https://www.nme.com/news/greta-thunberg-changes-twitter-bio-to-mock-donald-trump-tweet-currently-chilling-2586727

Rodrick, S. (2020, March 26). Greta's world. *Rolling Stone.* Retrieved from https://www.rollingstone.com/politics/politics-features/greta-thunberg-climate-crisis-cover-965949/

Rojek, C. (2012). *Fame attack*. London: Bloomsbury.

Rosen, J. (2019, December 12). Staring down Donald Trump, the same elephant in every room. *The New York Times Magazine*. Retrieved from https://www.nytimes.com/2019/10/16/magazine/the-same-elephant-in-every-room.html

Shohat, E., & Stam, R. (1994). *Unthinking eurocentrism*. London and New York: Routledge.

Sjoberg, B. (2020, March 1). *Greta Thunberg on cartoon depicting her being sexually assaulted: 'This shows that we're winning,' daily dot*. Retrieved from https://www.dailydot.com/irl/thunberg-cartoon-sexual-assault/

Thunberg, G. (2019, February 2). *Recently I've seen many rumors . . . . Facebook*. Retrieved from https://www.facebook.com/732846497083173/posts/767646880269801/

Turner, G. (2016). Celebrities and the environment. *Environmental Communication, 10*(6), 811–814. doi:10.1080/17524032.2016.1209327

Wamsley, L. (2019, December 12). After Greta Thunberg wins '*Time*' honor, Trump suggest she 'chill' and watch a movie. *NPR*. Retrieved from https://www.npr.org/2019/12/12/787488397/after-greta-thunberg-wins-time-honor-trump-tweets-chill-and-go-to-the-movies

Warren, R. (2019, April 25). Greta Thunberg's critics just want to be lucrative right-wing talking heads. GQ, Retrieved July 28, 2020 https://www.gq-magazine.co.uk/article/greta-thunbergs

Watts, J. (2019, March 11). Greta Thunberg, schoolgirl climate change warrior. *The Guardian*. Retrieved from https://www.scribd.com/article/401621366/Greta-Thunberg-Schoolgirl-Climate-Change-Warrior-Some-People-Can-Let-Things-Go-I-Can-t

Celebrity migrants and the racialized logic of integration in Germany

Kate Zambon

ABSTRACT
Since the turn of the millennium, "integration" has become a predominant floating signifier in discourse and policy regulating the place of immigrants and minorities in European societies. This study analyzes a self-described "integration campaign" that used celebrity exemplars to promote the German language to immigrants and their descendants. This case demonstrates the interrelationship between celebrations of new German diversity and discourses that frame immigrants-and especially Muslims-as a potential threat to national life. This campaign combines two potent sites of symbolic cultural politics: language and the body. It uses racialized celebrity exemplars to articulate normative whiteness symbolized by standardized German. The campaign targets the imagined figure of the perpetual migrant who is beyond the reach of the German language and, thus, outside the regulatory and disciplinary control of majority society. While it is self-styled as a playful invitation to learn German, the content of the campaign, its theme song, and the press discourse about it use racialized celebrity bodies to affirm colorblind meritocracy while devaluing the lives of racialized "migrants"who are unable or unwilling to conform.

Since the turn of the millennium, "integration" has emerged as a key concept in discourse and policy regulating the place of immigrants and minorities in European societies. Across the continent, countries that pioneered multiculturalism as a social and legal ideal have changed course, blaming multiculturalism for the supposed disintegration of society (Vertovec & Wessendorf, 2010). However, integration – the proposed successor to multiculturalism – has received comparatively little critical attention. This study examines how the media industry constructed integration in a celebrity-focused print media campaign that ostensibly encouraged German language learning. This state-supported media campaign purports to celebrate and support integration success. However, closer analysis reveals its presumptions of normative, white Christian Germanness and the social deficits of immigrants and minority Germans – groups that are conflated under the umbrella term "migrant." This case study analyzes how a campaign framed as a celebration of "migrant" celebrities forged a divide between normative white citizens and marked "Others" who must perpetually prove their value, generation after generation. Racialized bodies were displayed to affirm Germany's cosmopolitan, tolerant, and meritocratic character. However, this study shows that defining integration success through celebrity example constructs "integration failure" as a matter of individual choice. Moreover, in this campaign a successful life is only possible for those who "integrate" in ways that support white supremacist norms.

The campaign, titled "*Raus mit der Sprache. Rein ins Leben*"[1] (henceforth *Out with It*), featured photographs of prominent individuals "with immigration backgrounds" sticking out their black, red, and gold striped tongues to indicate their ability to speak German. Analysis of this case reveals an important theme in integration discourse: the supposed inadequacy of minority usage of the German language. This self-described "integration campaign," which claims "to encourage immigrants to learn German," argues that speaking the language is the key to a successful life in Germany.

There are two foundational problems with this premise. First, this campaign creates a fictional figure as its ostensible target: the "migrant" – a German of color who does not speak German. This figure inhabits imagined "parallel societies" where immigrant ways of life are preserved in amber over generations, untouched and unreformed by "Western values" (Malzahn, 2010), which are coded as white and Christian. Second, the fictional target of the campaign cannot logically be its audience. The campaign was distributed in 100 German-language periodicals and on 1,500 billboards nationwide. Readers of German newspapers and magazines typically already speak German. Understanding the ads and billboards requires linguistic fluency and knowledge of German public culture. This suggests that the true target is not German language learners, but rather the mainstream German public. The campaign promotes the myth of "permanent migrants" (El-Tayeb, 2011) who are beyond the reach of the German language and, thus, outside the regulatory and disciplinary control of majority society.

Despite the logical contradiction of the campaign's format and stated purpose, the campaign was widely praised and was honored with the prestigious German Language Culture Award (*Kulturpreis Deutsche Sprache*). This study analyzes the assumptions about immigrant and minority Germans communicated by the campaign. Furthermore, it explores how ideas about the German language construct the racialized category of the *candidate for integration* through an imagined form of standardized language defining valid citizenship and a "life worth living" (Agamben, 1998).

Using discourse theoretical analysis (Carpentier & De Cleen, 2007), this study analyzes the series of 27 print advertisements and the campaign theme song, "Just a Blink of the Eye" (*Nur ein Augenblick*) by the Afro-German rapper Harris, alongside press coverage of the campaign. A search of German press archive, WISO,[2] for the slogan, "*Raus mit der Sprache. Rein ins Leben,*" returned 33 articles discussing the campaign. Searches for coverage of the artist who wrote the theme song using *Harris* AND *Integration* AND *rapper* returned 20 articles, 18 of which appeared in late 2010 when the song was chosen. The two searches largely overlapped, resulting in 35 unique articles. This government and media industry campaign perpetuates second-class citizenship through integration discourse, using racialized celebrity bodies and a symbolic concept of language to bolster white Christian normativity.

The focus on German language acquisition among immigrants and their descendants coalesced around the turn of the millennium at the same time as the introduction of birthright (*jus soli*) citizenship. Like the concept of integration, according to David Gramling (2009), the multilingualism of foreign laborers was subjected to political debates since the mid-1970s. At the time, linguistic policy for labor migrants and their children prioritized the "readiness-to-return" (*Rückkehrbereitschaft*) by funding instruction in heritage languages. German instruction for language learners was neglected in government policy. Linguistic pluralism was promoted only after citizenship law changed to legally acknowledge immigration. Gramling (2009, 2016) identifies this "linguistic turn" as a new model of civic belonging based on "cosmopolitan monolingualism," which upholds the *idea* of "cultural diversity while discouraging the public use of multiple heritage languages" (Gramling, 2009, p. 131). In the early to mid-2000s, the government's "salutary neglect" gave way to new laws and policies tying social assistance and visa status to demonstrating progress in German language courses. In a remarkably fast turnaround, the center-right political coalition resignified the German language "not as an inherited ethnic possession but as a pan-ethnic *lingua franca*" (Gramling, 2009, p. 131) that could combat dreaded cultural relativism and "parallel societies."

In contemporary Europe, diversity is hailed as a cultural advantage in a global age. At the same time, persistent anxieties circulate about "poorly managed" diversity (Moore, 2015). Like the discourses around diversity and integration in policy and popular media, linguistic difference is understood through a "political economy of life" (Lemke, 2011) that sees it as both a force for growth through innovation and a potential threat from those who supposedly "opt out" (Wiese, 2015) of the national project. Symbolic language politics consolidate European monolingual norms against globalization and population mobility within the European Union. Not all vernaculars of the national language are valuable, however. A meaningful life in society requires "proper" speech (*Bildungssprache*). As the press discussions of *Out with It* show, the German vernacular *Kiezdeutsch* (neighborhood German) that developed in urban immigrant neighborhoods is separated from other informal and regional dialects and denigrated as incorrect, incomprehensible, and threatening, as are the people who use those dialects or "look" like they might.

"Out with it": language politics and celebrity exemplars

The *Out with It* campaign was a social marketing campaign created in 2010 by the German Foundation for Integration (*Deutschlandstiftung Integration*), an organization founded in 2008 by the Association of German Periodical Publishers (*Verband Deutscher Zeitschriftenverleger*) with government support. The foundation's board of trustees is chaired by media mogul Hubert Burda and the first German Commissioner for Integration, Maria Böhmer. Chancellor Angela Merkel is the organization's honorary patron. This organization reflects the private and public coordination behind the rise of integration discourse (see Schuster-Craig, 2017). According to its website, the Foundation for Integration aims to support the achievement of "equality of opportunity for people with a background of migration in Germany" (Deutschlandstiftung Integration: Deutschlandstiftung, n.d.). While this mission statement suggests an emphasis on structural issues, they primarily focus on so-called "information campaigns." They also maintain a scholarship fund for exceptional young people and an "integration award." Instead of acknowledging the conditions that produce racialized inequality, the foundation spotlights successful minoritized individuals and then narrates their stories to support the status quo.

The Foundation for Integration's first project, the *Out with It* campaign, gathered elite athletes, politicians, and entertainers with transnational or multi-ethnic backgrounds to "motivate migrants living in Germany to learn our language" (Kampagne für Integration:

Diese Promis werben für Deutsch-Kurse, 2010). The centerpiece of the campaign was print ads showing individual celebrities sticking out their tongues, which were digitally painted with the colors of the German flag. Below, in capital letters, the campaign slogan exhorts readers to speak (German) so that they can "start living." The ads primarily feature athletes and entertainers, but also included prominent Turkish-German politicians Aygül Özkan and Özcan Mutlu. Of the 27 models in the two runs of the campaign, I identified 20 prominent individuals with publicly available biographical information.[3] Of these individuals, 13 were born and raised in Germany, four immigrated before age 7, and only three immigrated after age 12. Less than half of the participants are immigrants and few learned German after early childhood. Of those pictured, all but one (Polish-German gymnast Magdalena Brzeska) are visible minorities. These details suggest that inclusion was not based on experience of immigration or German language learning, but rather the status as a person of color.

While the outstretched tongue could be read as a defiant gesture to break rules of decorum and claim the German language, the press primarily interpreted it as an exhortation to minorities to speak "good" German (for example, Kampagne für Integration: Diese Promis werben für Deutsch-Kurse, 2010). The most common term used to describe the gesture is *frech*, which translates to impudent, cheeky, or saucy. The undignified, infantile associations of this gesture problematize a straightforward empowering interpretation. Breaking norms of the "civilized body" (Elias, 2000) carries risks for racialized individuals. A racialized person's "corporeal schema" is not their own to construct from their experience. As Fanon contends, those schemas are given "by the other, the white man, who had woven [him] out of a thousand details, anecdotes, stories" (Fanon, 2008, p. 84). These representations hew closer to nature and the emotional, unconstrained body (Hall, 1997). At the same time, representations of minoritized people tend toward strongly polarized binary forms: "good/bad, civilized/primitive, ugly/excessively attractive….and they are often required to be *both things at the same time*" (Hall, 1997, p. 229). The celebrity exemplars in the campaign express a range of excessive affects, from serious and intense to joyful and irreverent, all looking directly at the camera with their mouths wide open and painted tongues outstretched. Most are exceptionally beautiful, their appearance clashing with the grotesque gesture. The representational incongruity peaks in the ads featuring Turkish-German politicians. It is difficult to imagine white German politicians, such as the campaign's official patron, Chancellor Angela Merkel, consenting to publicly perform this "uncivilized," childish gesture.

To what extent can this campaign be considered an act of free self-expression by the celebrity models? Certainly, campaign creators emphasize that people with transnational roots were involved at every level of campaign creation after its conception at a dinner Merkel hosted with top media executives (see Glück, Klein, Krämer, & Schöck, 2011). In the only scholarly critique of the campaign I found, Mita Banerjee (2011) astutely analyzes the question of agency and resistance. Banerjee observes that while the outstretched tongue may be shocking and perhaps defiant, it actually domesticates the subjects' foreignness, pushing them to justify themselves in state-sanctioned language. Banerjee rightly sees this as a campaign for normative whiteness but does not examine how Germans of color were active in its creation behind the camera. This campaign exemplifies the bind involved in celebrity power and agency more generally. Celebrity reflects and shapes social structures, collective identities, and national mythologies (Marshall, 1997; Redmond, 2018). For Rojek

(2001), celebrity is defined as the ability to impact public consciousness. While celebrities can use their voices as agents of change, they are more often agents of the status quo, both dependent on and supporting hegemonic institutions and discourses (Marshall, 1997). This campaign presents in the mode of celebrity as agent of change, but the change is a "return" to a (linguistically) homogeneous public sphere.

An integration song: ungrateful immigrants and innocent Germans

While celebrity power is concentrated in the amplification of the celebrity voice, this language campaign is conspicuously speechless. Instead, the images silence and brand their subjects' tongues the national colors, stripping celebrities of color of their power of voice. The exception is Afro-German rapper, Harris, who composed the campaign theme. Harris's lyrics proclaim Germany a just and meritocratic society while reinforcing negative stereotypes about transnational minority communities. Harris defends white German innocence by denying the impact of racism and condemning delinquent "migrants" who dare to criticize Germany. Harris presents a narrative of willful minority deficiency and white German benevolence. His devotion despite "superficial" racist slights proves that Germany is worthy of unconditional love. "Stars are, like characters in stories, representations of people. Thus they relate to ideas about what people are (or are supposed to be) like. However, unlike characters in stories, stars are also real people," lending their representations the authority of authenticity (Dyer, 1998, p. 20). Harris uses his "authenticity" as an Afro-German to act as a hegemonic enforcer, dismantling anti-racist critique. In choosing Harris as its emissary, the campaign promoted white supremacy without provoking public criticism.

The title of the campaign's theme song, "Just a Blink of the Eye," refers to the insignificance of racism in Germany. The song opens with Harris's claim to understand the persistent experience of prejudice.

> You are young, black hair, brown eyes, dark skin.
> Believe me, I know that shitty look too
> That particular "You, fucking K—–[4] look"
> But that's not Germany, that is just a blink of the eye[5]

This establishes Harris's minority credentials and acknowledges everyday racism. However, he dismisses these experiences of racism, arguing that they are ephemeral and not representative of the German nation. This discourse "unwitnesses racism" (Murakawa, 2019) by preemptively erasing it, protecting the nation by attributing racism to insignificant individuals. This discourse of "racial innocence" reframes racism as distant in time, space, or ideological extremity. James Baldwin (1998) identified innocence as a principal malady of the white American psyche, which escapes painful histories by displacing responsibility for inequality onto individual perpetrators or onto the afflicted themselves. Baldwin recognized that while the power and benefits are not equally shared, "the equal humanity of all Americans means that black Americans, too, are susceptible to the temptation to turn away from a bitter history" (Balfour, 2001, p. 91) and its ongoing reverberations. These observations resonate across European and colonial settler societies. Harris transforms his racialized status into armor in a crusade to uphold German innocence. Racism, here, is aberrant and inconsequential. It is not an inevitable byproduct of a political system that divides the population into normative nationals and perpetual migrants, nor is it a reason to criticize majority society.

Having invalidated critiques of systemic racism, Harris attacks intransigent, ungrateful immigrants:

> How is it that you've lived in this country for over 10 years?
> Maybe longer, and you still don't speak the German language?
> You say Germans are shit, German women are trash.
> Please do Germany a favor and get out!

Harris's imagined interlocutor is the stereotypical nightmare of failed integration. His alleged intolerance of "emancipated" German women correlates with stereotypes of Muslim men. The first sign of the immigrant's failure is his supposed lack of German language ability. It symbolizes his rejection of German society and invalidates any criticism he raises. After all, if he does not speak German, he cannot possibly understand German society. He holds no value to the nation, and Harris exhorts him to "get out." Harris even offers, "If you don't know where the airport is, I'll bring you. I'll pay for your ticket and souvenirs." The text is explicitly aimed at immigrants, but implicates all visible minorities who do not properly perform their appreciation for their place in Germany.

Harris condemns his interlocutor as infantile and self-segregating, suggesting that a poor attitude and work ethic are responsible for immigrants' problems, not racism, economic inequality, or systemic disadvantage. The audacity to critique Germany incites Harris, who assumes the role of pedagogue.

> But when I see and hear how they speak about Germany . . .
> If they can't go back to a war, that I can understand
> But you've got to behave yourself, that's just how it is!
> If you don't look German, that's just the way it is.
> Be proud of your roots, stick your chest out and walk tall
> But you can't live here and talk shit about everything
> And think that everyone should be nice to you too
> Above all, if you don't respect the Germans.

The immigrant's demand for respect is invalidated by his criticisms. This passage starts with Harris's anger at criticism of Germany, building on the familiar trope that if majority society is "all Nazis," then immigrants should simply leave. While conceding that some people cannot go back to war-torn homelands, Harris says they must "behave themselves." This stance resonates closely with American "respectability politics." In the words of Michelle Smith (2014), this approach proposes that "marginalized classes will receive their share of political influence and social standing not because democratic values and law require it, but because they demonstrate their compatibility" with mainstream society. Respectability politics are reinforced by mainstream discourses that blame social inequality on personal and cultural deficits. Harris acknowledges racial discrimination, "but that's just the way it is." This passage delegitimizes critiques of social exclusion, claiming that respect for majority society and pride in one's "roots" is the solution.

The demand for gratitude returns throughout the text. Harris says that "Germany is generous and has a big heart." He is offended by the interlocutor's laziness, "ignorance," and lack of appreciation for everything Germany provides. Harris rebukes and chides his interlocutor. "You're lucky, you're here now," Harris proclaims. "So, behave yourself, do your work, grow up, and don't be childish ... You should be ashamed to speak so badly of Germany!" Although Harris hears critiques of German inequality, he claims not to understand them. Harris demands an explanation from the foreign Other, only to ignore it when it is not delivered in standardized German.

> What is this shit all about? How ignorant do you have to be?
> You don't want to learn German, but you want to stay in Germany
> That is too much for me, I can't understand that
> Can you please explain it to me? Oops, I don't understand you
> And that's why you stay among yourselves, you can't speak German!

The supposed inability to speak German invalidates the claim to full political personhood including the right to political and social critique. Harris classifies language deficits as caused by intellectual deficits and a lack of will; he ties segregation to these deficits rather than decades of policies on guest worker housing, city planning decisions, and everyday racism in housing (see Mandel, 2008). Harris gleefully acknowledges the potential interpretation of his song as racist, rapping, "If I were blond with blue eyes, you would say that I am a Nazi," a sentiment he repeats in interviews (Harris, 2010).

For Harris – and apparently also for the media executives and politicians who chose this song for the campaign – his status as a visible minority makes it impossible for him to promote racism. This reveals a serious misapprehension of racism in the public sphere. If, building on Foucault's theories of biopolitics (Foucault, 2003, 2008), racism is a materially significant discourse that uses demographic features to fracture the population into *life that must be protected* and *life that poses a threat*, the logic of the discourse itself matters, not the demographic characteristics of its promoter. Celebrities play an important symbolic role in this process of ordering and fracture, as they "embody identity politics and give meaning to the imagined body of the nation state" (Redmond, 2018, p. 45) Harris uses his minority status to delegitimize anti-racist critiques, claiming that the nation is harmed by immigrants' disrespect of the majority population. By displaying himself as proof that racism is illusory, Harris becomes the ideal enforcer of white supremacist national hegemony.

Language and a life worth living

The *Out with It* campaign positions itself as a helping hand to "migrants" to encourage them to learn German and, thereby, become full citizens. Instead, it is an internal discussion involving normative German society and select celebrities of color to define national identity and the conditions on immigrant belonging. To understand the campaign, audiences must be familiar enough with the German public sphere to recognize the campaign models. Audiences must already speak German to understand the slogan and theme song. The campaign requires cultural and linguistic knowledge unavailable to the purportedly isolated population it claims to target. The relationship in Harris's song between language and politically legitimate personhood is elaborated further in the media coverage of the *Out with It* campaign. The remainder of this case study analyzes press reactions to understand the key role of language ideologies in integration discourse.

Language as both a means for and a measure of integration is a central theme in integration discourse. Arguments foregrounding the importance of speaking German appear frequently, whether in experiences of German-born minorities being praised for their "good German" (see Bota et al., 2012) or in complaints about the purported refusal of immigrants in "parallel societies" to learn German. Press discussion around the *Out with It* campaign shows how discourse about language divides the population into normative nationals and perpetual candidates for integration, regardless of personal history of migration. Although German language acquisition by first-generation immigrants differs greatly from language acquisition by children raised in the German school system and media sphere, integration discourse erases these distinctions. All candidates for integration, or "integrants" (Lentin & Titley, 2011), may be scrutinized and then praised or condemned for their use of German. Focusing on the purported unwillingness or inability to speak "proper German" places responsibility for social exclusion on integrants themselves, not on persistent educational and opportunity gaps.

Discussions of the *Out with It* campaign in the press were generally uncontentious. Press accounts mostly praised the campaign and uncritically conveyed its "preferred meanings„ (Hall, 2003, p. 172). A concept of integration emerges that proposes German language use as a metonym for full political personhood. This notion of language is portrayed as equally accessible to all who work for it. However, by using examples of minority celebrities raised in Germany, the campaign sets minority German speakers apart from white Germans. Although the featured celebrities have been exposed to German since childhood, their dominance of standardized German is portrayed as relevant for German language learners, or candidates for integration. The following press excerpts characterize the campaign's motivation and its imagined targets.

> With this campaign, the [Integration Foundation] seeks to make it clear how important it is for people with a migration background living in Germany to master the German language. (Rausch, 2010)

> In order to get, in particular, children and young adults to increase their willingness to learn German, celebrities with foreign roots have made themselves available for the second series of the Integration Foundation campaign. (Fietz, 2010)

> A poster campaign aims to move migrants to learn German .... The campaign primarily targets migrants and their children, who hardly speak German despite having been born in Germany. (Lachmann, 2010)

These quotes target the broad category of "people with a migration background," including those born and raised in Germany. All, here, are equally candidates for integration. Successful examples, embodied by celebrities, "motivate" those whose failure to integrate is signified by their inability or unwillingness to "speak German." By focusing on young people, these quotes delegitimate minority youth vernacular forms of German. They assume the existence of a correct, standard German language. This is framed as "our" language, the unmarked language of white Germans.

Crucially, "German" and "language" does not refer to actual speech, but to a symbolic ideal of "correct" standardized German. This point is driven home by the campaign's mode of representation. Celebrities are mobilized as bodies; their language is not heard, but is symbolized through the display of their tongues, branded with the national colors. Their bodies become symbolic nodes of integration discourse. In a distortion of the deliberative democratic model (Habermas, 1974), the communication of ideas for active citizenship is replaced by the silent tongue as a nationalist symbol. Language is a symbolic performance rather than a means of communication and contestation.

As in Harris's song, ideas communicated outside the proper register are dismissed as incomprehensible and illegitimate. The final quote above comes from a scathing opinion article, provocatively titled, "*Are Germans ashamed of their language?*" The column airs grievances about disrespect of the national language by minoritized and white Germans alike. Lamenting the disunity introduced by "migrants and their children," the author writes that

> Böhmer says to them, "Language is more than communication—it is a tie that binds us." It should be anyway ... But since that is still not the case today, we have this good and important poster campaign. After all, after five decades of immigration, young people in social combustion points [*soziale Brennpunkte*] in big cities stammer out a so-called "Kanak-Sprak" and are not capable of formulating grammatically correct sentences in German." (Lachmann, 2010)

The author stigmatizes minority German spaces and vernaculars as dangerous and claims that Germans lack the national pride required to suppress them. This essentially proposes ethnic cleansing; eliminating "unassimilable Others" is equated with national pride.

Across Europe, minority youth vernaculars are considered threatening to national language and majority culture (see Wiese, 2014). These vernaculars are associated with violence and sexism even while they are also often fashionable or "cool." The simultaneous devaluation and appropriation of minority sociolects resonates with debates around African American Vernacular English in the United States. Despite scholarly research to the contrary, deviations from standard German in minority vernaculars are mistakenly equated with errors made by German language learners (Wiese, 2015), rather than more accurately comparing them with regional dialects. Furthermore, this use of "flawed" German is perceived as threatening German norms and undermining social cohesion (Wiese, 2015, p. 356). Minoritized vernaculars are also associated with laziness and rejecting "proper" speech. Standardized "High German," in contrast, is a skill worthy of its elevated cultural capital (Wiese, 2014, 2015).

Through celebrity exemplars, *Out with It* uses a symbolic concept of standardized German to support a tautological definition of integration as the achievement of success. Language-as-integration defines the difference between success and failure, between life and mere existence. As one of the campaign's models, musician DJ Chino, explained,

> The German language is AWESOME! Only when you understand and are understood can you begin to live and not merely to exist. ("Bitte lernt Deutsch!": Stars starten neue Integrations-Kampagne, 2010)

This quote situates language at the base of the distinction between the politically qualified, valuable version of life (*zoe*) and bare life (*bios*) (Agamben, 1998). There is a persistent tension in the corpus from the intentional ambiguity surrounding language and communication. In this quote, DJ Chino discusses basic communication, to understand and be understood. However, the press coverage of this campaign explicitly denies language as simply, or even primarily, a matter of communication. As Böhmer stated, "language is about more than communication – it is the tie that binds us." The ambiguity around language and communication consolidates a normative notion of proper German in opposition to minority German vernaculars.

Proper language is legitimated as a fundamental requirement for valid and active citizenship. It is linked to the achievement of a "good" and valuable life.

> Whoever wants to become someone in Germany, and doesn't speak the language, has no chance.... Maria Böhmer said, "Good language knowledge opens the doors for a successful life in our country." (Integrations-Kampagne startet: Maria Böhmer wirbt für Sprachkurse, 2010)

> The message is clear: NO FUTURE WITHOUT A COMMON LANGUAGE! (*sic.*) (Herrmann, 2010)

Speaking the right form of German is an existential requirement for the future of society itself, as emphasized in capitalized text. Language-as-integration posits that normative belonging is equally accessible to all, since language learning is flexible and technically possible for all people. Those who refuse to speak properly cannot expect a place in society. In Böhmer's words, "whoever can't speak German is only an onlooker in our country" (Ehrenstein, 2010). Language-as-integration discourse erases discrimination and structural inequality, asserting that the solution to inequality lies with the individual. It revokes the agency of those without proper speech and declares them irrelevant.

The *Out with It* campaign publicizes the idea of language deficiency without addressing the chronically insufficient resources dedicated to instruction of German as a foreign language offered as part of "integration classes" (Haushaltsplan: Für Integrationskurse hat das Innenministerium kein Geld, 2014). In one of the only critical press articles on the campaign, award-winning journalist and author Mely Kiyak (2010) investigated the language course offerings aggregated on the website *ich-spreche-deutsche.de*, the only concrete service from the *Out with It* initiative. Kiyak searched for a language course that served populations with migration backgrounds, but found that the offerings targeted foreign students, business people, and newly arrived immigrants. Kiyak concludes that "the market has not reacted to the political demand on migrants to learn better German. Likewise, politicians have no solutions" (Kiyak, 2010). While four other articles in the corpus included skepticism about the campaign's purpose or effectiveness, only Kiyak's column seriously addressed the lack of resources for long-established immigrants to meet language standards of the German public sphere.

This campaign also obscures the reality that speaking German is already normal for multilingual youth (Gramling, 2009). Although they may speak another language at home, the overwhelming monolingualism of the media sphere and public life exposes young people to German long before they begin formal education. Still, code-switching multilingual youth are treated as though they learned German as a foreign language. They are congratulated when they speak with ease in formal registers or criticized for their "bad German" when they use informal youth sociolects. Thus, although most of the celebrity exemplars of *Out with It* are multilingual with German as a native language, they are commended not for their fluency in multiple languages but solely for their "proper" German. One campaign creator is paraphrased, saying, "the prominent ambassadors are living proof that in Germany everything is possible when you integrate yourself. And when you are good" (Fröhlich, 2010). The success of these celebrities is framed as a reward for "being good" by conforming bodies marked by transnational traces to social and economic norms that equate unmarked (white) Germanness with a fully human life.

Unlike the celebrity exemplars, the everyday minority Germans – actual or imagined – do not emerge well from scrutiny. In the *Out with It* corpus, characterizations of non-celebrity "migrants" were overwhelmingly negative. Minority hegemonic enforcers, like Harris, facilitate blame and condemnation of "integration refusers" (*Integrationsverweigerer*). They promote the trope of the "enemy of integration," typically described as a young urban Muslim male. In an interview about his new "integration song" with *Der Spiegel*, Harris condemns his own childhood friends:

> The excuse was always: Germany doesn't give us a chance. But that's not true. I myself was at a school for the "difficult to educate" (*Schwererziehbare*). There were remedial classes, there were extra remedial classes and remedial classes for remedial classes. No one can say that Germany doesn't do anything for these teens. They refuse! ... These criminal Alis[6] screw up the reputation of well-integrated Arabs and Turks. (Harris, 2010)

Here, Harris uses his own experience as a troubled young man who saw the error of his ways and achieved success to invalidate his friends who felt marginalized. In a profile of Harris in *Der Stern*, this reproach is echoed by self-identifying minority fans:

> "Yes, we are also at fault that things are the way they are"; fans who write "I am young. I am a Turk. I passed my A-levels and I'm completely integrated. And I hate these *K*—–, who can't behave themselves here." (Albers, 2010a)

The aggressively pejorative language in this quote is presented as acceptable. Likewise, Harris's casual and repeated use of pejoratives like "*K* – –," "black-head" and "criminal Ali" is not challenged, since, as a self-designated in-group member, Harris claims to be incapable of supporting racist projects. He expresses irritation with anti-racist critique. Referencing a contemporary national debate on racism, Harris posed the question, "why must the cudgels be brought out anytime anyone says anything about foreigners?" (Pham, 2010). This comment points to idea, common in integration "debates," that anti-racism abuses and victimizes normative Germans.

These themes of "migrant" deficiency and German innocence carry over into portrayals of actual transnational young Berliners. An article titled "*The Sad Reality of Integration: The Germans, They Are the Others*" (Albers, 2010b) follows Harris as he visits a majority-minority school in Berlin. A student wants to know about Harris's origins, and Harris insists that he is German. The journalist describes the scene: "A boy and a man. Both born and raised in Germany. Both marked as foreign by their dark hair, eyes, and skin. But only the boy feels foreign" (Albers, 2010b). Echoing themes from Harris's song, social exclusion as a matter of individual choice here, erasing the power differential between the celebrity and the child. The students are said to identify with Harris because of his status as a visible minority.

> They tell him stories from their lives as migrant children, of everyday racism, prescribed social roles, hateful Germans, of life in their own world and of the fear of life in the other world. Harris tries to destroy the clichés that a generation grew up with, that also serve a defensive function. However, he had to ask for clarification, since even though these children grew up in Germany, none of them speaks the national language perfectly." (Albers, 2010b)

The author does not specify which clichés Harris contested, but suggests that Harris responded to their accounts of discrimination by saying that their impressions of Germans were stereotypical and that they were using racism as an excuse for their problems. By characterizing their speech as incomprehensible, the author marginalizes the students and reproduces racialized deficit narratives.

The article displays the shame that students feel about inadequate speech in their community. Paraphrasing their comments, Albers (2010b) writes,

> It is "ungood" that the soccer star Mesut Özil was awarded the Bambi for Integration, since he couldn't speak correct German, says one boy. "My dad thinks that he can speak super good German, but when I hear him on the telephone, I think, what kind of talk is that," admits another. Encouraged, a pair of girls finally told of parents who can't speak German. "I am ashamed sometimes," said one quietly.

The author emphasizes the error in the first student's speech by direct quote. This adds humiliating irony to the student's criticism of German-born Mesut Özil's speech capacity, which he deemed disqualifying for the prestigious Bambi media award. The students' internalization of the national language ideology elicits shame for themselves, their families, and even the most celebrated members of their community. The article concludes with a quote from a student who resigns himself to social and economic failure if he cannot perform properly in the hegemonic linguistic register, saying "if I can't hack it – with the language and everything – then I won't make it here in Germany." This is the desired conclusion of Harris's visit, to push young minority students to ignore systemic racism and accept the narrative of personal responsibility and language normativity.

Conclusion

The celebrity exemplars in the *Out with It* campaign act as minority enforcers of the hegemonic norms of cosmopolitan monolingualism. Their success is attributed to their competence in standardized German, implying and sometimes explicitly stating that individuals not fluent in standard German cannot expect a dignified life in Germany. Racism "is just the blink of an eye," insignificant in comparison to the rejection of German society by non-German speaking transnational Others. The celebration of minority role models in *Out with It* was accompanied in equal or greater measure by condemnation of minority straw men and tropes of young Muslim males' antagonism toward majority Germans and their liberal democratic national project.

Celebrities are presented as successful integrants, proof that, as campaign model and women's national soccer team player Celia Okoyino da Mbabi put it, "there is equality of opportunity in Germany for children with a migration background too" (Fietz, 2010). Celebrities are portrayed as successful because they are integrated, and their success proves their integration. Forms of diversity that fit neatly into an imagined ideal of German and "Western" values – summarized in one article as "respect for civil society, democratic rules, the defense of human rights, the freedom to think differently" (Malzahn, 2010) – are positioned as a threat to the nation and to the "good immigrant." Only with a "German foreground" can candidates for integration hope to live. "If we are not successful in defending this [German] foreground, we will lose entire city sections forever – and with them the people" (Malzahn, 2010). In other words, threatening forms of difference embodied by enemies of integration must be eliminated to enable the life of successful candidates for integration as well as normative white Christian nationals.

In popular public narratives, diversity is valuable when it is well managed and contributes to national political and economic projects. Diversity is proof that "Western values" are tolerant and permit "the freedom to think differently." Difference is valuable when it adds "color" and inspires innovation, spurring growth. However, diversity that overflows or challenges hegemonic projects, that puts spaces and populations beyond the reach of the state, threatens the biopolitical power of the nation-state to regulate life.

Notes

1. Lit. "Out with language, into life." *Raus mit der Sprache* is an idiom, which loosely translates to "speak up" or "out with it."
2. WISO-net.de includes 188 local, regional, and national periodicals.
3. The first-run campaign also included a number of non-celebrity people of color who work in media and public relations.
4. Harris uses a highly pejorative term for foreigners that is associated with Turkish and Arab minorities. The term was partially "reclaimed" in the 1990s in the Kanak Attak movement (see Göktürk, Gramling, & Kaes, 2007).
5. All translations are the author's own.
6. The common Arabic name Ali is used as a racialized slur.

Disclosure statement

No potential conflict of interest was reported by the author.

References

Agamben, G. (1998). *Homo sacer: Sovereign power and bare life*. Stanford, CA: Stanford University Press.
Albers, S. (2010a, October 8). Deutschland vs. Türkei: Integration ist rund und hat einen beat. *Stern*. Retrieved from http://www.stern.de/kultur/musik/deutschland-vs-tuerkei-integration-ist-rund-und-hat-einen-beat-1611942.html
Albers, S. (2010b, November 19). Die traurige Realität der integration: Die Deutschen, das sind die anderen. *Stern*.Retrieved from http://www.stern.de/politik/deutschland/die-traurige-realitaet-der-integration-die-deutschen-das-sind-die-anderen-1625611.html
Baldwin, J. (1998). *James Baldwin: Collected essays*. T. Morrison (Ed.). New York, NY: Literary Classics of the United States.
Balfour, L. (2001). *The evidence of things not said: James Baldwin and the promise of American democracy*. Ithica, NY: Cornell University Press.
Banerjee, M. (2011). Race matters in cologne: Migration, aesthetics, and popular culture. In C. C. Waegner, P. R. Laws, & G. De Laforcade (Eds.), *Transculturality and perceptions of the immigrant other: "From-heres" and "come-heres" in Virginia and North Rhine-Westphalia* (pp. 196–214). Newcastle, UK: Cambridge Scholars Publishing.

"Bitte lernt Deutsch!": Stars starten neue Integrations-Kampagne. (2010, March 23). *Die Bild.* Retrieved from http://www.bild.de/politik/2010/lernt-deutsch-11911816.bild.html

Bota, A., Topçu, Ö., & Pham, K. (2012). *Wir neuen Deutschen: Wer wir sind, was wir wollen.* Reinbek, Germany: Rowohlt.

Carpentier, N., & De Cleen, B. (2007). Bringing discourse theory into media studies: The applicability of discourse theoretical analysis (DTA) for the study of media practises and discourses. *Journal of Language and Politics, 6*(2), 265–293. doi:10.1075/jlp.6.2.08car

Deutschlandstiftung Integration: Deutschlandstiftung. (n.d.). Retrieved May 10, 2016, from http://www.deutschlandstiftung.net/

Dyer, R. (1998). *Stars.* London, UK: Bloomsbury Publishing.

Ehrenstein, C. (2010, October 20). Zuwanderer zeigen Zunge und werben für Deutsch. *Welt Online.*

Elias, N. (2000). *The civilizing process: Sociogenetic and psychogenetic investigations.* E. Dunning, J. Goudsblom, & S. Mennell Eds.. Malden, MA: Blackwell Publishers.

El-Tayeb, F. (2011). *European others: Queering ethnicity in postnational Europe.* Minneapolis, MN: University of Minnesota Press. Retrieved from http://ebookcentral.proquest.com/lib/unh/detail.action?docID=765495

Fanon, F. (2008). *Black skin, white masks.* London, UK: Pluto-Press.

Fietz, M. (2010, November 4). Was sich vom Fußball lernen lässt. *Focus Online.* Retrieved from http://www.focus.de/politik/deutschland/integrationsdebatte-was-sich-vom-fussball-lernen-laesst_aid_568754.html

Foucault, M. (2003). *"Society must be defended": Lectures at the collège de France, 1975-1976.* D. Macy, Trans. New York, NY: Picador.

Foucault, M. (2008). *The birth of biopolitics: Lectures at the college de France, 1978-1979.* G. Burchell, Trans.). New York, NY: Palgrave Macmillan.

Fröhlich, V. (2010, October 22). Ohne Deutsch nur Zaungast. *Nürnberger Zeitung,* 4.

Glück, H., Klein, W. P., Krämer, W., & Schöck, E. (Eds.). (2011). *Kulturpreis Deutsche Sprache 2011: Ansprachen und Reden.* Paderborn, Germany: IFB Verlag Deutsche Sprache.

Göktürk, D., Gramling, D., & Kaes, A. (Eds.). (2007). *Germany in transit: Nation and migration, 1955–2005.* Berkeley, CA: University of California Press.

Gramling, D. (2009). The new cosmopolitan monolingualism: On linguistic citizenship in twenty-first century Germany. *Die Unterrichtspraxis/Teaching German, 42*(2), 130–140. doi:10.1111/j.1756-1221.2009.00047.x

Gramling, D. (2016). *The invention of monolingualism.* New York, NY: Bloomsbury Academic.

Habermas, J. (1974). The public sphere: An encyclopedia article (1964). *New German Critique,* (3), 49–55. doi:10.2307/487737

Hall, S. (1997). The spectacle of the "other". In S. Hall (Ed.), *Representation: Cultural representations and signifying practices* (pp. 223–290). London, UK: Sage.

Hall, S. (2003). Encoding/Decoding. In S. Hall, D. Hobson, A. Lowe, & P. Willis (Eds.), *Culture, Media, Language: Working Papers in Cultural Studies,1972–79* (pp. 117–127). London, UK: Routledge.

Harris, O. (2010, October 25). Wieso sind die bullen schuld? *Der Spiegel,* 43. Retrieved from http://www.spiegel.de/spiegel/print/d-74735320.html

Haushaltsplan: Für Integrationskurse hat das Innenministerium kein Geld. (2014, May 9). *Migazin.* Retrieved from http://www.migazin.de/2014/05/09/fuer-integrationskurse-hat-das-innenministerium-kein-geld/

Herrmann, D. M. (2010, October 20). Ministerin Aygül Özkan: Neue Werbe-Kampagne für Deutsche Sprache. *Die Bild.* Retrieved from http://www.bild.de/regional/hannover/neue-werbe-kampagne-fuer-deutsche-sprache-14358002.bild.html

Integrations-Kampagne startet: Maria Böhmer wirbt für Sprachkurse. (2010, March 24). *Die bild.* Retrieved from http://www.bild.de/politik/2010/maria-boehmer-wirbt-fuer-sprachkurse-11925022.bild.html

Kampagne für Integration: Diese Promis werben für Deutsch-Kurse. (2010, October 20). *Die bild.* Retrieved from http://www.bild.de/politik/2010/deutsch-sprechen-raus-mit-der-sprache-14356484.bild.html

Kiyak, M. (2010, October). Kolumne zu Deutschkursen: Liebe Aygül Özkan! *Frankfurter Rundshau*. Retrieved from http://www.fr-online.de/meinung/kolumne-zu-deutschkursen-liebe-ayguel-oezkan-,1472602,4767140.html

Lachmann, G. (2010, October 22). Schämen sich die Deutschen für ihre Sprache? *Welt Online*. Retrieved from http://www.welt.de/politik/deutschland/article10463938/Schaemen-sich-die-Deutschen-fuer-ihre-Sprache.html

Lemke, T. (2011). *Biopolitics: An advanced introduction*. New York, NY: NYU Press.

Lentin, A., & Titley, G. (2011). *The crises of multiculturalism: Racism in a neoliberal age*. New York, NY: Zed Books.

Malzahn, C. C. (2010 November 13). Der deutsche Vordergrund. *Die Welt*.Retrieved from http://www.welt.de/print/welt_kompakt/debatte/article10703316/Der-deutsche-Vordergrund.htmlv

Mandel, R. E. (2008). *Cosmopolitan anxieties: Turkish challenges to citizenship and belonging in Germany*. Durham, NC: Duke University Press.

Marshall, P. D. (1997). *Celebrity and power: Fame in contemporary culture*. Minneapolis, MN: University of Minnesota Press.

Moore, R. (2015). From revolutionary monolingualism to reactionary multilingualism: Top-down discourses of linguistic diversity in Europe, 1794-present. *Language & Communication, 44*, 19–30. doi:10.1016/j.langcom.2014.10.014

Murakawa, N. (2019). Racial innocence: Law, social science, and the unknowing of racism in the US carceral state. *Annual Review of Law and Social Science, 15*(1), 473–493. doi:10.1146/annurev-lawsocsci-101518-042649

Pham, K. (2010 November 19). Integration: Deutscher patriot. *Die Zeit*. Retrieved from http://www.zeit.de/2010/47/Rapper-Harris

Rausch, K. (2010, July 2). Schwarz-rot-goldene Zunge ist Anzeige des Monats Mai. *Berliner Morgenpost*, 177, pp. 15.

Redmond, S. (2018). *Celebrity*. London, UK: Routledge.

Rojek, C. (2001). *Celebrity*. London, UK: Reaktion Books.

Schuster-Craig, J. (2017). Integration politics as an apparatus. *German Studies Review, 40*(3), 607–627. doi:10.1353/gsr.2017.0096

Smith, M. (2014). Affect and respectability politics. *Theory & Event, 17*, 3.

Vertovec, S., & Wessendorf, S. (Eds.). (2010). *The multiculturalism backlash: European discourses, policies and practices*. London, UK: Routledge.

Wiese, H. (2014). *Voices of linguistic outrage: Standard language constructs and the discourse on new urban dialects*. Working Papers in Urban Language and Literacies.

Wiese, H. (2015). "This migrants' babble is not A German Dialect!": The interaction of standard language ideology and 'us'/'them' dichotomies in the public discourse on a multiethnolect. *Language in Society, 44*(3), 341–368. doi:10.1017/S0047404515000226

Turkey's TV celebrities as cultural envoys: the role of celebrity diplomacy in nation branding and the pursuit of soft power

Ece Algan and Yeşim Kaptan

ABSTRACT
With the increasing popularity of Turkish television dramas, actors from Turkish TV series have become global celebrities with hundreds of millions of fans worldwide. In this paper, drawing on a political economy of communication analysis, we investigate the ways in which the Turkish government utilizes Turkish TV series' actors' celebrity status to further its foreign policy agenda with respect to soft power. We argue that in the Turkish case, celebrity diplomacy or the instrumentalization of celebrities for state ambitions of soft power necessitates a reliance on commercial television exports for nation branding. This brings its own contradictions and consequences as the image and meaning desired by the Turkish government does not always align with what the TV industry creates when competing in the global TV marketplace.

Introduction

Global celebrities have tremendous media clout that can allow them to access and influence a wide range of audiences in ways that would be impossible for international institutions or heads of nation-states. Some are asked to lend their name, money and time for activist causes and others are enlisted as cultural diplomats or goodwill ambassadors by humanitarian organizations and politicians. Similarly, following the huge success since the late 2000s of Turkish TV exports in reaching transnational audiences and a number of Turkish TV series actors became global celebrities with hundreds of millions of fans worldwide, Turkish state officials and President Erdoğan himself sought to take advantage of their popularity to showcase Turkey and various aspects of modern and traditional Turkish culture. Not only could these TV series be utilized to help the Turkish state improve the image of the country in the world because they appeal to both Western and Eastern audiences, but they could also potentially make the case for Turkey's foreign policy ambitions ideologically through the plotlines. Therefore, starting in the 2000s, when the rise of Turkish TV exports coincided with the Justice and Development Party's (AKP) new foreign policy strategy of improving Turkey's soft power and investments abroad, the TV industry was pushed to take part in nation branding. This new strategy positioned the TV industry as a gateway for a Turkish presence in different regions, as expressed by Şekib Avgagiç, the chairman of the Istanbul Chamber of Commerce: "Our lifestyle and ways of consumption reach the countries abroad through TV series, then our products arrive …

They prepare the countries ready for our entrepreneurs to enter those markets" (Türk yapımları, Cannes dizi fuarında beğeniye sunuldu, 2018). With such instrumentalist logic, various Turkish state institutions, such as the Ministry of Culture and Tourism, the Ministry of Economics and several Chambers of Commerce, chose to take advantage of Turkish actors' global celebrity status by enlisting them in state nation branding and promotional efforts like attracting tourists, developing diplomatic relations, and expanding business opportunities.

However, the increasingly polarized context of Turkey's political and socio-cultural relations and the transnationalization of the Turkish TV industry in the competitive neoliberal context of international television have complicated the politics of representation and created various dilemmas for the TV celebrities and executives involved in nation branding. Not only are they faced with government demands and support for content that fits into the governments' ideas of how best to capture Turkish identity and culture televisually, but they also face the challenges posed by the competitive global television industry to create novel, contemporary and relevant content for diverse global tastes. In an increasingly repressed media environment in which a great majority of television channels belong to corporations with close ties to Erdoğan (Sözeri, 2015), some Turkish TV industry players and celebrities readily choose to lend a hand in the government effort to utilize TV exports for economic and political reasons. Others, fearing government intervention or direct targeting, choose to cooperate by changing plotlines, producing content for new digital platforms for niche audiences or rallying behind the official soft power discourse of the government (Algan, 2020).

Our paper aims to investigate the ways in which the Turkish government utilizes Turkish TV actors' celebrity status to further their foreign policy agenda with respect to soft power via a political economy of communication analysis. While the TV industry promotes them as global stars, the state institutions strive to present them as desirable representatives of the nation-state by highlighting their national identities. In order to engage in a nuanced analysis of soft power and nation branding from a media industry studies perspective, we analyze the larger power dynamics among Turkey's media and government institutions by illustrating how internationally known Turkish TV series actors such as Kıvanç Tatlıtuğ, Beren Saat, Can Yaman, Halit Ergenç, Özcan Deniz, and Songül Öden negotiate their celebrity diplomat roles as cultural representatives or "envoys," as they are referred to by the government. We argue that in the Turkish case, celebrity diplomacy or the instrumentalization of celebrities for state ambitions necessitates a reliance on commercial television exports for nation branding, which comes with its own contradictions as the image and meaning desired by the Turkish government does not always align with what the TV industry creates when competing in the global TV marketplace.

In this paper, we first review the relationship among celebrity diplomacy, soft power and nation branding while summarizing the Turkish government's neo-Ottomanist aspirations. Following the methodology section, we then discuss the rise of Turkish TV series abroad and government efforts to utilize TV celebrities in nation branding and the consequences of such demands on the TV industry and content created.

The uneasy role of celebrity diplomacy in nation branding and soft power

Marshall (1997) sees celebrities as "elevated individuals" (p. 3) who can epitomize "the empowerment of the people to shape the public sphere symbolically" (p. 7). This symbolic and affective power celebrities build with their fans is what attracts politicians and state officials to elicit their assistance. Wheeler (2016) defines celebrity diplomacy as "the employment of well-known or famous individuals to publicize international causes and to engage in foreign policy decision-making circles" (p. 530). According to Cooper (2008), to be considered celebrity diplomats, celebrities "must enter into the official diplomatic world and operate through the matrix of complex relationships with state officials." (p. 7). In the literature on celebrity diplomacy, which focuses mostly on Hollywood celebrities or famous musicians such as Bono, Jolie, Hepburn and Clooney working as UN cultural ambassadors or climate activists, the emphasis is on celebrities' "global reach in terms of problem solving" (Cooper, 2008, p. 3) and their ability to influence policy when taking on issues of global significance. While the Turkish case is slightly different from these because Turkish celebrities are enlisted to help achieve the government's foreign policy goals and enhance soft power instead of advancing global objectives, the very fact that these celebrities are seen as cultural ambassadors and in the official diplomatic world highlights the complex relationship among celebrity diplomacy, nation branding and soft power.

According to Aroncyzk (2013), who views nation branding as a form of soft power, governments resort to nation branding because 1. it can attract resources such as tourists, investments, or skilled labor and supports global competition as a result; 2. it helps nation-states gain legitimacy and authority in the international arena; and 3. it boosts international reputation, which can be used to foster consensus and patriotism in the domestic arena. However, Bolin and Miazhevich (2018) caution that the media should not only be seen as passive tools in orchestrating branding campaigns, for they play an important role in nation branding as institutions, systems and societal storytellers. Similarly, Kaneva (2018) also stresses that national brands are created within the transnational context of commercialism associated with popular cultural products. According to Volcic and Andrejevic (2011), the commercial nation branding trend of the neoliberal era "is characterized by unprecedented levels of state expenditure on branding consultants, the mobilization of private/public partnerships for promoting national identity, and the convergence of the state's use of commercial strategies for public and international relations with the private sector's use of nationalism to sell products" (p. 599). However, it is the private/public partnership, which requires the aid of TV series and celebrity diplomacy, that becomes a highly contested arena in Turkey, especially when the government wants to play an active role in the nation's brand to support the shift in Turkey's foreign policy toward reviving neo-Ottomanism.

The policy of neo-Ottomanist irredentism has been adopted soon after the neo-conservative Islamic party, the AKP, rose to power in 2002, and consisted of efforts to improve economic relations with Turkey's Muslim neighbors, which meant a decisive shift in the country's foreign policy goals from the West toward the Middle East and Asia (Kaptan & Karanfil, 2013). From a neo-Ottomanist perspective, the Middle East and Eastern Europe are the hinterland of the late Ottoman Empire, which explains Turkey's ambition to increase its cultural, political and economic leadership in these regions by projecting itself as a global leader and savior of Islam (Kaptan, 2013). Since soft power refers to the ability to entice and influence via the appeal and attractiveness of a national culture (Nye, 2004), and since the USA's lead in the export of films and television programming is considered partly responsible for its ideological power in the world, the success of Turkish TV series encouraged many governmental, non-governmental and corporate entities and actors, including TV executives, to rally around the idea that Turkish TV series could strengthen the image of Turkey and thus contribute to its soft power abroad.

However, finding ways to utilize the popular interests of global audiences and fans of television celebrities and employing different tactics to tap into political and economic priorities of the country is not unique to the Turkish government. For instance, according to Chua, the rise of regional and peripheral cultural industries, particularly in East Asia "led some governments in this region, notably Japan, Korea, and PRC, to think about using its pop culture exports as instruments of soft power, exercised in/on the export destinations and locations of consumption" (Chua, 2012, p. 67). As a result, those culture industries have been supported by the governments of their respective countries. In the case of Korea, Gibson (2020) says that while "Korean dramas continue to attract audiences around the world, the South Korean government wants to get actively involved in helping convert the country's powerful pop culture into true soft power", and that they achieve this by "bringing celebrities directly into traditional diplomatic events, enlisting them to record messages of support before major negotiations" (Gibson, 2020). As we will discuss below, even though celebrity diplomacy in Turkey reflects a larger foreign policy strategy, it is undertaken in a rather trial and error fashion and is not part of long-term cultural industry policy planning.

Methodology

In this paper, we take a political economy of communication approach when analyzing the instrumentalization of Turkish celebrities in globally circulated TV series in support of the government's foreign policy plans and soft power ambitions. The political economy of communication critically examines the power dynamics among media, market structures, institutions and political actors through an analysis of how media ownership, profit motivation, political power and government policies shape media industry structure and content. Also, this type of analysis can help illuminate how media development is affected at critical junctures, which are moments when media institutions, political direction and economic structures simultaneously change (McChesney, 2013). We particularly investigated the roles that celebrities were given by government officials and policymakers when ascribed the task of nation branding and considered the contemporary political environment defined by the critical juncture of the transnationalization of Turkish TV industry and the shift in Turkey's foreign policy.

Since the Turkish television dramas and celebrities generated significant attention in the national and global trade and popular press, for this research, we examined industry trade associations' websites, press releases and newsletters, such as those of MIPCOM (Marché International des Programmes de Communication) and ITO (Istanbul Commerce Chamber), over 80 news stories and op-ed columns from Turkish mainstream newspapers, as well as English editions of other industry trade magazines such as Variety. With a political economy analysis, we do not only identify and analyze policies and strategies but also investigate highly intricate national production processes that operate within the complexities of both transnational media industries and the political, cultural and economic impositions of the Turkish state on the industry. In the next section, we describe how Turkish celebrities reached global stardom and the significance of their worldwide appeal, as we elaborate on their role as celebrity diplomats or cultural envoys.

The global stardom of TV actors and emergence of Turkey's celebrity diplomats

The Turkish TV industry had to integrate into a neoliberal media environment after the 1980s due to market- and state-driven policies propelled mostly by US-based global media giants (Kaptan & Algan, 2020). By the mid-2000s, with the tremendous success of Turkish television series such as *Gümüş* (*Silver*), *Binbir Gece* (*1001 Nights*) and later *Muhteşem Yüzyıl* (*Magnificent Century*) in Europe, the Middle East and Asia, the Turkish TV industry started to become a visible and thriving global player in the global media industry. As a result, since 2014, the Turkish TV industry has maintained its status as the second highest exporter of scripted TV dramas in the world (Turkey world's second highest TV series exporter after US, 2014; Vivarelli, 2018) and since 2016 as the fifth largest TV program exporter worldwide (France & Turkey, 2016), bringing over 350 million USD in revenue and reaching over 500 million viewers (Sofuoglu, 2017). By 2023, the Turkish government hopes that television series will pull in 1 USDbn from exports (Bhutto, 2019). In order to mediate between the political economy of the larger domestic television production industry and global market imperatives, Turkey's TV industry resorted to a number of tactics that can help curb both global and domestic pressures in order to continue their production growth and global sales numbers. There are three main tactics employed by Turkey's TV industry to combat the socioeconomic and political challenges they face: (1) carefully managing the content to skirt government restrictions; (2) adopting the government's soft power discourse and public diplomacy aspirations by cooperating with government officials and businesses in their cultural promotion and nation branding efforts; and (3) adapting to global TV trends by undertaking rigorous marketing and branding campaigns (Algan, 2020).

In their efforts to tap into the soft power of these exports, government officials turned their focus on the TV series actors who reached global celebrity status, for these actors are assumed to represent Turkey positively via the characters they play. We particularly designate Turkish actors of exported TV series as global celebrities since their achievements and global celebrity status extend beyond the former Ottoman territories and neighboring countries, including the Middle East, Balkans and Europe. For instance, Tatlıtuğ's performance in the movie *Kelebeğin Rüyası* (*Butterfly's Dream*) was praised by the *Hollywood Reporter's* Boyd Van Hoeij, who wrote "acting is solid from top to bottom and it is the subtle and soulful work of Tatlıtuğ, a model-turned-actor, that impressed the most, and not only because he becomes the de facto lead in the film's second half" (Sirmoglu, 2017, para. 23). Similarly, *Kurt Seyit and Sura*, the first Turkish TV series premiered simultaneously in Turkey and the Middle East (on MBC) over two geographical areas covering 500 million people, achieved big success in Russia (Sirmoglu, 2017, para. 23), in the Baltic countries, and in the United States (on Spanish language TV channel Mundo Fox TV) (Amerika Kurt Seyit ve Sura, 2015). *Noor's* (*Gümüş*) "final episode attracted 85 million Arab viewers. MBC (a pan-Arab television channel) even launched a pay TV channel dedicated to *Noor* that allowed viewers to watch episodes around the clock" (Sirmoglu, 2017, para. 5). According to Sirmoglu, "the show's success was like no other in the Middle East and Kıvanç became a huge idol. Young men mimicked his moves and hairstyle (even bleaching their hair to look more like him) and women idolized him" (Sirmoglu, 2017, para. 5). He was even called "Halal Brad Pitt" by his Arab fans (Williams, 2013).

Similarly, many Turkish television actors, like Can Yaman to Songül Öden, Halit Ergenç and Tuba Büyüküstün, have also achieved global star status and are admired by millions on many continents. For instance, Can Yaman, a rising Turkish soap opera star, has 6 million followers on Instagram worldwide. Describing Yaman's fans' reaction during his visit to Spain, a news reporter wrote "he was totally surrounded by a sea of people, the vast majority women, jostling to get up close to the pin-up . . . a good number surged forward to try and touch the actor, tugging at his clothes and even managing to pull his hair out of his ponytail" (Elelman, 2019, para. 2). A Spanish fan's words in a blog dedicated to Turkish, Korean and American TV series further speaks to the fame that Turkish actors enjoy globally: "it only took a few hours of Can Yaman in Spain to turn an entire country upside down . . . . the Turkish actor became a mass phenomenon all over the world after starring in several TV shows that were a success on television and that is why his express visit to our country to do several interviews became a revolution" (Nano, 2020, para. 1).

Turkish soap stars becoming pop idols around the Arab world has boosted Turkish tourism, leading to a wave of Arab visitors booking special tours to the mansion by the Bosphorus where Noor was filmed (Yörük & Vatikiotis, 2013, p. 2364). The fact that these exports have brought economic value and ignited positive interest in the country has caused state officials to treat these series as a part of their foreign policy strategies. As a result, the popular actors from Turkish dramas started being enlisted to help with the publicity of the country and its economic interests, such as tourism and the promotion of Turkish brands and business abroad. For instance, Turkish TV actors were cast in ad campaigns, commercials and videos that promote Turkey's historical sites or Istanbul's vibrant shopping life, such as the Turkish Airlines commercial featuring Tatlıtuğ visiting Istanbul's landmarks (Artan, 2010). In an interview during his visit to Pakistan, the actor who plays Ertuğrul Gazi, Engin Altan Düzyatan, exemplified the soft power of TV series through tourism. He stated that watching *Diriliş: Ertuğrul (Resurrection: Ertugrul)* intrigued fans to visit Turkey and it became a popular tourist destination (Lodhi, 2020). By adding that "[this] is great. We are really glad it happened", he showed his gratification for making a contribution to the national economy.

Businessmen and government officials also take TV celebrities to various promotional events abroad, such as launch parties, openings and press conferences. While the actors are well compensated for these trips and appearances and they are good opportunities for self-promotion, the trips are mainly seen as cultural promotion and nation-branding exercises by government entities, and thus actors are expected to deliver certain messages about Turkish culture, businesses and products with the assumption that Turkish dramas' assumed soft power would translate into other realms of Turkish economy and socio-political relations. During these trips abroad, actors usually present themselves in a "cultural envoy" role– a phrase used by a special magazine issue published by the PR arm of AKP to refer to the TV actors (Kale, 2016). In professional, political or business activities, protagonists of globally popular Turkish TV series are presented as the representatives of the Turkish nation and have become (either voluntarily or involuntarily) "celebrity diplomats." As advocates of particular issues, celebrity diplomats practice unconventional forms of diplomacy via media campaigns and mass performances in staged events rather than in the conventional sites of diplomatic activity like embassies (Cooper, 2007, 2008).

The instrumentalization of celebrities and soft power

Cooperating with state institutions or attending the events organized by the government officials and business enterprises are considered regular activities of celebrity diplomats. In such economic and/or cultural events, Turkish celebrities' global fame is instrumentalized for nation branding purposes. For example, in 2012 after the unprecedented success of Noor in Arab countries, the CEO of İstanbul Shopping Fest, Füsun Sönmez organized a press conference with Kıvanç Tatlıtuğ and Songül Öden in Dubai to promote İstanbul Shopping Fest. Sönmez declared that promotional events for Turkey are organized by the Cultural Affairs and Information Offices abroad of the Ministry of Tourism and Culture in collaboration with other governmental and non-governmental institutions to attract tourists to the country (Kıvanç Tatlıtuğ ve, 2012). In this collaboration, Turkish TV celebrities take active charge in implementing soft power with the help of the affective bond they cultivated with the fans. During the press conference for the promotion of İstanbul Shopping Fest, both Tatlıtuğ and Öden stated that they were gratified to help publicize Turkey and endorse PR activities in the region (Kıvanç Tatlıtuğ ve Songül Öden Dubai'de, 2012). Tatlıtuğ was reported to state that as a global celebrity recognized abroad, he was honored to utilize his popularity in the Middle East to draw interest to Turkey and to contribute to its promotion (Kıvanç Tatlıtuğ ve Songül Öden Dubai'de, 2012). Tatlıtuğ's words suggest that celebrity endorsement, instrumentalization of the global fame of national actors by the state, and nation branding are closely interrelated and go hand in hand. Tatlıtuğ implicitly models to other Turkish celebrities a responsibility to partner with state institutions and private enterprises to promote the country. His words indicate that he ascribes this responsibility as a national duty.

Some Turkish TV celebrities even take on the role of the celebrity diplomat by themselves, especially if they believe such a role can help alleviate the historical antagonism that exists between Turkey and its neighbors. For instance, despite sporadic diplomatic problems and tensions that arise between Israel and Turkey's AKP government, one of the TV series exported in recent years, *İstanbullu Gelin* (The Bride from Istanbul) has been heavily watched in Israel. Özcan Deniz, the leading actor of the series, "has formed a significant fan base in Israel. Around 11 thousand people attended his concert held in Tel Aviv in April 2019" (Ökmen & Göksu, 2019, p. 261). In the concert, Deniz "told the Israeli crowd in Turkish, with an interpreter translating his comments into Hebrew: 'What politicians could not do, we could. Thanks to art, we will stay together forever'" (Stars of Turkish TV, 2019). Although he acknowledges political disputes between Turkey and Israel, Deniz positions himself outside the realm of everyday politics by constructing art as an impartial domain. Thus, Deniz ascribes himself the role of a celebrity diplomat who can bring people of hostile countries together peacefully, which, he claims, is a duty that politicians failed to accomplish. Considering the adverse political relationship between the two countries, this example shows that the politics of celebrity culture and celebrity diplomacy can work independently of the international politics of nation-states when celebrities are eager to perform the role of peacemakers. This might be a result of the celebrity's ideological stance or interests closely aligning with those of the current government.

However, not every Turkish drama celebrity is eager or actively enlisted to take part in the cultural envoy role. This is because, while in the Western world "there has been a 'push' in audience demand for celebrity activism" (Wheeler, 2013, p. 140), the practice of celebrity activism in non-Western contexts can be more contentious. Traditionally in Turkey, celebrities often refrain from actively taking part in political campaigns or being seen with politicians for fear of overblown public reactions from fans or reduce employability in future projects. For instance, when one of the internationally renowned actors of Turkish TV dramas, Beren Saat, tweeted her support for the Gezi uprising in 2013, which became a movement against Erdoğan's authoritarianism, fearing possible retaliation from the government officials or the public, TV executives would not cast her in another role until her tweet was forgotten. According to Vitrinel (2019), while politicized celebrities have been banned, investigated, detained or exiled throughout the history of Turkey, the targeting of very popular television personalities with little or no political involvement who find themselves being attacked for "expressing their point of view through tweets, for being critical of a political act, for their participation or even just for their appearance in a socio-political movement" (p. 223) is a new phenomenon in Turkey that has emerged with the international success of TV series.

While celebrities in dramas with plotlines supportive of the government's neo-Ottomanist foreign policy agenda are sought out as cultural envoys, the popular historical dramas that deviate from traditional conservative Muslim and imperial values can be directly targeted by government officials. The examples of historical TV dramas *Magnificent Century (2011–2014)* and *Resurrection: Ertugrul (2014–2019)* are illustrative of the conditions for inclusion of celebrity participation in soft power and nation branding efforts. After President Erdoğan openly criticized *Magnificent Century* for depicting the great Ottoman Sultan Suleyman's alcohol consumption and romantic/sexual involvement with concubines in his harem and accused its writers and producers of "show(ing) our history in a negative light to the younger generations" (Rohde, 2012, p. 18), the production team made adjustments to the plotline and added battle scenes showing the Sultan's mother praying. The show's directors and actors, including Ergenç who played Sultan Suleyman in the show, insisted that the show carried "no political message or any other cultural message" and emphasized that it was only a fictional soap opera (Rohde, 2012, para 19). The exchange between Erdoğan and the show's producers and actors resulted in Ergenç being targeted by AKP supporters in social media and the pro-government media when he was seen participating in the Gezi uprising. Complexities and discontent between the AKP government and the production crew became more apparent when the government withdrew permission from the producers to film in historical sites such as Topkapı Palace and a deputy from the AKP submitted a parliamentary petition to ban the show (Buttho, 2019 Also, according to Bhutto (2019), unlike other Turkish TV series, *Magnificent Century* has never been used by the government to project Turkish soft power to the world. Moreover, the Turkish government publicizing its soft power ambitions via Turkish dramas coupled with their direct targeting of *Magnificent Century*, whose content does not fit with its new foreign policy vision, has ultimately shaped expectations for the industry in terms of what "appropriate" TV content and celebrity cooperation should look like.

With its expensive production budget supported by the national public broadcaster Turkish Radio and Television Company (TRT) and content that reflects religious, conservative and nationalistic values, *Resurrection: Ertugrul* was applauded and praised by Erdoğan and prominent AKP figures for its successful portrayal of Turkey's ancestral history, traditions and national culture (Carney, 2018; Özçetin, 2019). Erdoğan visited the show's set to lend support and show his approval, and the show's theme song was used many times in his political campaigns. The show's producers also hosted heads of foreign states such as Nicolás Maduro, the President of Venezuela (Maduro visits set, 2018), and Ramzan Kadyrov, the Head of the Chechen Republic (Kadirov, Diriliş Ertuğrul, 2018). After the remarkable audience reception of *Resurrection: Ertugrul* in Kuwait, Erdoğan also took the cast of the series in his private plane to the opening ceremony of the Kuwait International Airport, a 4.5 USD billion project built by a Turkish contractor (Diriliş dizisi oyuncuları, 2017), to publicize the accomplishments of Turkey's construction sector.

The show's actors' engaging with political leaders, its memorabilia given as gifts during diplomatic visits, Erdoğan's visit to the show's set, and his promotional trips abroad with the show's actors all point to collaboration between the government and the media industry that only happens when the industry helps the government invoke soft power via the influence of celebrities, whose roles Erdoğan believes are representative of Turkish identity. Not only was *Resurrection: Ertugrul* created for the state's public broadcaster and in a way to sate Erdoğan's desire for a favorable popular visual representation of Turkish history and culture, but also its promotions carried the specter of the *Magnificent Century* case and the state's expectations of its actors' collaboration. Therefore, although Erdoğan's backing of a particular TV series and promotion of its cast corresponds to Turkey's foreign policy which "has strategically shifted from a Kemalist-nationalist (West-oriented) to a neo-Ottomanist paradigm" (Murinson, 2006, p. 946), these attempts appear as responsive and opportunistic rather than as a deliberate strategic and systematic approach to connect celebrity power with specific foreign policy goals.

Conclusion

The ripple effects of the Turkish TV industry's entrance into neoliberal global markets and the political implications in the domestic realm of its transformation into a global growth industry have been multifaceted. In this paper, we particularly focused on one significant aspect of this transformation, which is the instrumentalization of Turkish TV series as nation branding tools and their actors as celebrity diplomats. When the private TV sector's use of nationalism to sell products coincided with the government's foreign policy agenda, it allowed President Erdoğan and AKP officials to utilize the visibility of Turkish historical dramas and the popularity of its stars as invaluable sources of nation branding and much needed soft power. However, such a commercial nation branding trend, which requires nation branding to be offloaded onto the private sector (Volcic & Andrejevic, 2011, p. 600), creates its own dilemmas in an authoritarian neoliberal state such as Turkey.

In neoliberal forms of governance, the state transfers its responsibilities onto its citizens by way of privatization. Volcic and Andrejevic (2011) argue that "nation branding campaigns fit this logic insofar as they invite the populace to identify its own interests with active participation in building and promoting a national brand identity" (p. 602). In Turkey, the government's nation branding efforts via Turkish TV series and their celebrities require active participation of both the TV industry and audiences in a number of ways. In addition to producing content that casts Turkey in a favorable light, expectations from the TV industry also require its celebrities to take part in official state trips, articulate love for their country often, and reiterate how fortunate they are to have the chance to represent their country while carefully tailoring their nation branding role as being driven by patriotism and loyalty to the nation-state. The *Resurrection: Ertugrul* case clearly illustrates the economic and promotional rewards of such cooperation when the industry creates and brands its products as "Turkish" in a way that is in line with the government's nation branding ambitions. In this regard, the Turkish government and industry play an active part in harnessing the global celebrity power of Turkish TV stars by dictating how they should present themselves in the global arena and by enlisting them as celebrity diplomats and cultural envoys. These celebrities in turn can also elevate and cement their status as patriotic individuals by complying with the government's soft power ambitions. The audiences are also invited to embrace the shows that are supported by the government to provide a state-sanctioned representation of Turkey's ancestral history, and they're encouraged to protest and even attack the cast and crew of the shows that the government believes contradict the nation's desired brand.

Despite attempts of the government to control the nation branding and representations of celebrities, disconnects between the Turkish government's soft-power aspirations and what the commercial cultural exports designed to be competitive in the international TV markets manage to deliver can also happen, resulting in both TV production processes and the industry becoming intertwined with politics. The *Magnificent Century* case discussed in this paper is significant because it shows that content deemed unrepresentative of Turkey's image as a conservative nation and the protector of Islamic values and Eastern traditions could be targeted by the government. As a result, not only did the domestic crisis of representation caused by the show crystalize government expectations of the industry, but it also demonstrated the possible challenges and political pressure they could face if they failed to embrace their cultural envoy role. Thus, our research supports Vitrinel's (2019) findings that in Turkey, "celebrities may suddenly find themselves at the centre of political debates, be forced to take sides and put at risk their careers and even their lives" (p. 229). Internationally known Turkish television stars do not have the privilege to be what York (2018) calls "reluctant celebrities" and refuse to participate because their refusal can easily be interpreted as unpatriotic or supporting the other side of the political spectrum, and they could be banished or lose their jobs because of political interference.

Disclosure statement

No potential conflict of interest was reported by the author(s).

ORCID

Ece Algan http://orcid.org/0000-0002-8761-1052

References

Algan, E. (2020). Tactics of the industry against the strategies of the government: The transnationalization of Turkey's television industry. In S. Shimpach (Ed.), *The Routledge companion to global television* (pp. 445–457). New York, NY & Oxon, UK: Routledge.
Amerika, Kurt Seyit ve Şura'yı çok sevdi. (2015, April 30). *Milliyet Cadde*. Retrieved from https://www.milliyet.com.tr/cadde/amerika-kurt-seyit-ve-surayi-cok-sevdi-2052198
Aroncyzk, M. (2013). *Branding the nation: The global business of national identity*. New York, NY: Oxford University Press.
Artan, G. (2010, June 7). Tatlıtuğ'lu reklam filmi Ortadoğu'da gösterilecek. *HaberTurk*. Retrieved from https://www.haberturk.com/haber/haber/521478-tatlituglu-reklam-filmi-ortadoguda-gosterilecek
Bolin, G., & Miazhevich, G. (2018). The soft power of commercialised nationalist symbols: Using media analysis to understand nation branding campaigns. *European Journal of Cultural Studies*, *21*(5), 527–542. doi:10.1177/1367549417751153
Buttho, F. (2019, September 13). How Turkish TV is taking over the world. *Guardian*. Retrieved from https://www.theguardian.com/tv-and-radio/2019/sep/13/turkish-tvmagnificent-century-dizi-taking-over-world?CMP=share_btn_tw
Carney, J. (2018). Resur(e)recting a spectacular hero: Diriliş Ertuğrul, necropolitics, and popular culture in Turkey. *Review of Middle East Studies*, *52*(1), 93–114. doi:10.1017/rms.2018.6
Chua, B. H. (2012). Delusional desire: Soft power and television drama. In N. Otmazgin & E. Ben-Ari (Eds.), *Popular culture and the state in East and Southeast Asia* (pp. 65–81). Oxon, UK and New York, NY: Routledge.
Cooper, A. F. (2007). Beyond hollywood and the boardroom: Celebrity diplomacy. *Georgetown Journal of International Affairs*, *8*(2), 125–132.
Cooper, A. F. (2008). *Celebrity diplomacy*. Boulder, CO: Paradigm Publishers.
Diriliş dizisi oyuncuları Cumhurbaşkanı Erdoğan'ın uçağında. (2017, May 10). *Posta*. Retrieved from http://www.posta.com.tr/dirilis-dizisi-oyunculari-cumhurbaskani-erdogan-in-ucaginda-haberi-1294877
Elelman, C. (2019, November 26). Turkish pin-up soap star can Yaman mobbed at Madrid airport. *Euro Weekly News*. Retrieved from https://www.euroweeklynews.com/2019/11/26/surrounded-police-got-nervous-as-the-crowd-jostled-to-get-up-close-to-the-pin-up-credit-can-yaman-instagram-canyaman/

France and Turkey join biggest programme exporters. (2016, April 15). *Digital TV Europe.* Retrieved from https://www.digitaltveurope.com/2016/04/15/france-and-turkey-join-biggest-programme-exporters/

Gibson, J. (2020). *How South Korean pop culture can be a source of soft power.* Carnegie Endowment. Retrieved from https://carnegieendowment.org/2020/12/15/how-south-korean-pop-culture-can-be-source-of-soft-power-pub-83411

Kadirov, Diriliş Ertuğrul setinde: Oyuncuları Çeçenistan'a davet etti. (2018, November 28). *Sputnik Turkiye.* Retrieved from https://tr.sputniknews.com/kultur/201811281036367098-kadirov-dirilis-ertugrul-oyuncu-cecenistan-davet-etti/

Kale, İ. (2016). Secret cultural envoys: Turkish series. *Magazine of Culture of Turkey, 2* (July15th Exclusive Issue), 82–88.

Kaneva, N. (2018). Simulation nations: Nation brands and Baudrillard's theory of media. *European Journal of Cultural Studies, 21*(5), 631–648. doi:10.1177/1367549417751149

Kaptan, Y. (2013). Proximity or difference: Media representation of Turkish Melodramas in the Middle East and Balkans. *Global Media Journal: Mediterranean Edition, 8*(2), 1–10.

Kaptan, Y., & Algan, E. (2020). Introduction: Turkey's national television in transnational context. In Y. Kaptan & E. Algan (Eds.), *Television in Turkey: Local production, transnational expansion and political aspirations,* (pp. 1-24). Cham, Switzerland: Palgrave Macmillan.

Kaptan, Y., & Karanfil, G. (2013). RTU(°)K, Broadcasting, and the Middle East: Regulating the transnational. *International Journal of Communication, 7*(1), 2232–2340.

Kıvanç Tatlıtuğ ve Songül Öden Dubai'de. (2012, May 10). *Haber7.* Retrieved from https://www.haber7.com/yasam/haber/878541-kivanc-tatlitug-ve-songul-oden-dubaide

Lodhi, A. (2020, December 11). Would love to work in Pakistan, given the right opportunity: Engin Altan Düzyatan. *The Express Tribune.* Retrieved from https://tribune.com.pk/story/2275562/would-love-to-work-in-pakistan-given-the-right-opportunity-engin-altan-duzyatan

Maduro visits set of Turkish TV Series. (2018, July 11). *Hurriyet Daily News.* Retrieved from https://www.hurriyetdailynews.com/maduro-visits-set-of-turkish-tv-series-134444

Marshall, P. D. (1997). *Celebrity and power: Fame in contemporary culture.* Minneapolis: University of Minnesota Press.

McChesney, R. W. (2013). The political economy of communication. In A. N. Valdivia, Ed., *The international encyclopedia of media studies, Volume 1: Media history and the foundations of media studies,* (pp. 1–27). Malden, MA: Wiley-Blackwell. https://onlinelibrary.wiley.com/doi/full/10.1002/9781444361506.wbiems031.

Murinson, A. (2006). The strategic depth doctrine of Turkish foreign policy. *Middle Eastern Studies, 42*(6), 945–964. doi:10.1080/00263200600923526

Nano, R. (2020, April 13). Can Yaman's message to Jesusa, the grandmother he surprised on TV: "What a joy". https://www.riri-nano.com/2020/04/can-yamans-message-to-jesusa.html

Nye, J. S. (2004). *Soft power: The means to success in world politics.* New York, NY: Public Affairs.

Özçetin, B. (2019). 'The show of the people' against the cultural elites: Populism, media and popular culture in Turkey. *European Journal of Cultural Studies, 22*(5–6), 942–957. doi:10.1177/1367549418821841

Ökmen, Y. E., & Göksu, O. (2019). Kültürel diplomasi bağlamında Türk dizilerinin ihracatı ve kültür aktarımına katkısı: 'Diriliş Ertuğrul' örneği. In O. Göksu (Ed.), *Kamu diplomasisinde yeni yönelimler* (pp. 247–291). Konya, Turkey: Litertaütk Academia. https://onlinelibrary.wiley.com/doi/full/10.1002/9781444361506.wbiems031

Rohde, D. (2012, March 8). Inside Islam's culture war. *Reuters.* Retrieved from http://blogs.reuters.com/david-rohde/2012/03/08/inside-islams-culture-war/

Sirmoglu, A. (2017, April 25). *The domestic and global impact of Kivanc tatlitug's work–15 years strong.* Retrieved from https://www.kivancnorthamerica.com/post/the-domestic-and-global-impact-of-kivanc-tatlitug-s-work-15-years-strong

Sofuoglu, M. (2017, January 19). The giddying rise of Turkish television series. *TRT World.* Retrieved from https://www.trtworld.com/magazine/the-giddying-rise-of-turkish-television-series-4691

Sözeri, C. (2015). *Türkiye'de Medya-İktidar İlişkileri: Sorunlar ve Öneriler Raporu.* İstanbul, Turkey: İstanbul Enstitüsü Yayınları.

Stars of Turkish TV show brave death threats to perform in Israel. (2019, April 7). *The times of Israel.* Retrieved from https://www.timesofisrael.com/stars-of-turkish-tv-show-brave-death-threats-to-perform-in-israel/

Türk yapımları, Cannes dizi fuarında beğeniye sunuldu. (2018, October 15). *itohaber.com.* Retrieved from https://www.itohaber.com/haber/sektorel/208922/turk_yapimlari_cannes_dizi_fuarinda_begeniye_sunuldu.html

Turkey world's second highest TV series exporter after US. (2014, October 26). *Hurriyet Daily News.* Retrieved from http://www.hurriyetdailynews.com/turkey-worlds-second-highest-tv-series-exporter-after-us-73478

Vitrinel, E. (2019). Forced politicization of television celebrities in Turkey. *Journal of Balkan and near Eastern Studies, 21*(22), 222–233. doi:10.1080/19448953.2017.1367585

Vivarelli, N. (2018, April 8). Turkey experiences its own wave of peak TV. *Variety.* https://variety.com/2018/tv/features/turkey-experiences-its-own-wave-of-peak-tv-1202746009/

Volcic, Z., & Andrejevic, M. (2011). Nation branding in the era of commercial nationalism. *International Journal of Communication, 5,* 598–618. https://ijoc.org/index.php/ijoc/article/view/849

Wheeler, M. (2013). *Celebrity politics: Image and identity in contemporary political communications.* Cambridge, UK: Polity.

Wheeler, M. (2016). Celebrity diplomacy. In C. M. Constantinou, P. Kerr, & P. Sharp (Eds.), *The SAGE handbook of diplomacy* (pp. 530–539). Thousand Oaks, CA: Sage.

Williams, N. (2013, June 27). The rise of Turkish soap power. *BBC News.* Retrieved from https://www.bbc.com/news/magazine-22282563

York, L. (2018). *Reluctant celebrity: Affect and privilege in contemporary stardom.* Cham, Switzerland: Palgrave Macmillan.

Yörük, Z., & Vatikiotis, P. (2013). Soft power or illusion of hegemony: The case of the Turkish soap opera "colonialism". *International Journal of Communication, 7*(25), 2361–2385. https://ijoc.org/index.php/ijoc/article/view/1880

Micro-celebrity practices in Muslim-majority states in Southeast Asia

Siti Mazidah Mohamad

ABSTRACT
We have witnessed the growth and spread of celebrity culture worldwide, from A-list celebrities to ordinary individuals turned micro-celebrities. However, celebrity studies are still lacking in exploring celebrity culture in the global South that has recently seen growth in their micro-celebrities afforded by rising individualism, commodification, and social media penetration. This paper aims to address this gap by examining micro-celebrity practices in three Muslim-majority states in Southeast Asia, namely Brunei, Malaysia, and Indonesia. This paper reveals that celebrification and celebritization processes in these societies demonstrate context appropriation, adaptation, localization, and transcultural flow of celebrity culture. Through the examination of contextualized socio-cultural configurations brought by the micro-celebrities – namely rising local consciousness, development of new subjectivities, and young people's self-mobilities – this paper contributes to the celebritization process, which goes beyond the individual celebrity to consider the nature of celebrity and its social and cultural embedding in the Muslim-majority Southeast Asian societies.

Introduction

Celebrity practices, cultures, and audience engagement with celebrities in the Southeast Asian region have existed since the early twentieth century following the rise of the film and music industries. However, in recent years, the region has seen the development of a new form of celebrification process creating what is called micro-celebrities, an emerging group of celebrities made possible by their successful self-branding practices on social media (Abidin, 2016, 2017a; Khamis, Ang, & Welling, 2016; Marshall, 2006; Marwick, 2013; Senft, 2013, 2008). The proliferation of Southeast Asian micro-celebrities parallels the growing individualism, modernity, and digital development within the region, particularly its high Internet and social media penetration. As of January 2020, 63% of the region's total population are active social media users (Hootsuite & We Are Social, 2020). A continuous emphasis on individuality and self-expression, channeled via the self-disclosure of personal information on social media sites to audiences, has combined with technological advancement and transformed celebrity culture to allow it to move from the dependency on formal media institutions to a new level of independence for the individuals themselves.

Unlike the previous form of A-List celebrities, developed and marketed by entertainment agencies and who depended mostly on mass media to advertise themselves, extensive, large scale institutional efforts do not promote these micro-celebrities. They work independently, highlighting their personalities and identities and creating unique, personalized content on their social media platforms. These are ordinary individuals who use social media for self-disclosure and share seemingly banal everyday activities to connect with their audiences. These micro-celebrities work on a celebrity logic that is quite different from traditional (A-List) celebrities (Jerslev, 2016; Marshall, 2006). The micro-celebrity's celebrity logic encompasses the negotiation of public privacy (Jerslev, 2016) focused on a niche group of audiences on personalized platforms such as Instagram, YouTube, and TikTok; performing authenticity and intimacies (Abidin, 2015); as well the sharing of mundane life and the intentional display of rawness (Abidin, 2017b), which Abidin (2017b) refers to as "calibrated amateurism", within a participatory culture involving their audiences and their subjectivities (Marwick, 2016; Turner, 2010b). Their existence and visibility are further enhanced by the affordances new media offers in generating, personalizing, and circulating content for their audiences; affordances contribute to how the audiences makes sense of the micro-celebrities' presence and functions.

With the rising number of individuals gaining visibility and fame via persistent self-disclosure and performance of self online, matched with the growth in scholarly and public interest in micro-celebrities, the existence of micro-celebrities in the region cannot be dismissed. Despite the growing number and types of celebrities in the global South, there is not much known about how Southeast Asian celebrities – or specifically this new form of Southeast Asian micro-celebrities – differ from the dominant Anglo-American model (Driessens, 2013, 2018). Within this context of growing Southeast Asian micro-celebrities in the region, this paper aims to address this gap by examining micro-celebrity practices in three Muslim-majority states: Brunei, Malaysia, and Indonesia. These three states were chosen due to their relatively similar socio-cultural and religious roots, giving rise to celebrity cultures that may be similar while exhibiting their own unique contexts and patterns. For instance, Brunei's celebrity development is not as intensive and widely spread as Malaysia and Indonesia. While these latter countries have witnessed their celebrity cultures flourish, and their celebrities enjoy the audience's attention within and outside the region, Brunei celebrity development remains stagnant. This could be due to the slow rise of music, entertainment, and other creative industries as they are not yet recognized as profitable industries.

The apparent differences between these three states serve as a reminder that while seeing a similar form of micro-celebrity amongst these states, it is imperative to be cognizant of their diversities. In this case, I acknowledge micro-celebrities as a product of their national context while being influenced by transcultural flows from outside their locality and society. I take micro-celebrities as a unit of analysis to capture their local and transcultural practices to avoid offering a spatially bounded analysis of celebrity cultures based on national context alone, which have been cautioned by other studies (Driessens, 2018). This paper's empirical examples are drawn from research I conducted on young people's social media use and engagements between 2017 and 2020. These studies predominantly employed qualitative research methods such as semi-structured interviews, qualitative content analyses conducted on social media sites, and questionnaire surveys. Individually, these research studies examine Bruneian creatives' aspirations and affective labor on social media, Bruneian youth's social and economic mobilities via social media self-branding practices, and the celebrification process of *hijabi* micro-celebrities and the ways audiences make sense of their existence and their social media contents. Collectively, they provided more in-depth insights into young people's social (media) practices at a micro level, whereas at a more macro level, they allow a look at the transformation and localization of celebrity culture in the region that is somewhat inspired by those from Western and East Asian cultures.

Drawing from these studies and other celebrity-related studies in Malaysia and Indonesia, this paper builds on the existing knowledge we have of Southeast Asian micro-celebrities to contextualize and conceptualize micro-celebrity culture in the region. In this paper, the analyses of micro-celebrities' local appropriation of the Black Lives Matters phenomenon and the proliferation of *hijabi* micro-celebrities in the region demonstrate that micro-celebrities do not exist simply as a form of entertainment or only as brand and product ambassadors. The local micro-celebrities act as a conduit for their audiences to express their voices on local issues, raising local consciousness, and creating new subjectivities. In this context, I argue that micro-celebrities are functional entities that can offer self-identification and sense-making for their audiences. I further argue that the context appropriation, adaptation, localization, and the traces of transcultural flow of celebrity culture in the Southeast Asian micro-celebrities' practices, which are discussed in the subsequent sections, would further our understanding of celebrity culture as a socio-cultural formation beyond mere representation and a discourse (Turner, 2010a). In the penultimate section, I question the role of pseudo micro-celebrities who are seemingly without influence. Despite their questionable and insignificant celebrity status among the local audience, I argue that the local micro-celebrities' celebrification process has become a youth mobility practice that is affectively and strategically utilized by these young people for their social and economic mobility. This youth mobility practice in the form of celebrification of individuals signals the function and influence of micro-celebrities in the region.

Micro-celebrities' raising local consciousness and creating new subjectivities

The influence of celebrities goes beyond the relatable and identifiable self to include other aspects of everyday life such as politics, empowerment, social justice, and grassroots activism (Beta, 2020; Tsaliki, 2016). Celebrities play their role in highlighting specific issues and concerns (Drake & Miah, 2010) that may have been bypassed by mainstream media (Tsaliki, 2016). Celebrities act and are taken as moral leaders with authority to voice out pressing matters. Therefore, the audience's expectation of micro-celebrities advocating for social change in their societies via their position is not unusual; their celebrated position comes with responsibilities, making celebrity a functional entity. This expectation is commonly seen in Western celebrity culture and, to a lesser extent, has become common within Southeast Asian celebrity cultures such as Malaysia and Indonesia. My analysis of several Malaysian celebrities' social media postings revealed that they are quite careful about making public spectacle on politically related issues. In Brunei, it is uncommon to see an individual speaking out on pressing matters on public platforms at the same intensity we see with celebrities in Western countries. It has been only very recently seen among the young micro-celebrities (or influencers, the preferred label used in the country for micro-celebrities). These could be attributed to several reasons, including Brunei's collectivistic culture where cultural sensitivity and self-censorship are prevalent (Haji Mohamad, 2019), the fear of receiving backlash, and turning into the next "viral topic" in the country. In a small nation with over 400,000 population and high social media penetration (98% in 2020), online content is quickly circulated and consumed. Local content becomes viral or thought of as viral when it goes beyond word-of-mouth and is shared and scrutinized on social media platforms and discussion forums such as Reddit.

However, very recently, Bruneian influencers' appropriation and localization of one global phenomenon, the Black Lives Matter movement (hereafter, referred to as BLM), demonstrate how micro-celebrities and young people have taken to their social media sites to bring to the front and address the often ignored, somewhat underplayed, and normalized racial discrimination in Brunei. They problematized the use of the derogatory term *"Kaling"* to refer to a group of immigrants of South Asian descent (Indian, Bangladeshi, and Pakistani), who make up a large demographic of Brunei's immigrants often working in manual labor and blue-collar jobs. Such community response to this racist term is not new. However, it was recently sparked by George Floyds' upsetting death, and society's disapproval was made more apparent by the reachability and spreadability of social media content (more so on Twitter). These influencers (and other young people) were not only speaking to the general public. One particular Bruneian influencer, Bash Harry, "called out" other influencers on Twitter for their alleged lack of action in using their position, voice, and social media platforms to bring BLM to public attention and raise awareness of racism in Brunei. Such expectations of a celebrity are similarly seen in the case of Malaysian micro-celebrities. For instance, Vivy Yusof's Instagram upload of BLM content led to dissatisfaction amongst her audience, which sought equal attention for other global and Muslim-related issues such as the Syrians' misfortunes. Here, being a Malay Muslim micro-celebrity comes with an expectation that she must play her role as a Muslim and speak for the global Muslim community. Regardless of her position as a local (within Malaysia) and regional (within the Muslim-majority Southeast Asian states) micro-celebrity, she is expected to be cognizant of and responsible for voicing global issues. Vivy is expected to be concerned with issues close to her identity. If such expectations are not met, the audience will act as "social police" to monitor and reprimand these micro-celebrities.

The concern mentioned above and the appropriation of BLM content by the micro-celebrities is an example of the local appropriation of global and transnational contexts. George Floyd and his adversity are appropriated in Brunei's context to highlight the existing racism in the country and alludes to the rise in local consciousness of the country's issues and the new subjectivities of the audience. Via this phenomenon, we witnessed new ways of discerning the long existence of – but rarely deliberated – racism and discrimination issues in the country. Such mobilization of new subjectivities, or rather, such reproduction of old concerns in new forms in the region via social media exhibits the micro-celebrities' social functions. This local appropriation of global phenomena signals at least three significant socio-cultural configurations and realities brought about by micro-celebrities. First, micro-celebrities and young people are challenging previously taken-for-granted social practices, particularly the older generation's practices that they thought to have normalized, such as using the term *"Kaling"* and the different forms of discrimination the immigrants received. This contestation also suggests intergenerational tension between older and younger generations, felt more by the latter who are trying to challenge the predominant socio-cultural norms and practices imposed by the former. To some extent, micro-celebrities' presence offers young people an outlet to convey their thoughts and normalize new social behavior and practices.

Second, this local appropriation of BLM's context reveals a transfer of power to micro-celebrities and power-sharing between the micro-celebrities and their audiences. Enabled by new media's affordances, enhanced multi-directional participation and engagements, audiences are more involved with the content micro-celebrities portray on their platforms. The expectation of Bruneian influencers (from their audiences, the general public and fellow influencers) in BLM's context reveals a power transfer and power-sharing between celebrities and their audience, which confirms the performativity of a celebrity body as a site of production, consumption (Hearn & Schoenhoff, 2016; Marshall, 2006; Marshall, 2010; Mohamad & Hassim, 2019) and contestation as shown via Bash Harry's and Vivy Yusof's cases earlier. Here, an influencer's position is not reduced to merely showcasing their personalities, identities, and brands (such as in product reviews). They are expected to be proactive and take a stand on issues of concern, and at the same time shape cultural values. Related to the previous point on young people challenging norms, they use micro-celebrities to reflect or voice their concerns. In this instance, we can see a two-way engagement between the audience and the micro-celebrity. The audience uses the micro-celebrity as a functional entity to make their voices heard and to make sense of themselves and their identity through self-identification. For their part, the micro-celebrity gains the power of their platform; the transfer of power to micro-celebrities is visible in these celebrities' ability to speak up for a cause without the need for institutional endorsement, as their celebrated position allows for this to happen. Nevertheless, the micro-celebrities' relatability, authenticity, and celebrated identity somewhat became a double-edged sword; they rely on individuality, relatability, and rawness to springboard their status, but these same qualities tie them down with audiences' expectations to speak up for specific causes as they are perceived as self-regulated and authentic individuals.

Finally, this local-global contextualization also points to the transnational and transcultural nature of celebrity culture; local influencers are learning from global celebrities and the roles they play as indicative in the justification used by Bash Harry in the use of influencers' position, voice, and platforms to bring BLM to public attention. One prominent feature I observed in the region's celebrity culture is the influence of Western (celebrity) cultures and in recent years, East Asian culture such as the Korean Wave (*Hallyu*) due to their cultural proximity (Peichi, 2013; Shim, 2013). It has become common to see Korean cultural elements in the Muslim societies in Southeast Asia, suggesting cultural hybridity and recontextualization of other celebrity cultures in the region (Mohamad, in press; Syed, Azalanshah, & Kwon, 2019) and making it imperative to look into how celebrity culture in the region is shaped by transnational cultural flow and the interplay between different local and transnational institutions and agents in creating today's micro-celebrities. Despite micro-celebrities ostensibly not needing institutional support (as they are self-generated via individualized online content sharing), they are nevertheless influenced by transnational corporations and institutional systems.

Via the local appropriation of BLM phenomena by micro-celebrities and their audiences, I have shown how micro-celebrities reconfigure socio-cultural realities in Brunei. Using micro-celebrities as a medium to voice their concerns, the audiences are challenging local socio-cultural norms and practices. We have also seen the transfer and sharing of power between audiences and the micro-celebrities and traces of transcultural influence in

Southeast Asian celebrity cultures, revealing the social functions and the localized and contextualized forms of micro-celebrification in the region. Such consciousness of local issues and realities examined in this section are not that different from those of the global North. Nonetheless, what has been discussed so far demonstrates local experiences within the underlying socio-cultural landscapes in the region that are continuously shaping the celebrification process and the region's celebrity cultures and vice versa. The function of micro-celebrities can be analyzed in another form of celebrification that recently garnered the attention of scholars in the region due to its apparent social-cultural and political implications, which is discussed in the next section.

Hijabi micro-celebrities: *Hijab* practices and women empowerment

The region has seen impressive growth of another type of celebrification – the proliferation of Muslim *hijabistas* or *hijabsters* and the rise of self-made *hijabi* micro-celebrities following the resurgence of Islam in Muslim-majority Southeast Asian countries since the 1970s (Osman, 1985; Saat, 2018; Weintraub, 2011) as well as the high social media penetration in the region. The presence of Muslim *hijabi* celebrities (that is, celebrities who are often characterized by their use of the *hijab* or Muslim headscarf), such as the prominent micro-celebrities Dian Pelangi (@dianpelangi, Indonesian, 5.1 million Instagram followers), and Vivy Yusof (@vivyyusof, Malaysian, 1.8 million Instagram followers), is one of the noticeable features of celebrity culture in the Muslim-majority Southeast Asian countries. Such presence is not particular to the Southeast Asian contexts, as young Muslim women worldwide are taking advantage of the social media affordance to share the latest fashion, trends (not necessarily Islamic), self-presentation, and to perform religious piety. For instance, let us consider the well-known London-based British Muslim Dina Tokio. What Dina offers via her YouTube videos is the life of a Muslim woman living within neoliberal and Western contexts. Dina attempts to tackle the preconceived notion of Muslim women as oppressed, subjugated, and the foreign "other" through her #youraveragemuslim YouTube series (Islam, 2019). Beyond the hijab styling, make-up tutorials, and mundane beauty styling tips shared on her YouTube accounts, she is significantly altering how Muslim women are viewed in her respective community (or even globally).

In this region, Brunei, Malaysia, and Indonesia have seen a fair share of *hijabi* micro-celebrities of different natures. Via the examination of these two different types of *hijabi* micro-celebrities practices, I posit that these *hijabi* celebrities function as markers for their audiences to make sense of their hijab practices and their identity. In this context, *hijabi* micro-celebrities include those empowering hijab-wearing micro-celebrities who are not involved with preaching religious knowledge on their social media and those who are considered religious social media influencers. The hybridity of these *hijabistas* or *hijabsters* emerged through the intersectionality of culture, religion, modernization, and consumption as the growth of luxury hijab retail brands heightened the veil as a statute of class (Mohamad & Hassim, 2019; Williams & Kamaludeen, 2017). The consumption of hijab from well-known brands and hijab practices in the region is not merely for covering-up and fulfilling religious obligations. However, for the *hijabi* micro-celebrities, hijab consumption is associated with identity creation, a middle-class marker, a symbol of modernization, and progress while keeping to their religious obligations (Mohamad & Hassim, 2019).

Hijabi micro-celebrities act as brand ambassadors or brand reminders, and at the same time, they become conduits for audiences to make sense of their own hijab practices and their own identities as Malay and Muslim women. They also provide a sense of belonging as part of a fashionable group of women via owning and donning headscarves from the brands promoted by the micro-celebrities (Hassim & Mohamad, 2020). Vivy, as I have examined in another work, offers her audience self-identification through her authentic identity, relatability, and "everydayness", and is acknowledged as a role model for her audience to reshape their own life (Mohamad & Hassim, 2019). In contrast to the Indonesian *hijabi* influencers (as can be seen later), Vivy does not offer explicit religious knowledge. She does not label herself as a *Muslimah* (a pious Muslim women). Nevertheless, her Malay Muslim identity is apparent in the social media content she shares (wearing headscarves and the use of captions and hashtags such as *Alhamdulillah* and *InsyaAllah*). Vivy, as the face of The dUCk Group brand selling hijab amongst other products, is used to promote women's empowerment and hijab practices via her dUCk products and the narrative created for each of their collections.

A case in point is The dUCk Group's *Barbie X dUCk* collaboration. This collection with Vivy as the local model raises questions of what *hijabi* Malay represents and a *hijabi* celebrity's function in society. If assessed by their Western/Eastern and non-*hijabi*/*hijabi* binaries, Barbie's and Vivy's identities contradict one another. Using Barbie dolls as models and inspiration, the company (The dUCk Group) aims to inspire young girls (and women) to be ready to pursue their dreams. Vivy was selected as the local role model for this *Barbie X dUCk* collaboration based on her impressive and inspiring career for many in Malaysia and across Asia (Cheong, 2018). Her career trajectory, from a law graduate from the London School of Economics to the co-founder and Chief Creative Officer of FashionValet, the region's leading e-commerce platform, epitomizes Vivy as a symbol of inspiration and women empowerment for girls and women alike. Beyond the cultural and religious contexts, and the contradictions mentioned, Vivy and Barbie share similarities in success and empowerment. Here, Vivy's life is used as a model for success and as the local Barbie, she functions as an illustration of "girl power", suggesting that anyone can achieve success. She exists as an inspiration, and her celebrated existence embodies the audience's desire for progress.

Aside from inspiring audience consumption of hijab, being a channel for audiences' self-identification and acting as a middle-class marker, *hijabi* micro-celebrities, as shown by Beta (2019) and Nisa (2018), can operate as religious social media influencers. Nisa (2018) in her study on Indonesian female Muslim *hijabi* influencers, demonstrated that these influencers through creative and lucrative *Dawa/Dakwah* (religious preaching) on Instagram are reaching out to their audiences, usually Muslim (young) women, to entice them toward religious transformation (for instance, to practice hijab as a religious obligation). These religious micro-celebrities are using fame (contrary to religious expectations on women to keep their gaze down and not attract attention), and the affordances of social media (multi-modal features and spreadability, to name a few) to spread Islamic teachings in the country. Fame is seemingly used as a tool and a strategy by these *hijabi* celebrities to be seen and heard for a more significant religious cause. This religious sharing practice by the Indonesian *hijabi* celebrities/influencers signals the transfer of religious authority from religious institutions to individuals and the transformation in the form of religious content sharing, which was previously mass conducted at religious hall and mosques. This phenomenon has also been observed in Brunei (Haji Mohamad, 2018) and Malaysia. Unlike the mass broadcasted Islamic teaching, in this new form of religious social media sharing, the audience receives content they willingly signed up (and follow) for.

As Nisa (2018) revealed, the creative content of *Dakwah* is not merely about sharing Islamic content. Similar to the self-identification and relatability Vivy offers her audience, these religious influencers use their own progressive or "*hijrah*" journey toward becoming virtuous Muslims, their religious knowledge, and ethical disposition as content for their *Dakwah* to build their (para-social) relationships with their audiences and effectively become active religious agents and role models for the young people. As a result, Instagram has recently become a space for Indonesian female Muslim youth to educate each other in becoming virtuous Muslims (Nisa, t2018). Religious self-cultivation and *hijabi* celebrification could continue to transform the landscape of political Islam in Indonesia. The rise of digital religious activism is a significant progression recently seen in Indonesia due to this new form of religious social media practices (Beta, 2020).

Brunei has also seen the emergence of aspiring *hijabi* religious influencers such as Hanisah Othman and Hanisah Lia. They have utilized their Instagram accounts to share religious knowledge and to use their self-transformation narrated in an affective way to capture their audiences' attention. However, I must point out that these religious influencers in Brunei do not have the same level of exposure, engagement, and size of following as those shown in Beta's (2020, 2019) and Nisa's (2019) work. This could have been caused by young people's lack of interest in portraying themselves as religious influencers. For an Islamic state, surprisingly, Brunei has more generic influencers (fashion enthusiasts, fitness enthusiasts, singers, actors, and lifestyle influencers) than religious influencers.

From these two different types of Southeast Asian *hijabi* celebrities, we can also observe growing local consciousness and the development of new subjectivities in rethinking Islamic practices, individual self-transformation and empowerment, and changing religious landscapes in the three Muslim-majority states. Via the examples of Vivy and the Indonesian religious social media influencers, *hijabi* micro-celebrities can function as an inspiration and push for more progressive women who continuously work on reinventing and mobilizing themselves as cosmopolitan Malay Muslim women, global in outlook while rooted to their socio-cultural and religious belief and practice (Mohamad & Hassim, 2019). As can be seen in this context, *hijabi* micro-celebrities in the Muslim majority Southeast Asian countries play a significant role in local socio-cultural practices and follow the modernization progress in their respective states and region. They also act as conduits for their audiences to reframe themselves according to gender (women empowerment) and religion (self-transformation), while potentially bringing wider socio-cultural configurations in the region. This phenomenon has been considered by Marshall and Redmond (2016, p. 2), who posited celebrities as conduits for audiences to "comprehend cultural values around gender, youth, or class". While being cognizant of the micro-celebrities' functions, in what follows I will examine the existence of less significant or less functional celebrities.

The pseudo micro-celebrities? Making sense of Southeast Asian micro-celebrities

From these celebrated bodies analyzed and discussed in the previous sections, we witnessed the autonomy in creating oneself in today's digital and neoliberal times and the rise of individuals who are always searching for the best, most appropriate self for the current context. As Howard (2010, p. 118) aptly points out, "instead of building their biographies, individuals now purchase ready-made components of self-identity, choosing from a range of options"; these micro-celebrities are creating their own identity based on their interests and personal dispositions. Often, as I have observed and discussed in the previous sections, micro-celebrities refocused their online personae to fit into the current trend and the expectation of their audiences. Notwithstanding this autonomy, the participatory and collaborative features of social media sites open up space for the audience to actively respond and contribute to the celebrities' production of self and identity online. In this new culture of self-promotion, consistent, edited, and perfected self-disclosure via social media sites becomes essential to maintaining the audience's interest and ensuring continuous consumption of the content creator's daily life (Marwick, 2013). I posit that it is within these audience subjectivities that the celebrity's sense-making practices can be further understood.

Via the two examples above (local contextualization of the BLM phenomenon and *hijabi* celebrification), micro-celebrities have raised local consciousness and developed new subjectivities within the region. While cognizant of their function and socio-cultural configurations, we also need to consider micro-celebrities without social function or influencers without influence, which resonates with Rojek's (2001) "Celetoids" or short-lived celebrities. Would pseudo micro-celebrities, those with low audiences (number of followers) and without distinct social function still be considered celebrities? In this section, through the analysis of audience responses to local celebrities in Brunei, I argue that micro-celebrities are subjected to audience subjectivities and expectations and that these pseudo micro-celebrities, regardless of how they are viewed by the audience, exist as an identifier of young people's mobility or at least, an aspiration for future mobilities. In one of my studies of Brunei's social media influencers, most survey respondents claimed that the so-called Bruneian influencers should not be called "influencers" because they do not generate positive and life-changing impacts on the public (apart from doing product reviews). It is important to note that there is an apparent negative connotation of influencers in the country due to what could be labeled as culturally and religiously insensitive actions of a few local influencers in recent years. A case in point – in 2018 several local influencers were publicly criticized for posing in an inappropriate manner at the soft opening of a well-known fast food joint's second branch in the country. One of the photos marked as "social media marketing gone wrong" was of one influencer posing barefoot on a restaurant table. Many locals considered such an action disrespectful and unacceptable in their culture.

Surprisingly, local audiences are more receptive of global celebrities; Western (traditional and micro-celebrities) and East Asian (K-Pop idols, South Korean celebrities and influencers) personalities are thought to have more impact on local audiences, which seemed to be evident in the participant responses to the survey where they were asked to name five Social Media Influencers (within or outside Brunei) that they follow on Instagram. Only a few mentioned several local influencers (such as RanoAdidas, Kurapak, Lipstickmyname, Thanis Lim, Rozan Yunos, and Jeeradoesfashion) and those who did also included non-local influencers in their list. This does make one wonder why local audiences are less able to relate to local influencers who share the same culture, language, and social practices. Although this somewhat lukewarm response cannot be used to generalize local influencers' audience reception, it offers a picture of the triviality of local celebrity culture in the public's eyes. In this situation, where celebrity culture is almost absent or celebrities are considered non-celebrated individuals, what kind of celebrity culture do we have?

At this juncture, I would like to postulate two notions concerning the contextualization of the celebrification process and celebrity culture. Firstly, within the context of these Southeast Asian societies and taking into consideration audience responses to local influencers, I argue that a critical aspect in understanding celebrity culture is audience-subjectivities, as the audience can contribute to the creation, spread and reinforcement of local consciousness and new subjectivities and the co-creation of celebrity. Celebrity as a category is not only democratization in the number and types but also in its nature that is now open to audiences' contestation (Van Krieken, 2019). Audiences play a role in circulating and spreading media relevant to them (Jenkins, Ford, & Green, 2013), which substantiates and further extends Driessens (2014, p. 115) conceptualization of celebrity culture as sense-making that comprises the celebrities, the industries that produce them, the commodities they represent and what audiences do and say about celebrity.

In the case of micro-celebrities, the spreadability of celebrity content, images, and ideas needs to be analyzed from the view of the audiences who are the persons making sense of their existence, the need for micro-celebrities in their everyday lives, and the role in shaping the micro-celebrities' content as I have discussed in the earlier sections. This approach in audience inclusion and engagement in studying celebrity culture, as underlined by other scholars (David Marshall, Graeme Turner, and Philip Drake), offer what I would imagine to be an attempt at factoring in celebrities, audiences, and contexts together in understanding contextualized celebrification and celebritization processes. Contexts are significant in the celebritization process as they provide the landscape for the celebrification of their celebrity and localized celebrity culture.

Empirically speaking, the region's micro-celebrities are subjected continuously to their audience's critiques and contestation. Aliff Syukri, a Malaysian celebrity who gained his fame via the marketing of his beauty and cosmetic products, his narratives of failure and success, everyday life, and the controversial videos he uploaded on his Instagram and YouTube channels, is a good example of a micro-celebrity whose actions are constantly under scrutiny and contested by his audience. An observation of his social media content I conducted between 2017 and 2020 permits me to condense his controversial "marketing" style. He capitalizes on viral culture to amplify his presence and repeatedly creates controversies which usually contradict the society's socio-cultural norms. To appease the audience, he then apologizes for his insensitive actions. In 2017, Aliff's single "Bobo Dimana" with Nur Sajat (another Malaysian celebrity) and Lucinta Luna (an Indonesian singer) was labeled as culturally and religiously inappropriate due to its provocative content and dance performance (Mokhtazar, 2018a, 2018b). He later released an Islamic song "Agama Kedamaian" with his wife to recover from the backlash he received over "Bobo Dimana". Similarly, the Bruneian influencer Jeeradoesfashion's online presence is not without her audience's rejections and criticisms. She was challenged by the lack of acceptance from the audience (society) when she first started her Outfit of the Day (OOTD) posts and creative styling on her Instagram, which was characterized as "over the top." Those negative responses were directed toward her fashion style (layering different clothes, thick fabric, and high heels), which are considered non-practical and not suitable for everyday wear in the country. Getting such responses from local society is not unexpected given that Brunei during that time (circa 2015–2018) was still new to the work of social media influencers and their creative expressions.

These micro-celebrities' presence and self-performance are laden with struggles, conflicts, contestations, and negotiation. While emphasizing their individualities via self-expression and self-disclosure, these micro-celebrities continue to negotiate their celebrated selves in their respective societies. Following this audience-subjectivity as part of a micro-celebrity's celebrity logic, I suggest that celebrification is not an isolated process where ordinary individuals transform themselves into celebrities by solely using the content generated on social media. Their self-disclosure and self-selectivity processes are grounded in their contexts and to some extent, depends on audience-subjectivity. In this case, the creation of a micro-celebrity is never a one-way process. As I have argued elsewhere (Mohamad & Hassim, 2019), a micro-celebrity functions as a relatable individual capable of influencing the audience's self-worth and self-development and the micro-celebrity work on reconfiguring these Malay Muslim societies. Audiences are always actively reworking the images shared by celebrities and micro-celebrities, and these celebrities, in turn, are working to meet audiences' expectations.

Secondly, in the Southeast Asian context, with an ongoing celebrification process and democratization of celebrity among social media users, this celebrity status assessed by visibility and fame could become a new normal and celebrification could become a youth mobility practice. Such normalization of celebrification, and gaining fame and "celebrity" status due to online visibility, is supported by performance of mundaneness as part of celebrity logic. Coming back to the earlier question I posed on local micro-celebrities without function or of a lesser influence, I argue that their presence would be good enough to signal potential in self-mobilities for other aspiring individuals. Those local micro-celebrities' scale and audience may not be as large as other micro-celebrities worldwide, but they act as a reference point for those in their society (Marshall, 2016).

In the remainder of this paper, I would like to bring forward the notion of celebrity culture as part of youth culture and practice to further understand micro-celebrities' social function. Linked to this possibility of a new normal in relation to youth practice is a question of whether the term or existence of micro-celebrities would be useful if one day more young people become ordinary/micro "celebrities" online (with or without influence). Would we see the banalization of celebrification and micro-celebrities? Quite similar to Theresa Senft's camgirls' saturation due to an overabundance of webcam and digital technology (Turner, 2013), would we see similar saturation in micro-celebrities? Of course, by asking this, I risk downplaying the significance of micro-celebrity culture, a culture with its own logic and mechanisms. Nonetheless, if celebrification becomes banal, how would celebrity and celebrity culture in this context be conceptualized?

I would like to draw on the local situation in Brunei to illustrate this point. Making oneself visible on social media, while quite a recent practice in Brunei, is gaining traction among the youth as can be seen in a few Bruneian influencers such as Jeeradoesfashion (a fashion enthusiast and art director), Aj_fithetics (a fitness enthusiast turned bodybuilder), and Ninjatutul (an edutainer), as well as some non-influencers (including those with potential but who are not yet recognized as influencers). They effectively and affectively utilize social media sites to share their aspirations, volunteering activities, experiences, skills, and of course, to make their presence known for future needs such as seeking employment. Furthermore, with the growing creative industries in the region, it is common to see creatives' presence online to self-promote their work. Here, local micro-celebrities could become what Couldry (2016) calls celebrity as the role model for the culture of self-promotion itself.

However, by this, I am not implying that everyone on social media would become micro-celebrities or seek for this celebrification of self to attain social and economic mobilities, as Van Krieken (2019) rightly cautions. We have to be cognizant of existing issues: equality, power, esthetics, (Driessens, 2013; Van Krieken, 2019), and audience reception. As Hearn and Schoenhoff (2016) argued,

> While the mechanisms for attaining high visibility and celebrity value may be widely accessible today, under contemporary socialized capitalism, so far, they have completely failed to bring about any real material improvement in people's lives and managed only to exacerbate already existing class inequality. (p. 208)

Failure to realize one's aspirations despite such visibility and celebrification is possible. Nevertheless, these individuals' practice of self-disclosure (leading to promotion and branding) on social media could signal the potential and utilization of the celebrification process as part of young people's self-empowerment and mobility strategies in the region. In such an instance, it would make sense to relate micro-celebrities' celebrification processes to young people's aspirations for social and economic mobility, especially in today's rising unemployment in the region where Brunei ranked top on the list of unemployment statistics with 9.2% of unemployment in 2018 (The ASEAN Secretariat, 2019). Affective (or aspirational or hope) labor in the form of self-disclosure and self-branding (Duffy, 2015; Kuehn & Corrigan, 2013) and transforming oneself into a micro-celebrity may become expected and necessary to negotiate the current precarious conditions.

Conclusion

While Brunei, Malaysia, and Indonesia have their own micro-celebrities and influencers, the level of fame and exposure and the socio-cultural configurations they bring to their societies differ significantly. This paper has offered an examination of micro-celebrities' practices in three Muslim-majority states to demonstrate the social function of micro-celebrities through which we could start to understand the localized celebrity culture, celebrification, and celebritization processes in the region. Knowing the social functions and significance of these micro-celebrities in these Southeast Asian societies would go beyond the representation of these celebrated individuals. They offer insights into the societies' current socio-spatial practices, a contextualized understanding of their celebrification, and the socio-cultural implications they bring to their societies as part of the celebritization process. Notwithstanding my attempt to contextualize celebrity culture in the Southeast Asian region, I acknowledge these countries' diverse characteristics, leading to their localized celebritization process, local-national-regional awareness of new subjectivities, and creating progress and development unique to the region. While the localized celebrification and celebritization process reveal celebrity cultures specific to the region, these processes also allude to the wider and significant phenomena such as existing and growing transcultural hybridity. Beyond the localized and contextualized analyses of the celebrification of micro-celebrities, the key arguments made in this paper could advance the conceptualization of a celebrity, celebrification, and the celebritization process that goes beyond celebrity culture to focus on "a meta-process involving changes in the nature of celebrity and its social and cultural embedding" (Driessens, 2013, p. 7).

Disclosure statement

No conflict of interest reported by authors.

ORCID

Siti Mazidah Mohamad http://orcid.org/0000-0003-1243-4554

References

Abidin, C. (2015). Communicative intimacies: Influencers and perceived interconnectedness. *Ada: A Journal Of Gender, New Media, & Technology*, 8. http://adanewmedia.org/2015/11/issue8-abidin/
Abidin, C. (2016). Visibility labour: Engaging with influencers' fashion brands and #OOTD advertorial campaigns on Instagram. *Media International Australia*, *161*(1), 1–15.
Abidin, C. (2017a). Influencer extravaganza: Commercial "lifestyle" microcelebrities in Singapore. In L. Hjorth, H. Horst, A. Galloway, & G. Bell (Eds.), *The Routledge companion of digital ethnography* (pp. 158–168). Routledge. New York.
Abidin, C. (2017b). #Familygoals: Family influencers, calibrated amateurism, and justifying young digital labor. *Social Media + Society*, *3*(2), 1–15.
Beta, A. (2019). Commerce, piety and politics: Indonesian young Muslim women's groups as religious influencers. *New Media & Society*, *21*(10), 2140–2159. doi:10.1177/1461444819838774
Beta, A. (2020). The Muslimah intimate public: Re-considering contemporary Da'wa activists in Indonesia. *Asiascape: Digital Asia*, *7*(1–2), 20–41. doi:10.1163/22142312-BJA10002
Cheong, B. (2018, October 21). *Duck releases limited edition scarves for Barbie dolls*. The Star. Retrieved April, 20, 2019, from https://www.thestar.com.my/lifestyle/style/2018/10/21/duck-scarf-barbie-limited-edition
Couldry, N. (2016). Celebrity, convergence, and the fate of media institutions. In P. D. Marshall & S. Redmond (Eds.), *A companion to celebrity* (pp. 98–113). Wiley Blackwell. West Sussex.
Drake, P., & Miah, A. (2010). The cultural politics of celebrity. *Cultural Politics*, *6*(1), 49–64. doi:10.2752/175174310X12549254318746
Driessens, O. (2013). The celebritization of society and culture: Understanding the structural dynamics of celebrity culture. *International Journal of Cultural Studies*, *16*(6), 641–657. doi:10.1177/1367877912459140
Driessens, O. (2014). Theorizing celebrity cultures: Thickenings of celebrity cultures and the role of cultural (working) memory. *Communications: European Journal of Communication Research*, *39* (2). doi:10.1515/commun-2014-0008

Driessens, O. (2018). Celebrity in the age of global communication networks. In A. Elliott (Ed.), *Routledge handbook of celebrity studies*(pp. 245-254). Routledge. London.

Duffy, B. E. (2015). The romance of work: Gender and aspirational labour in the digital culture industries. *International Journal of Cultural Studies, 19*(4), 441–457. doi:10.1177/1367877915572186

Haji Mohamad, S. M. (2018). The performance of religiosity on social media: Three future research directions. *IAS Working Paper, 39*.

Haji Mohamad, S. M. (2019). Self disclosure on social media in Brunei Darussalam. In M. Caballero-Anthony & M. Sembiring (Eds.), *Resilience in the face of disruptions. RSiS monograph* (pp. 46–56), S. Rajaratnam School of International Studies. Nanyang Technological University. Singapore.

Hassim, N., & Mohamad, S. M. (2020). Hail hijabis: Celebrification of influencers by postmodern Malay-Muslim women in Malaysia. In T. Kananatu, J. Goh, & S. Sharon Bong (Eds.), *Effecting gender and sexuality justice in Asia: Finding resolutions through conflicts*(pp.17-30). Springer. Singapore.

Hearn, A., & Schoenhoff, S. (2016). From celebrity to influencer: Tracing the diffusion of celebrity value across the data stream. In P. D. Marshall & S. Redmond (Eds.), *A companion to celebrity* (pp. 194–212). Wiley Blackwell. West Sussex.

Hootsuite & We Are Social. (2020). *Digital report 2020*. Retrieved August 1, 2020, from https://wearesocial.com/global-digital-report-

Howard, C. (2010). Individualization. In A. Elliott (Ed.), *Routledge handbook of identity studies* (pp. 112–128). Routledge. London.

Islam, I. (2019). Redefining #YourAverageMuslim woman: Muslim female digital activism on social media. *Journal of Arab & Muslim Media Research, 12*(2), 213–233. doi:10.1386/jammr_00004_1

Jenkins, H., Ford, S., & Green, J. (2013). *Spreadable media: Creating value and meaning in a networked culture*. New York University Press. New York.

Jerslev, A. (2016). In the time of the microcelebrity: Celebrification and the Youtuber Zoella. *International Journal of Communication, 10*, 5233–5251.

Khamis, S., Ang, L., & Welling, R. (2016). Selfbranding, 'micro-celebrity' and the rise of social media influencers. *Celebrity Studies, 8*(2), 191–208. doi:10.1080/19392397.2016.1218292

Kuehn, K., & Corrigan, T. F. (2013). Hope labor: The role of employment prospects in online social production. *The Political Economy of Communication, 1*(1), 9–25.

Marshall, P. D. (2006). New media - New self: The changing power of celebrity. In P. D. Marshall (Ed.), *The celebrity culture reader*(pp.634-644). Routledge. New York.

Marshall, P. D. (2010). The promotion and presentation of the self: Celebrity as marker of presentational media. *Celebrity Studies*, 1, 35–48.

Marshall, P. D. (2016). Exposure: The public self explored. In P. D. Marshall & S. Redmond (Eds.), *A companion to celebrity* (pp. 497–518). Wiley Blackwell. West Sussex.

Marshall, P. D., & Redmond, S. (Eds.). (2016). *A companion to celebrity*. Wiley Blackwell. West Sussex.

Marwick, A. (2013). *Status update: Celebrity, publicity & branding in the social media age*. Yale University Press. New Haven.

Marwick, A. (2016). You may know me from YouTube. In P. D. Marshall & S. Redmond (Eds.), *A companion to celebrity* (pp. 333–350). Wiley Blackwell. West Sussex.

Mohamad, S. M. (in press). Hallyu 2.0 in Brunei Darussalam: Audience affective engagement with Korean culture on social mediascape. In K. H. Kim & S. Y. Rou (Eds.), *The Korean wave and Islamic Southeast Asia (pp.140-157)*. Universiti Kebangsaan Malaysia. Kuala Lumpur.

Mohamad, S. M., & Hassim, N. (2019). Hijabi celebrification and hijab consumption in Brunei and Malaysia. *Celebrity Studies*, 1–25. doi:10.1080/19392397.2019.1677164

Mokhtazar, S. (2018a, December 20). *#Showbiz: 'Bobo Di Mana' is most trending local song in Malaysia*. New Strait Time. Retrieved January 29, 2021, from https://www.nst.com.my/lifestyle/groove/2018/12/442419/showbiz-bobo-di-mana-most-trending-local-song-malaysia

Mokhtazar, S. (2018b, September 12). *#Showbiz: Aliff Syukri to sing nasyid songs after 'Bobo Di Mana' controversy*. New Strait Time. Retrieved January 29, 2021, from https://www.nst.com.my/lifestyle/groove/2018/09/410635/showbiz-aliff-syukri-sing-nasyid-songs-after-bobo-di-mana

Nisa, E. F. (2018). Creative and lucrative Daʿwa: The visual culture of Instagram amongst female Muslim youth in Indonesia. *Asiascape: Digital Asia*, 5(1–2), 68–99. doi:10.1163/22142312-12340085

Osman, T. (1985). Islamization of the Malays: A transformation of culture. In A. Ibrahim, S. Siddique, & Y. Hussain (Eds.), *Readings on Islam in Southeast Asia*(pp. 44 -47). ISEAS. Singapore.

Peichi, C. (2013). Co-creating Korean wave in Southeast Asia: Digital convergence and Asia's media regionalization. *Journal of Creative Communications*, 8(2–3), 193–208. doi:10.1177/0973258613512912

Rojek, C. (2001). *Celebrity*. Reaktion Books. London.

Saat, N., Ed.. (2018). Introduction. In N. Saat (ed.), *Islam in Southeast Asia: Negotiating modernity*(pp 1-12). ISEAS Yusuf Ishak Institute. Singapore.

Senft, T. (2008). *CAMGIRLS celebrity and community in the age of social networks*. Peter Lang Publishing.

Senft, T. (2013). Microcelebrity and the branded self. In J. Hartley, J. Burgess, & A. Bruns (Eds.), *A companion to new media dynamics* (pp. 346–354). Wiley-Blackwell. West Sussex.

Shim, D. (2013). The Korean wave in Southeast Asia: The case of Singapore. *Journal of Southeast Asian Studies*, 23(1), 277–311.

Syed, M., Azalanshah, M., & Kwon, S.-H. (2019). Hallyu and strategic interpretation of Malaysian modernity among young Malay women. *Asian Women*, 35(3), 1–24. doi:10.14431/aw.2019.09.35.3.1

The ASEAN Secretariat. (2019). *ASEAN key figures 2019*. Retrieved from https://www.aseanstats.org/wp-content/uploads/2019/11/ASEAN_Key_Figures_2019.pdf

Tsaliki, L. (2016). "Tweeting the good causes": Social networking and celebrity activism. In P. D. Marshall & S. Redmond (Eds.), *A companion to celebrity* (pp. 235–257). Wiley Blackwell. West Sussex.

Turner, G. (2010a). Approaching celebrity studies. *Celebrity Studies*, 1(1), 11–20. doi:10.1080/19392390903519024

Turner, G. (2010b). *Ordinary people and the media*. Sage. London.

Turner, G. (2013). *Understanding celebrity* (2nd ed.). Sage. London.

Van Krieken, R. (2019). *Celebrity society: The struggle for attention*. Routledge. London.

Weintraub, A. (Ed.). (2011). Introduction: The study of Islam and popular culture in Indonesia and Malaysia. In A. Weintraub (Ed,), *Islam and popular culture in Indonesia and Malaysia* (pp. 1–17). Routledge. London.

Williams, J. P., & Kamaludeen, M. N. (2017). Muslim girl culture and social control in Southeast Asia: Exploring the hijabista and hijabster phenomena. *Crime, Media, Culture*, 13(2), 199–216. doi:10.1177/1741659016687346

Symbolic bordering: The self-representation of migrants and refugees in digital news

Lilie Chouliaraki

ABSTRACT
In this article, I combine theorizations of the selfie as an aesthetic and technological practice of digital self-representation with a theatrical conception of spectatorship, inspired by Adam Smith, in order to argue that the selfie has the potential to operate as a significant ethico-political spectacle in the spaces of Western publicity. I exemplify my argument by using the remediation of migrant and refugee selfies in mainstream news as a case study of "symbolic bordering"—as a technology of power that couples the geopolitical bordering of migrants in the outskirts of Europe with practices of "symbolic bordering" that appropriate, marginalize, or displace their digital testimonies in Western news media.

Introduction

Despite the extensive engagement of Western media with the 2015 migrant crisis, we saw little of migrants' and refugees' own personal stories and images (Gillespie et al., 2016). An exception to this has been photographs of migrants taking selfies; selfies of migrants with Angela Merkel or the Pope; selfies of celebrities-as-migrants. What does it mean for the selfie to be used as a recurrent media genre for the representation of migrants? What news value do these selfies bear? And what do they tell us about the role of Western media not only as news platforms but also as political and moral spaces? In addressing these questions, I propose to re-theorize the selfie in line with Adam Smith's theory of public spectatorship as a moral invitation to witness, within a journalistic environment of digital re-mediations that organize Western structures of public visibility—of who we see, how, and why. The aim of this approach is to construct a preliminary typology of the migrant-related selfie as an act of witnessing and to explore how such an act complicates existing narratives of the selfie as digital self-representation. The migrant selfie, I argue, expands existing literature, by showing how the selfie operates as a technology of power that contributes to orientalist agendas that "other" migrants and refugees; it does so by coupling the geopolitical bordering of migrants stuck in the outskirts of Europe (Vaughan-Williams, 2009) with practices of "symbolic bordering" that appropriate, marginalize, or displace their digital testimonies in Western news media.

Theoretical and empirical context

Definitions of the selfie

When a 25-year old Syrian traveling to Europe was asked by *TIME* journalists what was the most important thing in his journey, he answered: "Charging my phone" (Laurent, 2015). Indeed, as Gillespie et al. (2016) assert, the migrant smartphone is the single most essential traveling tool for migrants. They use it to keep in touch with family, navigate unknown landscapes, communicate in emergencies, collect information, and network with others like them: "In this modern migration," Matthew Brunwasser (2015) writes in *The New York Times*, "smartphone maps, global positioning apps, social media and WhatsApp have become essential tools … the first thing many do once they have successfully navigated the watery passage between Turkey and Greece is pull out a smartphone and send loved ones a message that they made it." Their social media use notwithstanding, however, the migrants' own photos and stories hardly figure in Western news—despite the celebration of citizen journalism as a driving force in contemporary crisis reporting (Allan, 2013). An exception to this has been the extensive visibility of migrant-related selfies—for instance, when migrants arrive at the European coast, wet, tired, and often traumatized, or when they meet with authority, politicians, or celebrities, or when others photograph themselves as if they were migrants in a spirit of solidarity.

It is this heterogeneous genre of the migrant-related selfie that I focus on here. I draw on Levin's definition of the selfie as "not a *self*-portrait … but rather the *representation* of the *self* as a product of the system of interpersonal relationships though which it is articulated online" (Levin, 2014; emphasis in original). This definition enables me to approach the migrant-related selfie as a digital trace of self-representation by or about migrants, which circulates in undefined networks of digital publicity that constantly redefine its interpersonal relationships—who sees it, how, and why (Senft, 2015). While such networks are usually conceptualized horizontally, as consisting of other equivalent users who may like or share selfies across social media (Dean, 2016), my interest lies in the vertical movement of migrant selfies from social to mainstream media—from their "intermediation" across (relatively) symmetrical user circuits to their "remediation" in the powerful spaces of global broadcasting (Chouliaraki, 2013b).[1] What does it mean for migrant selfies to circulate on Western news platforms? In which ways are they inserted in "our" dominant visual economies? How is their news value justified? And what do these justifications tell us about Western media not only as news platforms but also as moral and political spaces? I explore these questions by constructing a concise typology of migrant-related selfies on Western news, namely, (a) selfie-taking photographs, (b) solidarity selfies of migrants with Western figures of authority, and (c) celebrity selfies of support to migrants; and by analyzing the communicative potential of this typology in terms of the affective and the moral connections each category seeks to establish with its news publics.

Aesthetic and sociotechnical approaches to the selfie

Despite the significance of "remediation" questions for our engagement with the ethico-political challenges of our times, including the migrant crisis, these have hardly been explored

---

[1] I draw on Bolter and Grusin's "remediation" (1999) so as to extend the term to refer not only to the embeddedness of one medium into another but also to the resignifications of aesthetic content that occur in this process of technological embeddedness.

in existing work on digital self-representation. Rather, literature on the selfie is divided in two strands: the selfie as performative practice, and the selfie as sociotechnical process.

The study of the selfie as performative practice draws on sociological accounts of linguistic self-presentation, by Goffman (Hess, 2015) and Austin (Jerslev & Mortensen, 2015), and on semiotic approaches to aesthetics (Iqani & Schroeder, 2016; Koffman, Orgad, & Gill, 2015) so as to foreground three dimensions of digital self-representation. The first focuses on the self-reflexivity involved in the public staging of the private self; this dimension draws attention to the civic, political, and cultural potentialities of "vernaculars of performativity" in social media (Papacharissi, 2011), approaching them as "cultures of connectivity"—sites of individuation, bonding, and memory, rather than simply as "networks" (van Dijck, 2013). The second focus falls on the narrative practices of users' self-representations in social media; this draws attention to new forms of "digital story-telling" (Vivienne & Burgess, 2013) and explore their implications for new forms of sociality and public connection—for instance, in institutional contexts (Thumim, 2009) or familial relations (Vivienne & Burgess, 2013). The third focus is on the historicity of self-portraiture as an artistic genre that inscribes the selfie in long-term trajectories of aesthetic, technological, and cultural change in the public presentation of the self (Hall, 2014; Tifentale & Manovich, 2015).

If this triple focus on "performativity" situates meaning-making at the heart of what the selfie is and how it should be studied, the second theoretical strand offers a different, though not necessarily incompatible, epistemology of digital self-representation. It claims that rather than approaching the selfie as a performative system of significations of the self, we should instead conceptualize it as a technological gesture—a material trace devoid of representational meaning (Gómez & Thornham, 2015). In its capacity as techno-trace, the significance of the selfie derives not from its discursivity or its historicity but from its systemic simultaneity, that is, by the very fact that it always-already appears within existing circuits of other traces like itself. Variations within this literature, consequently, reflect different research foci on the social and technological dimensions of the selfie. On the one hand, emphasis falls on the political economy of the selfie; research here highlights the selfie as technomaterial process embedded in networks of consumption-driven communication that reproduce the power relations of neo-liberal capitalism—what Dean (2005) refers to as "communicative capitalism." Her more recent argument reworks Walter Benjamin's political economic view of culture into the selfie, reading the latter as a new "auratic" object no longer endowed with "exhibition" but with "circulation value": "Accessibility and transportability" Dean explains, "don't just increase, they become ends in themselves," and "photos are less singular objects or images to be contemplated than they are temporary and replaceable elements" (Dean, 2016). On the other hand, there is literature on the relationship between selfies and nonhuman agents, such as software codes and digital affordances, focusing on the algorithmic dimensions of self-representation and their social effects (van House, 2009, 2011). This is because nonhuman agents not only organize the vast quantities of online imagery into durable patterns of visuality but also shape the social practices through which such patterns open up to individualized consumption, for uploading, sharing, liking and so on. A comparative study of the distribution of LGBTQ (lesbian, gay, bisexual, transgender, and queer) celebrity selfies on two social media platforms (Duguay, 2017), for instance, shows "the relevance of platforms in shaping selfies' conversational capacity," insofar as different algorithmic configurations across the platforms "influence whether selfies feature in conversations reinforcing dominant discourses or in counterpublic conversations."

Emerging out of these distinct bodies of literature is a dualist ontology of the selfie as either a meaningful practice of self-representation or a techno-economic practice of (re-) distributions. If the former highlights the textualities embedded in the performative acts of photographing oneself, the latter foregrounds the broader social and technological networks wherein such performative acts circulate. What remains marginal in both these strands of research is the ethico-political dimension of the selfie as a witnessing act that raises important questions of identity, voice, and otherness in the digital media (but see, partly, Koliska & Roberts, 2015). It is the attempt to acknowledge this dimension that informs my dialectical approach to the selfie introduced in the following.

A dialectical approach to the selfie

Rather than exclusively focusing on either strand of research, I opt for a dialectical approach, which views the selfie as a meaningful trace of the self, moving across connected environments—as both "human connectedness" and "automated connectivity," in van Dijk's terms (2013). In a similar move, Frosh's theorization of the selfie as "gestural image" conceives of the selfie both as an "aesthetic and representational innovation, requiring the analytical tools of visual communication," and as a "technocultural circuit of corporeal social energy" that gives rise to "kinaesthetic," rather than hermeneutic, sociability. This approach, Frosh argues, challenges the traditional visual analytics of the selfie in favor of an integrated analytics of the body—the "broader somatic and sensory dimensions of cultural experience and practice" that constitute the "mediated phatic body" (Frosh, 2015, p. 1623). While I concur with the significance of this dialectical approach, my study seeks to address a different, overlooked dimension of selfie analytics: the relationship of the selfie not with the somatic body and its kinaesthetic capacity but with the body politic and its ethical responsiveness. Without attention to the ethical nature of the selfie as a technology of power that regulates collective affect and judgment, I contend, it is impossible to address remediation as a question of digital visuality, publicity, and power and to reflect on the stakes that remediation, as a key journalistic process, entails.

I next offer my theorization of the communicative environment of the migrant-related selfie: its meaning-making capacity as a testimonial act and the media networks within which it is remediated. I argue that such networks of journalistic remediation reclaim the contemplative quality of images, their capacity to be gazed at objects of emotion and evaluation, and insert them into a nexus of theatrical relationships of viewing. These relationships, I claim after Adam Smith's theory of spectatorship, are primarily moral; that is, they stage the figure of the migrant into various testimonial narratives and thus invite a range of ambivalent engagements with her/his predicament. I subsequently present a preliminary typology of the theater of the selfie in order to explore its theatricality both as a stage for affective engagements and as a site of power relationships that produces hierarchical classifications of humanity—what I discuss as "symbolic bordering."

Conceptual context

My interest in an ethics of the selfie and its remediations raises questions about the nature of the selfie not only as a form of self-representation but also as a techno-aesthetic component of digital journalism. What does it mean to make news about migrants through the aesthetic of the selfie? Which specific remediations of the selfie are deemed newsworthy and why? What do these selfies tell us about the human status of migrants? And what relationships do they seek to establish between "us" and "them"? Insofar as this set of questions involves a complex assemblage of mutually embedded relationships of viewing, including the selfie-taking migrant, their personal online circle and the publics of online journalism, we need to develop an understanding of the selfie as a network of "theatrical" relationships of viewing. Even though the theatrical metaphor has already been used to frame the selfie as a new form of "the presentation of the self in everyday life," along Goffman's lines, what is still missing is an account of digital self-representation as an encounter with human vulnerability that requires a response. Let me outline this conceptual approach and its analytical possibilities.

The selfie as theater

The selfie interrupts the flow of mainstream news reporting in order to insert fragments of "the other's" face into this flow. It is this fleeting encounter between them and us, framed by digital narratives on "our" various screens, which introduces the structure of theatricality in the online remediations of the selfie. Theatricality here refers to a communicative structure that does not necessarily belong to the traditional scene of the theater but operates in line with the conventions of theatrical performance—namely, by distancing the spectator from the spectacle of the other through the objective space of a framing device and, at the same time, enabling proximity between the two through narratives that invite our emotion and judgment on the other: "More than a property with analyzable characteristics," as Féral and Bermingham argue, "theatricality seems to be a process that has to do with a 'gaze' that postulates and creates a distinct, virtual space belonging to the other" (2002, p. 97).

While for Adam Smith the theatrical metaphor conceives of society as a stage, where seeing others inevitably invites a moral response, "who are they and who am I as a consequence of meeting them?," the selfie partakes this theatrical structure insofar as it fulfills two criteria of theatricality. First, it establishes a mode of spectatorship that is based on the staging and framing of the self for purposes of being seen and responded to by others—Smith's "sympathetic spectator"; and second, this staging of the self simultaneously presupposes not only an immediate audience of intended addressees but also the imaginary spectatorship of an uninvolved public that is implicitly invited to take a stance toward this staging—what Adam Smith refers to as the "impartial spectator" (Marshall, 1984).

In order, therefore, to understand how the migrant-related selfie operates in the Western media landscape, we need to understand both dimensions of theatrical spectatorship: how the selfie produces meaning through practices of self-representation that stage the self so as to be seen and responded to by a select group of others (the aesthetic performance of the self), and how the selfie is inserted into broader institutional structures of news journalism that connect us all as undefined publics of "impartial" spectatorship (the hierarchical remediations of the selfie in Western media). Let me examine each dimension, in turn.

Sympathetic spectatorship: The selfie as performance of the self

As performance, the selfie is inscribed onto two technologies: the oldest, the face, and the newest, the digital screen (Pinchevski, 2016). The face operates as a testimony of our universal commonality and, in evoking what we all profoundly share, it gestures toward authentic presence.[2] The digital screen maximizes the reach of the face, enabling distant others to appear to us as fully present and to confront us with their own humanity. Through this performative duality of face and screen, the selfie articulates and circulates claims to the self as authentic presence and, in so doing, simultaneously acts as an invitation for us to engage with this presence in various modalities of sympathetic spectatorship: empathy, solidarity, suspicion, or disapproval. It is in this capacity to confront us with the humanity of the other in its here-and-now mode that the selfie recovers its moral dimension—its theorizations as "mundane" or "narcissistic" (e.g., Lüders, Prøitz, & Rasmussen, 2010) being part of this moral regime of sympathetic spectatorship that any selfie belongs to. For if, as Levinas puts it, "the face to face" is the par excellence mode of ethical address, because it "addresses humanity at large," then the selfie is a radical intensification of this address, both in that it digitally "presences" the other's face to us (Senft, 2015) and in that it expands the scope of our face-to-face relationships—through what Frosh (2015) terms the "corporeal sociability" of the selfie (its likes, shares, comments, etc.).

Migrant-related selfies, in particular, are a paradigmatic case of digital self-representation as ethical address, because they are aesthetic performances of the face under conditions of risk. Selfies of migrants who just reached the Greek shores perform authenticity through the affective grammar of the face and the body, which articulates euphoric affect. This "being here" is a moral address insofar as arrival here also signifies survival of a deadly sea crossing in the Mediterranean. The digital screen brings, in this case, the face of the migrant closer through acts of "presencing" that are, simultaneously, also appeals for sympathetic spectatorship—an invitation for us to connect to its affective grammar. In order to study the selfie as aesthetic performance, therefore, I propose to engage with its two dimensions of sympathetic spectatorship: the authentication of the selfie, through a semiotic reading of the "face" as visual meaning-making that produces various narratives of humanity; and, the presencing of the selfie, through a reading of the moral relationships it enables between the subjects and objects of digital self-representation.

Impartial spectatorship: The re-mediation of the selfie

The global visibility of migrant-related selfies, however, depends on their circulation beyond horizontal networks, such as the social media, to vertical ones, such as professional news organizations (CNN, BBC, DW, or *The Guardian*). This shift simultaneously means that the selfie gives up some of its "circulation" value in favor of what we may call "contemplative" value: a form of value that draws attention to the selfie as an object to be focused on, gazed at, and responded to by an undefined body of "impartial" spectators—the Western body politic.

In this "contemplative" conception, however, the selfie cannot be understood simply as a diffused techno-trace accumulating meaning-free "circulation" value. It should instead be seen as a matter of theatrical re-mediation, where multiplatform journalism selects, reassembles, and, importantly, resignifies other media according to its own logics—impartial

---

[2]For a discussion of selfie authenticity see Senft (2015).

spectatorship here referring not to a position from nowhere but to the "naturalized" visual narratives of "us" and "them" that routinely contextualize the selfie-as-news (Schudson, 1993). While such remediations were, in the past, a matter of professional authorship, citizen testimonies now turn re-mediation into an editing activity, where nonprofessional content is subject to processes of "recontextualization" (editing, reframing, renarrativizing) and "remoralization" (reinvesting it in moral discourses suitable to the news platform) (Chouliaraki, 2015). In contrast, then, to disintermediation accounts (Fenton & Downey, 2003) that link social media with the breaking down of news intermediaries, it is, I argue, precisely through the regulative work of journalistic remediation that social media news ultimately reaches mass global audiences (Al-Ghazzi, 2014).

The analysis of the migrant-related selfie in the news, I propose, should thus focus on both dimensions of the theater of the selfie: the aesthetic performance of the self, which constitutes sympathetic spectatorship through authenticity and presence, and its re-mediation in news journalism, which constitutes "impartial" spectatorship through recontextualization and remoralization, in line with the ethico-political logics of various journalistic institutions. How do different types of migrant selfie perform the self as an authentic "here I am"? How are these claims to authenticity and presence recontextualized in Western news sites? What are the moral discourses of such recontextualizations and what do these tell us about the news as moral and political spaces?

Analytical context

My theatrical approach to the selfie draws on two key aesthetic and technosocial insights of the relevant literature, namely, the narrativity of digital self-representation and the "circulation value" of the selfie. It complicates the former by introducing vertical remediation as constitutive of the visual narrativity of the selfie, while it expands the latter by demonstrating that, far from free-wheeling, the "circulation value" of the selfie is embedded in techno-institutional relationships of power, as in global news journalism.

The choice of the migrant-related selfie as the empirical material of this study is motivated by an interest in understanding how the visibility of migrants is regulated in Western media, in particular during the 2015 migrant crisis. Studying how migrants appear in our news matters because it helps us better comprehend the broader communicative environment of the crisis. This was a versatile environment marked by an originally positive rhetoric of reception that enjoyed a wave of compassion after the death of 3-year-old Aylan Kurdi, but eventually turned into suspicion, following the November 2015 Paris attacks; it was the latter that legitimized Europe's exclusionary politics of bordering and blocked 58,000 migrants in Greece with mass deportations to Turkey on the agenda, in March 2016 (Gillespie et al., 2016). Focusing, therefore, on the time span of the crisis, June 2015–March 2016, enables me to analyze this period as a "peak" moment in migrant self-representation, which has something important to tell us not only about migrants themselves but crucially about Western journalism as a site of regulation for "our" moral sensibilities.

The choice of the term "migrant-related selfie," instead of "migrant selfie" reflects the fact that only some of those images were actually selfies taken of and by migrants; the others were images about migrants, but neither by nor of them. Indeed, the three key types of migrant-related selfies that appeared in global news networks, such as BBC, CNN, DW, or *The Guardian*, during the "peak" moment were (a) migrants being photographed to take selfies, (b) migrant selfies with celebrities, and (c) celebrities taking selfies as if they were migrants. There are variations within each category, but they are all three characterized by what Wittgenstein (1958) terms a "family resemblance" in their aesthetic and technosocial qualities. I examine each in the sections "The selfie as performance" and "The selfie as remediation" in the following.

Selfie-taking photographs: Self-representation as celebration

Celebration selfies are almost exclusively shot on the beaches of Lesbos—one of the migrants' main entry points into Europe from the Turkey coast. They portray migrants taking selfies smiling and making the V-sign, alone or in groups. We never see these selfies as such, however. What we see is photojournalistic pictures of migrants taking selfies. CNN's video link (there is a similar one by the BBC), for instance, is a 1-minute-long piece entitled "The migrant selfie," which begins with a migrant explaining the significance of celebration selfies and continues with a sequence of selfie-taking instances on the beach (CNN, 2015).

Selfie as performance

Even though all selfies have a strong locative dimension, "I am right here, right now" (Hess, 2015), this category of selfies with its smiling faces and V-signs situates the locative within a particularly intense authenticity of affect (Thumim, 2012): the euphoria of arrival; hence the term "celebration" to describe them. "Of course yes, as you are VERY happy you're here," confesses the migrant interviewed by CNN, "the first thing that you did [sic] is a selfie yeah and we send it to our families yeah." Having dreamed of reaching Europe against all odds, migrants' extreme emotions upon arrival render these selfies not simply occasions for self-presentation but "visual proofs" of the extraordinary event of reaching Europe—what Reading calls "mobile witnessing" (2009, p. 69). It is the force of emotion inherent in mobile witnessing that simultaneously foregrounds presencing as an ethical force in these selfies. This is insofar as the selfie's locative claim ("I am *here*") also entails a strong existential dimension ("*I am* here"). Far from indexing just any random location, the deictic function of the celebration selfie goes beyond arrival to connote survival, the fact of having endured a deadly sea crossing in the Mediterranean. It is this deixis of arrival-as-survival, the selfie's "I've made it" moment, that mobilizes its corporeal sociability, its likes, comments, and shares, as an occasion of online jubilation (Frosh, 2015).

The theatricality of the celebration selfie, it follows, can be reduced neither to its purely locative content ("I am *here*") nor to a playful assertion of the self ("this is *me*"). It consists in staging the euphoria of survival both as descriptive and as a normative moment. Beyond its denotative value of signifying survival, the selfie's normative meaning connotes hope. It captures a moment of pregnant possibility, as projects of the migrant self that were previously unthinkable now come within reach—what Ernst Bloch has termed the utopian "not yet" (1995, xxviii). The sympathetic spectator of the celebration selfie is invited to relate to the aesthetic performance of the celebratory selfie as a "yet to come."

Selfie as remediation

The remediation of the celebration selfie relies on estrangement, on turning the ordinary act of selfie-taking into extraordinary. By focusing on selfie-taking as curious or rare,

Western news platforms recontextualize the selfie from an occasion of corporeal sociability on social media to an invitation of ethical appraisal, open to public commentary and judgment: Who are they? Why are they owning mobile phones? Why are they taking selfies? Should they be taking them? Situating these questions at the heart of their stories, "our" news simultaneously turns mobile witnessing into meta-witnessing: It is the fact that "they" take selfies, not their faces, that we are invited to contemplate.

Two consequences follow from this. The authenticity and presence effects of meta-witnessing no longer reside in the deictic and existential functions of the selfie but in the narrativity of the news about the selfie. The moral mechanism of theatricality, consequently, also changes: No longer about the authenticity of euphoric affect, the selfie is now remoralized as an ambivalent practice, suspended between sympathy, as in the CNN piece, and suspicion, as in a series of other press outlets. Authenticity, to begin with, relies on journalistic authority and is about attaching a professional jurisdiction of validity to the news; CNN, for instance, achieves sympathy through the inclusion of a firsthand testimonial (the migrant) and the sequence of selfie-taking visuals, all of which avoids overt judgment yet seek to raise awareness around the issue. By the same token, presence is no longer about existential deixis, the subjectification of space through the selfie's "here *I am*," but about invitations to contemplate the migrants' selfie activity itself—"see what they are doing." CCN features the piece in its "Edition," a series of brief videos for swift consumption without in-depth content. In contrast to the selfies' aesthetic performance of presence as survival, migrants are here recontextualized as "present absences": Rather than human agents reaching for their "not yet," they are the objects of our curiosity and suspicion.

While empathetic curiosity informs the majority of mainstream news outlets, including CNN, *TIME*, BBC News, *The Independent*, and the *New York Times* (BBC News, 2015), evidence of suspicion is present in certain right-wing outlets, such as *The Daily Mail* and *The Sun*, and social media platforms. Remoralization here produces a more ambivalent narrative, where the use of headline language stirs xenophobia ("they are among the thousands to have flocked to Lesbos" [Smith, 2015]; "smartphones are the secret weapon fuelling the great migrant invasion" [Lawson, 2015]; "Police discovered hundreds of disturbing images of executions on phones images included ISIS flags, dead children and victims of war and terrorism" [The Muslim Issue, 2015]), Social media responses to this coverage are more explicit, pointing to an "incompatibility" between being a refugee and being a social media user ("With an Otter Box! RT: Poverty stricken Syrian migrant takes selfie with her $600 smartphone" [Near Chaos, 2015]).

This hate discourse is evidently attached to extreme right-wing news, yet, I argue, the misrecognition of migrants is inherent in all remediations of the celebration selfie. This is for two reasons. First, remediation as estrangement already presupposes that selfie-taking as digital agency can only be associated with people like "us," not "them." Informed by this orientalist presupposition, narratives of estrangement ultimately represent the migrants' selfie-taking activity in ways that, at once, assert and undermine their humanity. Even though affirming the digital literacy of migrants may be useful, in that it challenges stereotypical views of "backward" non-Europeans (O'Malley, 2015), the news status of such an affirmation is simultaneously an act of "othering," insofar as such it invites us to contemplate migrants' selfie-taking as extraordinary. The meta-witnessing of celebration selfies could, in this light, be seen as the contemplation of those rare public occasions when those who have no voice attempt to speak. And yet our media give this voice no stage.

The second reason, therefore, why these remediations are a form of misrecognition is that no migrant selfies are present in our media. Migrants do not represent themselves in Western news, "others do the representing for them" (Malkki, 1996). If selfies are, in Frosh's words, "reflexive texts" where the self operates "as a deictic shifter, fluctuating between the self as an image and as a body" (2015, p. 1621), then the remediation of migrants' selfie-taking in Western news chooses to keep its focus on the image, photographing the act that represents the body, not the body itself. At the same time, it is not just the corporeal being of the migrants that is missing but, crucially, also their historical existence. While the news may inform us on why refugees take selfies, it leaves out the core question of what might have driven them away from home (Gillespie et al., 2016). In keeping migrants' voice and historicity outside the regime of remediation, then, Western news may thematize their digital activity but ultimately fail to humanize them. The sympathetic spectatorship of mobile witnessing mutates here into an "impartial" spectatorship of meta-witnessing that objectifies the figure of the migrants and puts their status as human at stake.

Solidarity selfies: Self-representation as recognition

This category consists of selfies that migrants have taken with celebrity figures standing in solidarity with them at detention camps around Europe. Celebrities are here defined as public figures with a surplus of symbolic capital that endows them with recognizable brand value (Chouliaraki, 2013a)—for instance, Angela Merkel or Pope Francis.[3] Because of this symbolic capital, then, solidarity selfies, unlike celebration ones, are fully remediated in Western news.

Selfie as performance

The authentication of solidarity selfies is established through an aesthetics of immediacy. Borrowing from the photographic snapshot, the migrant-with-celebrity selfie mimics the informality of "kodak" family pictures (Iqani & Schroeder, 2015) and bears connotations of "performed intimacy, authenticity and access"—all key markers of unstaged, imperfect self-expression (boyd & Marwick, 2011, p. 140). The authenticity of spontaneity, however, primarily benefits the celebrity, whose public presentations suffer from what boyd and Marwick call an inherently "indeterminate 'authenticity'" (2011, p. 139): Does celebrity mean what she/he does or is it all show business? This is because the selfie's compositional structure, which sets celebrity and migrant side-by-side as equals, conceives of solidarity as an arrangement of co-presence, where the celebrity's physical positioning next to the migrant is symbolically displaced onto moral positioning. By virtue of appearing there and photographed next to the vulnerable, she/he is seen to possess the emotional depth and virtuous character to stand by the migrants and commit to their cause.

If authentication is about the transfer of truth value from migrant to celebrity, presencing is about the transfer of symbolic value from celebrity to migrant. While ordinary selfies largely generate "phatic" exchanges, performative acts with little meaning transfer beyond the locative function of "*here* I am" (Frosh, 2015), solidarity selfies, I argue,

---

[3]On the celebrification of politicians, such as Merkel, see Wheeler (2012); on the celebrification of religion, see Lofton (2012).

tactically use the "here *I am*" of the celebrity to shed light on the presence of the migrant. It is, again, the compositional arrangement of co-presence that produces effects of presencing, as the side-by-side visually juxtaposes the migrant, unknown and powerless, with the celebrity, established and powerful, and, in an act parallel to product endorsement, associates the latter's brand value with the former—what Fuqua terms "human branding" (2011). Presencing, in this context, means that even though the migrant does not become famous, he/she acquires a potential for "recognizability" (Cavarero, 2000), for legitimate presence and for public acknowledgment in the spaces of Western news.

The combination of authenticity and presence in solidarity selfies establishes what Schudson (1993) calls the "celebrification" of the migrant cause. Celebrification refers here to a synergetic configuration of theatrical relationships, whereby the selfie capitalizes on the figure of the migrant so as to stage the celebrity as a "true" brand of benevolent activism, while it reciprocally transfers the symbolic value of celebrity onto the migrants, endowing them with a potential for recognizability. The sympathetic spectator of the solidarity selfie is, thus, invited to engage in what we may call "humanitarian" witnessing—a mode of witnessing that construes migrant news as a hybrid between the "truth" of suffering others and the legitimacy of "our" own public personas.

Selfie as remediation

It is precisely the theatrical relationship of celebrification, albeit now reduced from reciprocal synergies of value to a unidirectional transfer of value from the migrant to the celebrity, that renders the remediation of solidarity selfies in "our" news possible. Newsworthiness, in other words, is attached to the authentic performance of humanitarianism attached to the celebrity brand, as she/he stands beside the migrant, and becomes evident in the systematic prioritization of Merkel or the Pope, in news stories that feature these selfies—a prioritization that is simultaneously correlative to the full silencing of the migrants' self-representation, in these same stories. Both CNN and BBC recontextualize the solidarity selfie as an illustration on stories about the politics of the Western figures: Merkel's open migration policy (Dewan & Hanna, 2016; Hill, 2015), or the Pope's visit to the Greek islands in DW (AFP & Reuters, 2016), and CCN's "Edition" (Social Action, 2016).

Even though news networks favor the promotion of celebrity-driven pieces for their own benefit, this celebrification of the solidarity selfie has, as I have already insinuated, a cost. Rather than being placed at the heart of the migration story, as a victim of European politics and a potential carrier of rights to safety and residence, the migrant remains absent. Despite having important stories to tell about why and how he/she has turned up in Europe, he has, in Arendt's words, lost "the relevance of speech" (1998, p. 297). The impartial spectator of the solidarity selfie news, consequently, is not invited to be the witness of a humanitarian story, where solidarity is about engaging with the migrant's face and taking responsibility to reflect on and act on the crisis, but the monitorial witness of "our" own familiar public figures: following up on routine news stories of "our" German Chancellor or the Catholic Church leader.

This celebrification of the solidarity selfie further remoralizes the migrant cause in ambivalent news narratives: Should we receive them or close our borders? Notice, for instance, CNN's headline "Germany's Merkel stands by refugee policy despite 'terrifying' attacks" or *The Independent* that fuses migrant and terrorist in one headline (Fenton,

2016). Just as celebration selfies open up a space where the human status of migrants is ultimately undermined, even if it is rhetorically asserted, so solidarity selfies introduce a rupture in the symbolic status of migrants, whereby even if they may be entitled to rights of residency and protection, they are ultimately denied public recognition. Recognizability, the universal moral right to be acknowledged as a legitimate public presence, is marginalized in favor of monitorial witnessing. The migrant, it follows, only figures in the news as a by-presence, a presence auxiliary to the stories about our leaders, our politics, our controversies.

Celebrity selfies: Self-representation as erasure

This category consists of a sequence of widely circulated images from one particular event, a star-studded Cinema for Peace gala, part of the 2016 Berlin Film Festival. Organized by world-known activist artist Ai Weiwei, this selfie sequence was part of a series of solidarity tokens, such as covering of the building's façade with plastic lifesavers from sea rescue operations, that the artist staged to protest against Europe's negative response to the migration crisis. The selfie depicts celebrities impersonating migrants by wearing thermal blankets—another emergency aid item used in sea rescue operations. As before, celebrities are defined as public figures with a transferable surplus of symbolic capital, yet, unlike the solidarity selfie, these are not political or religious figures of authority but film and music stars (e.g., Charlize Theron, Pussy Riot's Nadya Tolokonnikova). Importantly, there is no co-presence to mobilize celebrity–migrant value transfers. The migrant is now absent.

Selfie as performance

If solidarity selfies celebrify the migrant cause in contexts of co-presence, here the celebrification of the cause erases the presence of the migrant. Authentification works instead through impersonation: Celebrities act out the part of the migrant, by covering themselves in a thermal blanket while attending the gala. The selfie's truth claim, its "*I am here*," is thus not based on verisimilitude, the claim to "reality-as-it-is," but the "as-if" of stage acting: The celebrity, bearing the blanket as an acting prop, stands for the migrant. Insofar as it relies on the suspension of disbelief, the authenticity of the celebrity selfie is thus par excellence theatrical.

In line with the theatrical model, presencing also presupposes an imaginative mobility of positions, insofar as the anguished refugee is evoked, not visualized, through the metonymic placing of a gala-attending celebrity in his/her position. The "I am *here*" claim, in other words, denotes the migrant only insofar as the symbolic meaning of the blanket momentarily resignifies the celebrity as a sufferer. As with solidarity selfies, here, too, the performance of celebrity selfies works to "celebrify" the migrant cause. Unlike solidarity selfies, however, celebrification now entails none of the reciprocal synergies of value between the two. Instead, given that the celebrity is the only one on stage, the symbolic value of acting out the refugee through metonymical displacement onto the celebrity entails an ambivalent potential—it is both about "human branding" and about a critique of inauthenticity. The sympathetic spectator of the celebrity selfie is, in this sense, invited to engage in what we may call "ironic" witnessing—a mode of witnessing that, seriously as it may take the cause of refugee suffering, remains profoundly suspicious of the spectacles of popular culture and their "ventrilocation" of human suffering through the glamorous voices of show business (Chouliaraki, 2013a).

Selfie as remediation

It follows that, similarly to the solidarity selfie, it is celebrification that catalyzes the newsworthiness of the celebrity selfie, too: the presence of Charlize Theron, the glamorous context of the actors' gala, and the occasion of a world famous cultural event. Yet unlike the solidarity selfie, we no longer see the selfie itself but a photojournalistic shot of the act of selfie-taking. While this is reminiscent of celebration selfies, their recontextualization is different. If celebration selfies derived their newsworthiness from the estrangement of the migrants' digital agency, celebrity selfies are newsworthy precisely because they rely on intimacy-at-a-distance: a form of mediated agency that, according to Thompson, maintains the celebrity's proximity to her/his fan base, through the para-social interactions of mass and digital platforms (Thompson, 1995).

Each type of selfie was consequently remoralized in different narratives of ambivalence. While the celebration selfie, let us recall, opened up narratives of curiosity and suspicion around the very legitimacy of celebration selfies (why are they doing it and should they be doing it?), the celebrity one is remoralized as a story of both fascination and critique. For instance, *The Guardian*'s (February 16, 2016) title and subtitle on the subject are "Celebrities don emergency blankets at Berlin fundraiser for refugees" and "Charity event at art installation designed by Ai Weiwei outrages Berlin's culture secretary," while the rest of the article is about the "obscene" aspects of celebrity activism: the thermal-blanket impersonations, as well as Ai Weiwei's earlier initiative of photographing himself as a dead Aylan Kurdi. In contrast to the declared intentions of selfie activism, it follows, the impartial spectator of the celebrity selfie news is here invited to focus on an internal controversy of "our" own popular culture: the inauthenticity of "our" celebrity figures as communicative platforms for transnational solidarity, rather than the troubling absence of the migrant face across news platforms. This, I argue, is a "narcissistic" form of witnessing that, while it capitalizes on the glamorous voyeurism around celebrity culture, simultaneously approaches celebrity humanitarianism as a terrain of "our" self-reflexivity for its authenticity deficits, without, however, touching on a more fundamental question—the systematic marginalization and displacement of the migrant's face in Western spaces of public visibility.

Indeed, despite its reflexive critique, the implication of the remoralization of the celebrity selfie is the full erasure of the migrant from the news narrative. If earlier news narratives relied on the authenticity of the migrant to articulate either ambivalent discourses of compassion and suspicion or a potential for recognizability, here there is a total eclipse of the migrant as an agent in the celebrity selfie. In a manner reminiscent of both celebration and solidarity selfies, the impartial spectator of the celebrity selfie is thus also confronted with a fundamental ambivalence in witnessing the migrant face. Unlike the previous cases, however, this is a compound form of ambivalent witnessing. This is because witnessing now relies not only on the news' gesture to open up a space of visibility for the migrant only to immediately close it down, as before, but on doubling this process through "post-humanitarian critique," where the misery of others is taken up but only in order to serve as the stage where "we" debate "our" own personas, events and moral practices. This is a form of "post-humanitarian" witnessing that may increase the visibility of a cause but does not help us understand it or humanize its actors (Chouliaraki, 2013a).

Conclusion: The selfie as "symbolic bordering"

In August 2015, a BBC news story broke. It was about an advertising campaign based on selfie-taking by an actor who posed as a refugee, documenting his sea crossing to Europe. The story featured illustrations of these fake selfies, pointing to signs of fakeness in the campaign and reflecting on the blurring of boundaries between authentic and nonauthentic refugee self-representations. What is significance about this selfie story is that it is the only one where the migrant face appears in full frontal view (BBC Trending, 2015). It is, in my view, this impossibility, in our media, to encounter the faces of migrants as staged and photographed by themselves, that is, as a sovereign act of self-representation rather than as forensic material for the study of digital authenticity, that emerges as the most significant insight of this analysis.

It is this insight that I here define as "symbolic bordering": the systematic elision of the other's face as an authentic and agentive presence in Western spaces of publicity. While "symbolic" references the selfie as a techno-aesthetic practice of theatrical performance that articulates ethical proposals for connectivity as it circulates across platforms, "bordering" refers to the geopolitical regime of security that keeps migrants outside Western zones of safety and prosperity (Vaughan-Williams, 2009). Symbolic bordering gestures to the doubling of this geopolitical regime onto digital journalism, as a practice of the latter that consolidates the securitizing logic of the former, by consistently excluding migrant visualities from its spaces of visibility. Symbolic bordering can, in this sense, be approached as a regulative mechanism of global journalism that is operative in and through "our" news platforms, thereby also regulating who appears, how, and why, in the spaces of Western publicity.

The migrant-related selfie, I have shown, produces effects of symbolic bordering insofar as it selectively participates in the circulation flows of "our" news contexts. In so doing, it becomes embedded in different techno-aesthetic configurations of the other and the self, each of which enables different modes of witnessing between "us" and "them." While the face of the migrant figures in digital self-representations of celebration and recognition, its journalistic recontextualizations situate these selfies in ambivalent and open-ended moral registers: empathy and suspicion, in celebration (why are they taking selfies? should they?) or doubt and fear (are our politicians right or wrong? should we open the borders?). Even though both curiosity and doubt may be regarded as legitimate concerns in the age of mass human mobility, their fully hegemonic status in the news allows for no other moral registers to contextualize and resignify these selfies for us.

As a result, neither the triumph of survival and its politics of hope (the migrants' "not yet") nor their appeal to inclusion and its politics of legitimacy (the migrants' appearance next to "our" politicians) has a chance to emerge as a valid ethico-political claim in Western media. What these media do choose to include and debate, instead, is celebrity claims that "ventrilocate" the migrants, by "speaking their voice" in glamorous self-representations of distant suffering. The ambivalent contextualizations of these selfies between voyeurism ("here is Charlize Theron looking good!") and disapproval ("it's wrong to 'play' the refugee") granted, neither argument thematizes the voice and predicament of the migrant cause itself; both reproduce the local concerns of "our" commodified popular culture. As a consequence, the remediation of migrant-related selfies in Western news confirms what Arendt has long ago observed; as a marginal figure without rights, she has argued, the refugee ends up "representing nothing but his own absolutely unique individuality which, deprived of expression within and action upon a common world, loses all significance" (1998, p. 302).

Symbolic bordering is, I would argue further, more than simply a regulative mechanism that operates through norms of journalistic appropriateness and newsworthiness about who, how, and why we witness in the news. Rather, I have also shown that by selecting which faces, bodies, and voices are "appropriate" and "newsworthy," symbolic bordering operates as a crucial form of sovereign power that defines the norms of humanity (who is human?), recognition (who is included?), and voice (who can speak?) in our public life: a form of power that, paraphrasing Vaughan-Williams (2009), we might call "bio-political sovereignty." If, as Hannah Arendt has put it, Western publicity is a space of world-disclosing action through which individuals reveal their humanness in the presence of equals (Arendt, 1976), then the power of symbolic bordering lies in restricting precisely this fundamental act of world-disclosure. In so doing, it reduces "our" spaces of publicity to "post-humanitarian" spaces: ethico-political spaces that may allow for forms of empathic, humanitarian witnessing yet, at the same time, thrive in voyeuristic and ironic encounters of migrant others, which are ultimately unable to move beyond the fears, doubts, and concerns of ourselves.

References

AFP & Reuters. (2016, April 5). Pope Francis to visit Lesbos to review refugee crisis. *DW*. Retrieved from http://www.dw.com/en/pope-francis-to-visit-lesbos-to-review-refugee-crisis/a-19165871

Al-Ghazzi, O. (2014). "Citizen journalism" in the Syrian uprising: Problematizing Western narratives in a local context. *Communication Theory*, 24(4), 435–454. doi:10.1111/comt.2014.24.issue-4

Allan, S. (2013). *Citizen witnessing: Revisioning journalism in times of crisis*. Cambridge, UK: Polity.

Arendt, H. (1976). *The origins of totalitarianism*. New York, NY: Harvest Books.

Arendt, H. (1998). *The human condition*. Chicago, IL: University of Chicago Press.

BBC News. (2015, September 7). The 'vital' role of mobile phones for refugees & migrants. *BBC News*. Retrieved from https://www.youtube.com/watch?v=DWTFG-x1dnk

BBC Trending. (2015, August 3). 'Migrant' hoax: The selfies that fooled the internet. *BBC News*. Retrieved from http://www.bbc.co.uk/news/blogs-trending-33764636

Bloch, E. (1995). *The principle of hope*. Cambridge, MA: MIT Press.

Bolter, R., & Gursin, D. (1999). *Remediation. Understanding new media*. Cambridge, MA: MIT Press.

boyd, d., & Marwick, A. (2011). *Social steganography: Privacy in networked publics*. Boston, MA: International Communication Association.

Brunwasser, M. (2015, August 26). A 21st-Century migrant's essentials: Food, shelter, smartphone. *The New York Times*. Retrieved from https://www.nytimes.com/2015/08/26/world/europe/a-21st-century-migrants-checklist-water-shelter-smartphone.html?_r=1

Cavarero, A. (2000). *Relating narratives: Storytelling and selfhood*. London, UK: Routledge.

Chouliaraki, L. (2013a). *The ironic spectator: Solidarity in the age of post-humanitarianism*. Cambridge, UK: Polity.

Chouliaraki, L. (2013b). Remediation, intermediation, transmediation. *Journalism Studies*, 14(2), 267–283. doi:10.1080/1461670X.2012.718559

Chouliaraki, L. (2015). Digital witnessing in conflict zones: The politics of remediation. *Information, Communication & Society*, 18(11), 1362–1377. doi:10.1080/1369118X.2015.1070890

CNN. (2015, August 21). Selfies you won't forget. *CNN*. Retrieved from http://edition.cnn.com/videos/world/2015/08/21/migrant-selfie-kos-mediterranean-orig.cnn

Dean, J. (2005). Communicative capitalism: Circulation and the foreclosure of politics. *Cultural Politics*, 1(1), 51–73. doi:10.2752/174321905778054845

Dean, J. (2016, February 5). Images without viewers: Selfie communism. *Fotomuseum*. Retrieved from http://www.fotomuseum.ch/en/explore/still-searching/articles/26420

Dewan, J., & Hanna, J. (2016, July 28). Germany's Merkel stands by refugee policy despite 'terrifying' attacks. *CNN*. Retrieved from http://edition.cnn.com/2016/07/28/europe/germany-merkel-security-refugee-policy

Duguay, S. (2017). Dressing up Tinderella: Interrogating authenticity claims on the mobile dating app Tinder. *Information, Communication & Society, 20*(3), 351–367.

Fenton, N., & Downey, J. (2003). Counter public spheres and global modernity. *Javnost—The Public, 10*(1), 15–32. doi:10.1080/13183222.2003.11008819

Fenton, S. (2016, March 29). Angela Merkel selfie with Syrian refugee goes viral after he is wrongly named as Brussels bomber. *The Independent*. Retrieved from http://www.independent.co.uk/news/world/europe/syrian-refugees-selfie-with-angela-merkel-goes-viral-after-he,-is-wrongly-named-as-brussels-bomber-a6958371.html

Féral, J., & Bermingham, R. P. (2002). Theatricality: The specificity of theatrical language. *Substance: A Review of Theory & Literary Criticism, 31*(2/3), 94–108. doi:10.2307/3685480

Frosh, P. (2015). The gestural image: The selfie, photography theory, and kinesthetic sociability. *International Journal of Communication, 9*, 1607–1628.

Fuqua, J. V. (2011). Brand Pitt: Celebrity activism and the Make It Right Foundation in post-Katrina New Orleans. *Celebrity Studies, 2*(2), 192–208. doi:10.1080/19392397.2011.574872

Gillespie, M., Ampofo, L., Cheesman, M., Faith, B., Iliadou, E., Issa, A., ... Skleparis, D. (2016). *Mapping refugee media journeys: Smartphones and social media networks*. Retrieved from http://www.open.ac.uk/ccig/sites/www.open.ac.uk.ccig/files/Mapping%20Refugee%20Media%20Journeys%2016%20May%20FIN%20MG_0.pdf

Gómez, E., & Thornham, H. (2015). Selfies beyond self-representation: The (theoretical) f(r)ictions of a practice. *Journal of Aesthetics & Culture, 7*, 28073. doi:10.3402/jac.v7.28073

Hall, J. (2014). *The self-portrait: A cultural history*. London, UK: Thames and Hudson.

Hess, A. (2015). The Selfie Assemblage. *International Journal of Communication, 9*, 1629–1646.

Hill, J. (2015, October 1). Migrant crisis: How long can Merkel keep German doors open? *BBC News*. Retrieved from http://www.bbc.co.uk/news/world-europe-34402001

Iqani, M., & Schroeder, J. E. (2016). #selfie: Digital self-portraits as commodity form and consumption practice. *Consumption Markets & Culture, 19*(5), 405–415. doi:10.1080/10253866.2015.1116784

Jerslev, A., & Mortensen, M. (2015). What is the self in the celebrity selfie? Celebrification, phatic communication and performativity. *Celebrity Studies, 7*, 249–263. doi:10.1080/19392397.2015.1095644

Koffman, O., Orgad, S., & Gill, R. (2015). Girl power and 'selfie humanitarianism.' *Continuum, 29* (2), 157–168. doi:10.1080/10304312.2015.1022948

Koliska, M., & Roberts, J. (2015). Selfies: Witnessing and participatory journalism with a point of view. *International Journal of Communication, 9*, 1672–1685.

Laurent, O. (2015, October 8). See how refugees use selfies to document their journey. *TIME*. Retrieved from http://time.com/4064988/migrant-crisis-selfies

Lawson, D. (2015, September 28). Smartphones are the secret weapon fuelling the great migrant invasion. *The Daily Mail*. Retrieved from http://www.dailymail.co.uk/debate/article-3251475/DOMINIC-LAWSON-Smartphones-secret-weapon-fuelling-great-migrant-invasion.html

Levin, A. (2014). The selfie in the age of digital recursion. *InVisible Culture, 20*. Retrieved from http://ivc.lib.rochester.edu/the-selfie-in-the-age-of-digital-recursion/

Lofton, K. (2012). The celebrification of religion in the age of infotainment. In D. Winston (Ed.), *The Oxford Handbook of Religion and American News Media* (pp. 421–438). Oxford, UK: Oxford University Press.

Lüders, M., Prøitz, L., & Rasmussen, T. (2010). Emerging personal media genres. *New Media & Society, 12*(6), 947–963. doi:10.1177/1461444809352203

Malkki, L. H. (1996). Speechless emissaries: Refugees, humanitarianism, and dehistoricization. *Cultural Anthropology, 11*(3), 377–404. doi:10.1525/can.1996.11.3.02a00050

Marshall, D. (1984). Adam Smith and the theatricality of moral sentiments. *Critical Inquiry, 10*(4), 592–613. doi:10.1086/448266

The Muslim Issue. (2015, December 15). Daily archives. *The Muslim Issue*. Retrieved from https://themuslimissue.wordpress.com/2015/12/15/?iframe=true%26theme_preview=true

Near Chaos. (2015, September 5). With an Otter Box! RT @DefendWallSt: Poverty stricken Syrian migrant takes selfie with her $600 smartphone. Retrieved from https://twitter.com/near_chaos/status/640247516596842496

O'Malley, J. (2015, September 7) Surprised that Syrian refugees have smartphones? Sorry to break this to you, but you're an idiot. *The Independent*. Retrieved from http://www.independent.co.uk/voices/comment/surprised-that-syrian-refugees-have-smartphones-well-sorry-to-break-this-to-you-but-youre-an-idiot-10489719.html

Papacharissi, Z. (2011). Introduction to themed issue, On convergent supersurfaces and public spheres online. *International Journal of Electronic Governance*, 4(1), 9–17. doi:10.1504/IJEG.2011.041704

Pinchevski, A. (2016). Screen trauma: Visual media and post-traumatic stress disorder. *Theory, Culture & Society*, 33(4), 51–75. doi:10.1177/0263276415619220

Reading, A. (2009). Mobile witnessing: Ethics and the camera phone in the "war on terror." *Globalizations*, 6(1), 61–76. doi:10.1080/14747730802692435

Schudson, M. (1993). *Advertising, the uneasy persuasion: Its dubious impact on American society* (New ed., Communication and society). London, UK: Routledge.

Senft, T. (2015) The skin of the selfie. In A. Bieber (Ed.), *Ego Update. The History of the Selfie*. Dusseldorf, Germany: Koenig Books.

Smith, J. (2015, September 6). Selfies on the shore: Refugees in lifejackets celebrate on the beach after reaching Greek island where thousands are waiting to enter Europe. *The Daily Mail*. Retrieved from http://www.dailymail.co.uk/news/article-3224305/Selfies-shore-Refugees-lifejackets-celebrate-beach-reaching-Greek-island-thousands-waiting-enter-Europe.html

Social Action. (2016, March 25). *Pope Francis welcomes refugees to Rome*. Retrieved from https://twitter.com/i/moments/713421646883737600

Thompson, J. B. (1995). *The media and modernity: A social theory of the media*. Cambridge, UK: Polity.

Thumim, N. (2009). 'Everyone has a story to tell': Mediation and self-representation in two UK institutions. *International Journal of Cultural Studies*, 12(6), 617–638. doi:10.1177/1367877909342494

Thumim, N. (2012). *Self-representation and digital culture*. Basingstoke, UK: Palgrave Macmillan.

Tifentale, A., & Manovich, L. (2015). Selfiecity: Exploring photography and self-fashioning in social media. In D. M. Berry, & M. Dieter (Eds.), *Postdigital aesthetics: Art, computation and design* (pp. 109–122). London, UK: Palgrave Macmillan.

van Dijck, J. (2013). *The culture of connectivity: A critical history of social media*. Oxford, UK: Oxford University Press.

van House, N. A. (2009). Collocated photo sharing, story-telling, and the performance of self. *International Journal of Human-Computer Studies*, 67(12), 1073–1086. doi:10.1016/j.ijhcs.2009.09.003

van House, N. A. (2011). Personal photography, digital technologies and the uses of the visual. *Visual Studies*, 26(2), 125–134. doi:10.1080/1472586X.2011.571888

Vaughan-Williams, N. (2009). *Border politics: The limits of sovereign power*. Edinburgh, UK: Edinburgh University Press.

Vivienne, S., & Burgess, J. (2013). The remediation of the personal photograph and the politics of self-representation in digital storytelling. *Journal of Material Culture*, 18(3), 279–298. doi:10.1177/1359183513492080

Wheeler, M. (2012). The democratic worth of celebrity politics in the era of late modernity. *British Journal of Politics and International Relations*, 14(3), 407–422. doi:10.1111/j.1467-856X.2011.00487.x

Wittgenstein, L. (1958). *Philosophical investigations* (2nd ed.). Oxford, UK: Blackwell.

Refugee testimonies enacted: voice and solidarity in media art installations

Karina Horsti

ABSTRACT
This article examines how two media art installations in which celebrity actors enact refugee storytelling create awareness of the complexities of representation and solidarity with refugees. The celebrity actor produces familiarity, or "audibility," for contents of the stories. Yet at the same time, the familiarity of the actor alerts the visitor to the politics of listening. The artworks therefore produce the potential for ethical listening, which requires interrogation into the privileges of the listener. The artworks produce a kind of sociality different from that of typical celebrity advocacy. Instead of being at the center of attention, the actors' presence draws critical attention to the politics of listening.

Introduction

Stories of refugees and asylum seekers have proliferated in recent years in the European cultural field, particularly during and after the "European refugee reception crisis" of 2015. Artists, theater directors, authors, and filmmakers have been at the forefront with journalists and activists to document one of the most catastrophic situations in recent years. This article explores how listening to the stories of refugees in and through contemporary art could produce solidarity between those who have to flee and those who do not. Attention to the critical potential of the arts is particularly important in present-day Europe, where political and popular visions of human rights and seeking refuge are becoming more and more narrow.

There is a long tradition in Europe of seeing the arts "as the source of an 'ethical vision' and a repository of human values" (Belfiore & Bennett, 2008, p. 10), and the creative attention paid to the conditions of refugees in contemporary art can be understood as a continuation of this. The conceptualization of the arts as a socially impactful practice requires artists and museums to provide communicative spaces and cultivate sociality across differences.

Documentary arts, which work with the material of real-life events, are a broader recent trend in the creative arena. However, documentary art has long roots, with one notable phase being the Great Depression of the 1930s, when a group of artists in the United Kingdom began to document people's suffering and struggles through realistic aesthetics as a countermovement to abstraction and surrealism. More recently, after the attacks of September 11, 2001, several novelists turned from fiction to essays; in the words of V. S. Naipaul, they believed that "fiction is no longer adequate to make sense of the world" (Webb, 2009, p. 67). The documentary approach in the arts, therefore, could be seen as a response to events that disturb the social order and artists' sense of ontological security. Artists who engage with real-life events feel a responsibility and an obligation to search for the "ethical vision."

Storytelling has been one of the main strategies for artists working with refugee experiences. While the notion of the "subaltern voice" has been critically interrogated since Gayatri Chakravorty Spivak's (1988) seminal essay "Can the Subaltern Speak?" and rethought in the context of recent practices of self-narration in the digital era, the theorization of *voice*—the capability to speak and to be heard—remains an unfinished matter (in media and cultural studies, see, e.g., Husband, 1996; Sreberny, 2006; Couldry, 2010; Dreher, 2009, 2012; Ong, 2014; Rovisco, 2015; Musarò, 2017). The notion of "refugee voice" needs careful reflection: It assumes that there is one voice rather than many, and the idea of "giving" a voice to refugees (through art, for example) involves a power dynamic between the party who has resources to "give" and the party who accepts the opportunity to speak in the context provided to it. Moreover, the public to whom the story is narrated is often imagined as the White middle class (Ong, 2014, p. 189).

Furthermore, scholars of performance such as Catherine Wake and Saidiya Hartman have brought attention to the ethics of repeating narratives of violence, suffering, and pain. In Saidiya Hartman's terms, the problem is how to replay "scenes of subjection" without creating more of the same. In such scenes, the person who repeats his or her own story or the fictionalized story of an abstracted refugee may again be objectified and defined predominantly in terms of suffering (Wake, 2009).

Within media studies, Tanja Dreher (2009, 2012) has addressed the hierarchies of voice and audibility by focusing on the position and practice of the one who listens. Listening requires opening oneself up to the possibility of change and vulnerability. Dreher (2009)[1] has developed a model of ethical listening across difference at the intersection of feminist and critical race studies that requires horizontal engagement with the one who is listened to. In this approach, the ethical imperative of listening is to be attentive to one's own privileges and complicities. Therefore, ethical listening is not an attempt to cognitively understand and explain the Other or that which is different, but to understand unequal relationships and power dynamics. Instead of explanation, listening means presence and openness to recognizing the incompleteness and unsettledness that emerge in encounters across differences.

This ethical approach to listening is helpful in thinking about solidarity in the context of the relationship between refugees and Western publics. This relationship is complex and needs to be defined in relation to such humanitarianism that does not carry reciprocity but is instead based on a hierarchical relationship between one party who has the resources to help and the other who receives generosity. Rights-based solidarity, on the contrary, is an emotionally and morally motivated practice that strives for mutual support (Ticktin, 2011; Fassin, 2012, pp. 2–4; Horsti, 2013; Chouliaraki, 2013, pp. 11–13). Social philosophy shows how solidarity is often produced through shared experience and the feeling of belonging together, such as forms of sociality based on shared civic life or struggles to overcome injustice (for an overview, see Laitinen, 2013). However, solidarity can also refer to a universal ethical responsiveness to humanity (Laitinen & Pessi, 2015; Rorty, 1989; Scholtz, 2008) that goes beyond "we-thinking"—thinking that produces opposition between "us" and "them." In this sense, solidarity can also refer to a basic ethical concern for others: a moral, global or human solidarity.

Through an examination of two media art installations, this article discusses the potentiality of contemporary art to produce solidarity between the (presumed Western) public and refugees through storytelling and listening. I have examined the two artworks, with their situated aesthetics and the debates surrounding them, and have analyzed the scripts of the refugee narratives used in the artworks, as well as additional materials provided by the artists on their websites and social media. I have also examined how the artists have described their work in public. Contemporary art as a context for the study of mediated storytelling and listening brings forward the role of the artist (as the one who listens and retells) and the situatedness of the telling in a more apparent way than most other genres of media and popular communication.

In this article, I draw attention to the ways multiple voices are presented and connected in the artworks, as well as to how the pieces position the listener. The stories are first listened to by the artists, then by the actors who enact the stories in the installations, then by museum curators, and finally, by the visitors. Moreover, I study the multidirectional potential of producing solidarity through art by considering the references and connections to histories, identity positions, cultural signs, and experiences that might produce mutual understanding and invite reciprocity. I also discuss the role of celebrity actors in the two pieces and examine the ways they shape the politics of listening and voice and position the refugee story in the cultural sphere. Both installations use celebrity actors who enact the storytelling of refugees, and in doing so, the installations appear not only in the sphere of contemporary "high" art but also in the sphere of popular culture. The actors, familiar to museum visitors from television and film, potentially appeal to a wider public than contemporary art institutions tend to reach.

Research on celebrity advocacy in the humanitarian field has been critical of how the emotions of the celebrities themselves often become the centre of attention and point of identification. Although celebrities attempt to bring attention to humanitarian causes and transform or "authenticate" distant suffering for domestic settings, celebrities, their glamour, and their feelings are arguably substituted for the voice of the sufferer. Thus, while celebrities "give their popular voice" to the refugees, they often end up becoming the centre of attention (Chouliaraki, 2012; Driessens, Joye, & Biltereyst, 2012; Goodman & Barnes, 2011). In contrast to the role of celebrities in humanitarian advocacy, I argue in this article that the celebrities in the artworks I examine perform a different social relationship and offer the potential for a different kind of sociality. While the "glamour" of the popular actors attracts the attention of the public, the media art installations invite the visitor to reflect on the politics and ethics of listening and telling. The installations invite the visitor to consider whose suffering affects the viewer and whose storytelling receives attention. The pieces explicitly interrogate their metarepresentation by creating awareness of the complexities of representation and of solidarity with refugees.

First, I examine Finnish artist Timo Wright's audio installation *The Long Journey Home* (2012/2017), which combines eight stories told to the artist by present-day refugees, internally displaced people from Finnish Karelia (in 1939–1945) and Finns who had been evacuated to Sweden as so-called "war children" during World War II. The stories amalgamate into one in the voice of a familiar Finnish actor, Vesa Vierikko, who performs the different experiences without mentioning any names or places. Wright first exhibited the sound installation in 2013 in Galleria Rajatila, a Finnish art gallery, but I saw the piece in 2017 in a Finnish history museum (Lotta Museum) exhibition *Open your heart* about humanitarian aid in Finland in 1941–1952, during and after the war with the Soviet Union.

The second work I examine is a multichannel installation, *Love Story*, by South African artist Candice Breitz, which I experienced in 2017 at the National Gallery of Victoria in Melbourne, Australia. It was first shown at the Kunstmuseum Stuttgart, Germany, in 2016 and subsequently has been shown around the world in museums such as the Arken Museum of Modern Art in Denmark and the Museum of Fine Arts, Boston. The installation is divided into two spaces. In the first space, Hollywood actors Alec Baldwin and Julianne Moore reenact stories told by present-day refugees. The script is cut from transcripts of six refugee testimonies in a fast-paced montage. In the second space, the visitor is invited to sit across from each of the six refugees, who simultaneously perform their testimony on six television screens equipped with headphones. At the National Gallery of Victoria, Breitz renamed her work as *Wilson Must Go* as a protest against the gallery's contract with Wilson Security, which has been accused of human right violations in Australia's offshore detention centres.

The long journey home

> The day I left was an ordinary day of the week. We lived in (*muted*) and suddenly we heard the bombings. The war was starting. The neighbours got together to discuss what was going on, and my mother was confused. My mother said "now you need to leave" because the buildings across the street were bombed. We took only our shoes. (*The Long Journey Home*, 2017)

The familiar voice of Finnish actor Vesa Vierikko recounts this story of fleeing a home. He articulates the tragic experience clearly and with concentration. I hold the installation's old-fashioned telephone receiver to my ear and recall Vierikko's role as one of the soldiers in the well-known film *Talvisota/The Winter War* (published in 1989). It is comforting to listen to this voice, which is so recognizable—almost like a family member speaking to me. I maintain my concentration as the story changes; without interruption, another person's experience of being forced to flee begins. I don't know where or when these events took place, but all the stories recall the moment a person had to leave his or her home. The repetition of the different, yet similar, memories of leaving amalgamate into one story; it is both one story and multiple stories at the same time. I can tell that the names of the places that had to be abandoned were included in the original script but omitted from the enacted version. Wright has not deleted the whole sentence, only the name of the place. Even the prepositions "in" and "from" (indicated by the suffixes *-ssa, -sta* in Finnish) are still there, which serves to draw the listener's attention to the absence of the place names.

Through the similarity of the testimonies, the installation potentially produces solidarity among museum visitors toward present-day refugees—but only in cases where the visitor already identifies with Karelian evacuees and Finnish war children. However, most visitors, like myself, have not themselves lived through evacuations and war. The installation assumes that Finnish museum visitors are connected to these experiences through "prosthetic memory" (Landsberg, 2004): memory of an event that has not been lived through, but has been experienced only through mediation, for example, in literature or film. The mediation can still produce a deeply felt experience, which then creates a personal and intimate "memory." The installation implicitly addresses visitors that identify as Finnish (or Karelian) and whispers the possibility that fleeing could have happened to you, too, if times were different, or that the story could be your grandmother's.

The installation presumes that the visitor "knows" the stories of the Finnish refugees and through them may be able to cultivate an ability to listen to and produce solidarity with present-day refugees. In doing so, the work produces a multidirectional potential to understand past and present experiences of war. Historian Michael Rothberg (2009) suggests that "we consider memory as multidirectional: as subject to ongoing negotiation, cross-referencing and borrowing: as productive and not private." The interaction of different histories in Wright's installation illustrates what Rothberg terms "multidirectional memory," that is, the "productive and intercultural dynamic" of memories (Rothberg, 2009, p. 3). The amalgamation of memories that takes place through the erasure of details and narration by a familiar and popular voice is productive. However, rather than producing a new multidirectional memory or a new vision of the past and present, I argue that the installation produces the potential to recognize the multidirectionality of memory. Wright's installation is not a storehouse from which memories are consumed; rather, memory "needs to be invoked, conjured, made" (Neumann, 2000, p. 8). The installation makes certain presumptions for the making of memory and solidarity that, however, are rather unproblematized and nation centered. The visitor is presumed to identify with Karelian evacuees and Finnish war children, which are underlined as being "Finnish experiences," and only though this premise is the visitor able to hear the experience of the present-day refugee. The situational setting of the installation emphasizes this reading.

The situational aesthetics (Papastergiadis, 2010)—the place and space of the work—are as important as the work itself in the practice of conjuring memory and making something out of the multidirectional potential of the installation. *The Long Journey Home* originates from 2012, and was a political statement in response to the Finnish parliamentary elections of 2011, when anti-immigrant candidates obtained seats in the Finnish parliament and racist speech in online spaces had become a widely discussed issue. Alarmed by the rising anti-immigration movement, the artist felt obliged to create a position from which a gallery visitor could feel solidarity with present-day refugees through temporal similarities (Wright, 2018).

I experienced the installation at a different time and in a different setting, however. As I listened to the audio installation *The Long Journey Home* in the Lotta Museum in Tuusula, Finland, my gaze wondered around the surrounding exhibition. This was not a contemporary art museum, but rather a small museum presenting a specific narrative of the wars Finland fought with the Soviet Union. Lotta Svärd, the focus of the museum, was a Finnish auxiliary organization for women that was established in 1918 during the Finnish Civil War. Lottas, as the women of the organization were called, supported the conservative White Guard in the Civil War. During the Second World War, when Finland fought the Soviet Union, the Lotta Svärd organization mobilized women to replace the men who had been conscripted into the army.

Lottas served in hospitals, at air raid warning posts, and in other auxiliary tasks in close cooperation with the army. Lotta Svärd also carried out voluntary social and humanitarian work. However, after the war, the Soviet Union demanded that Lotta Svärd and all the other paramilitary organizations be banned as "fascist" organizations. The funds of Lotta Svärd were transferred to a new humanitarian organization called the Finnish Women's Aid Foundation, which was to continue the humanitarian and social work of the Lottas. Only after the fall of the Soviet Union in 1990–1991 were the former Lottas able to make their history and memory public, and the museum was opened in 1996. Within the permanent exhibition documenting the history of Lotta Svärd, a special exhibition about the organization's humanitarian and social work, titled *Spaces of love —Open your heart!*, opened in 2017. This was the context in which Timo Wright's audio installation appeared, among historical photographs, documents, objects, and audio clips recounting the humanitarian work carried out by many civic organizations in 1941–1952 under the broader umbrella organization Finnish Relief.

The *Spaces of love* exhibition had two sections. The first recalled memories of the journeys of the 400,000 people evacuated from the ceded territories in Eastern Finland. Because the new border with Russia was drawn further west, the Finnish population in the ceded regions had to leave their homes and livelihoods and relocate elsewhere in war-torn Finland during and after the wars with the Soviet Union in 1939–1945. The other section of the exhibition—where Timo Wright's work was located—documented and honored the member organizations of Finnish Relief. The organizations' aid was directed to orphans, widows, those disabled during the war, and to what the exhibition refers to as *siirtoväki*—internally displaced populations.

Timo Wright's sound installation was surrounded by a spectacle of Finnish solidarity in the past. The photographs in the exhibition depicted equitable and unconflicted caregiving, and the factual explanations gave the impression that humanitarian support from the international community and the Finnish public was well organized and practical. Social inequalities were nowhere to be seen. The exhibition presented a harmonious and morally stable past. A Finnish visitor could feel proud and take the position of a moral agent: This is a nation that resettled more than 400,000 people—this was the message the exhibition conveyed.

The exhibition was unveiled soon after 2015, the year in which the number of asylum seekers in Finland rose almost 10-fold compared to the previous year, to 32,000. The country had become divided between those who wanted to offer assistance to asylum seekers and those who responded with fear and even hate, attacking the people seeking protection. The juxtaposition of Wright's installation, which also pointed to the present, with a spectacle of the seemingly harmonious solidarity of the past produced an uncomfortable question: How did Finland manage to relocate 400,000 people into the country in the war-torn past when 32,000 asylum seekers were now considered a crisis dividing the nation?

The spatial arrangement of the artwork encouraged the visitor to listen to the narratives and look at present-day refugee conditions from the perspective of the war generation. The work is premised on the idea that memories of events can be evoked by other events: the multidirectionality of memory (Rothberg, 2009). A collection of different narratives of history brought together in one space may surprise the visitor and prompt him or her to consider the present and the past from new perspectives. The arrangement creates an incentive to carry on the legacy and sense of responsibility that the exhibition seems to suggest is essential to Finnish citizenship. Therefore, in addition to the installation's invitation to listen to the stories of refugees, the positioning of the installation invites the visitor to listen to past generations of Finnish humanitarians.

The museum accomplishes this, however, by sanitizing and revising the history of postwar Finland, failing to listen to the unsettling, controversial, and uncomfortable voices of the past. While the past is evoked as a potential reference point for solidarity, the sanitizing of the past nevertheless risks to distance it. The narrative of resettling more than 400,000 people, 12% of the population at the time, is told as one of responsibility and solidarity—as a response to the call for "elävä kansallinen yhteistunto," "vibrant national solidarity," that president Kyösti Kallio made in his 14 March 1940 speech after the Winter War peace treaty was signed. However, as many scholars have argued, the resettlement of Karelian evacuees was not unproblematic (e.g., Raninen-Siiskonen, 1999; Sallinen-Gimpl, 1994). The locals across Finland were not always willing to assist the Karelians and often treated the newcomers with suspicion. There was also resentment over the fact that many Finnish landowners had to sell their land to the state for a nominal fee as part of the resettlement project.

In addition to temporal solidarity, the installation also attempts to produce spatial solidarity by underlining how memories travel with people (Erll, 2011). It therefore complicates the idea of territorially bound national memory and treats refugees as subjects in national history-making: Finnish history can be regarded as cumulative history (Neumann, 2016), as a hybrid and multivoiced collection of the memories people carry with them.

Interestingly, the museum did not explicitly direct the Finnish visitor's attention to the multidirectional potential of the artwork or to its placement in the exhibition about the journey of the displaced Karelian population and the Finnish relief efforts. However, the page describing the exhibition on the museum's English-language website did draw visitor's attention in this direction by adding a reference to the so-called "refugee crisis" of the present. To underline the connection, where the Finnish Ministry of the Interior uses the term "asylum seekers," the museum website used the term "refugees": "This year, the Ministry of the Interior estimates that between 25,000 and 30,000 refugees will arrive in Finland, and a majority of them may stay in Finland permanently as immigrants. Time will tell whether we can handle it. Will there be enough love in Finland in 2017?"

The lack of an explicit connection drawn for Finnish speaking visitors between past and present forced mobilities was a conscious decision. Curator Maria Andersin (2017) told me that the museum did not want to draw an explicit parallel between Karelian displaced persons and present-day refugees. There was a risk that such a historical parallel could be uncomfortable for the museum's core group of visitors. Some Karelian evacuees do not want to be referred to as "refugees," as the term may imply foreignness and bring into question whether they belong in Finland. Others, however, are active in the present-day Refugees Welcome movement precisely because they feel a connection to the experience of refugees arriving in Finland.

However, by putting these two mobilities into dialogue with each other, the museum is not only drawing from the past to make sense of the present. By making this connection, the museum is also seeking new audiences and new relevance for the past that it archives and exhibits. As Andersin (2017) points out, few members of the core museum audience—the former Lottas—are alive anymore, and the war children who were sent to Sweden as unaccompanied minors are also getting old. The museum is concerned with the question of how the experiences of the Lottas can remain relevant for future generations. Present-day refugee issues offer another kind of audience and topicality to the Lotta Museum.

Love story

> Okay, I'm ready. So, her name is Julie? Start? Okay. Hi Julie! I'm Sarah and first, I want to thank you for doing this for us. People think about refugees in bad and horrible ways. They think we came here to steal their country, money, jobs and even their homes. We didn't come here to have another war. We just came to have a good future. My dream is to be a doctor and to swim in the national team. In Syria I can't do this. The message I want to give to the world is that we refugees are human, like every girl or guy in Germany. (Sarah Ezzat Mardini, 18 October 2015, in *Love Story*)

Love Story is a video installation created in 2016 by South African-born and Berlin-based artist Candice Breitz, which I saw in the NGV Triennial at the National Gallery of Victoria in Melbourne in 2017. Via a large projection, Hollywood actors Alec Baldwin and Julianne Moore perform the stories of six refugees who had been interviewed by Candice Breitz in Berlin, Cape Town, and New York. In the next room, the visitor can sit at eye level with the refugees, who appear on six flatscreen monitors, and listen through headphones to their interviews, each of which lasted 3 to 4 hours. Four of the six interviews are also available on Vimeo.[2]

For the opening in Melbourne, Breitz renamed her work *Wilson Must Go* in protest of the gallery's use of Wilson Security's services.[3] All publicity material related to the work had to use the new name until the gallery dropped its security provider, Breitz decided. In February 2018, 2 months after the Triennial was opened, NGV selected a new security company. Wilson Security had provided guards for Australia's offshore detention centres on Nauru (since 2012) and on Manus Island (from 2014 until October 2017), and its staff had been accused of or been implicated in human rights violations, as was reported in *The Guardian*'s Nauru files (Evershed, Liu, Farrell, & Davidson, 2016). Candice Breitz (2017a) therefore felt that "it would be morally remiss, in light of the above knowledge, for me to remain silent in the context of the current conversation that is taking place around the Australian government's ongoing and systematic abuse of refugees." The local Artists' Committee in Melbourne had already protested NGV's security contract before the Triennial, but the gallery had not responded seriously. The committee had then contacted the international artists participating in the Triennial, hoping that the status of these artists would force the gallery to address the ethical problem.

Sitting in front of an audience including NGV curators during the opening weekend event, Breitz (2017b) acknowledged the hierarchical relations at work in the protest:

> I need to say that in terms of the protests this week, the Artists' Committee have done all the leg work. Of course it's very easy for a foreign artist to parachute in and have an immediate platform. I have an automatic level of visibility as a result of being an artist in this exhibition. I want to use that visibility to thematize what is going on at the NGV and to make it a little less likely that Wilson or a likeminded company will be selected when it comes to the

permanent security contractor. The Artists' Committee has already staged compelling protests. They are the individuals who have the most to lose in this context. They have neither the prominence nor the security that I have. They have nevertheless insisted on conducting an ethical political dialogue with this very powerful institution.

The decision to rename the installation, Candice Breitz said, was made in solidarity with three different institutions or groups of people: with the gallery that had commissioned her work and that she believed was not going in the right ethical direction by contracting Wilson Security, with the Melbourne based Artists' Committee, and with the refugees she had interviewed. It also threatened Breitz's artwork:

> The same eyes that watched over murder, rape and child abuse in the detainment centres where refugees are held would be watching over my work, these same people would be providing care for my work. This scene became repulsive to me. I felt a responsibility not only to my practice, but also to the interviewees [who are featured in the artwork] and to this museum, which has been so generous to me. (Breitz, 2017b)

The quotes show how Breitz was simultaneously concerned about her own installation, the ethics of the gallery that had partly commissioned it, and her responsibility to the refugees who had shared their testimonies. Breitz acted on the premise of rights-based solidarity, on a moral practice that aims to over come injustice (Laitinen, 2013). She chose to take a position that was compatible with the ethics of her work and with the political position that she shared with the refugees who she had interviewed. Therefore, her ethics of listening (Dreher, 2009) to refugee experiences included the responsibility to care for the relationships she had with the refugees and to recognize her own privileged position as a well-known artist and the audible "voice" that came with it.

However, the protest was also a gesture toward the publics who might find the presence of Wilson Security an offense to their experience of the museum. Breitz's protest opened a critical position for members of the public to identify with so that they could continue to engage with art that immerses the viewer in the conditions of refugees. Moreover, the Triennial exhibition could go on to become a legitimate space for conversation about the treatment of refugees by the Australian government and in other contexts beyond Australia. The exhibition included several other works that engaged with the topic of refugees, and some of the artists followed Breitz in participating in the Wilson Security protest, while others did not (see more details in Neumann & Horsti, 2017).

Photo courtesy of Candice Breitz. Stills from *Love Story* (2016). Featuring Alec Baldwin and José Maria João. Commissioned by the National Gallery of Victoria (Melbourne), Outset Germany (Berlin). and the Medienboard Berlin–Brandenburg.

The first room of the *Wilson Must Go* installation resembles a movie theatre: In a projection in a dark room, Hollywood actors Alec Baldwin and Julianne Moore reenact refugee narratives. The script is cut from transcripts of six testimonies in a fast-paced montage. The script that Baldwin and Moore perform is in first-person singular. The refugee tells his or her story to the artist, Candice Breitz. The artist as listener is explicit in the script in the form of address, such as "Candice, I didn't understand." But the script also reveals that the refugee is aware that his or her story will be re-mediated by Baldwin or Moore. The refugees address them, too, which is a discursive strategy that adds some humor and lightness to the viewing experience: "First of all, I want to thank Alex for being part of—Oh, Alec! The name is Alec."

The piece establishes a sense of reciprocity and mutual recognition between the refugees, the celebrities and the artist. First, the script reveals how both the refugees and the celebrities are actors in Candice Breitz's work. Second, the connection between the two groups of actors is mediated through objects. Each of the refugees has given Breitz a piece of jewellery or personal object that Moore and Baldwin then wore as they re-performed the relevant person's story. The object is a sign of the individual who is speaking through the voice of the Hollywood actor. For example, in the re-performance of José Maria João, an Angolan refugee in South Africa, Alec Baldwin wears José Maria João's copper bangle and says: "I just want to tell Mr. Alec—when this guy Alec tells my story, he has to get it right. Mr. Alec, you must be happy that Candice is giving you this opportunity to give the people my story, to tell them about my life." As José Maria João sees it, Baldwin is privileged to be able to tell his story, and therefore, Baldwin holds a certain responsibility toward him.

Another refugee reflection is enacted by Julianne Moore: "I know when she [Julianne Moore] will listen to the story and share it with the world, I know it wouldn't be the same as if it was just me, coming to stand here, just me sharing my story, because I don't think that all those nice people would come and listen to my story." Here, the audience becomes the fourth agent in the installation—along with the Hollywood actors, the refugees and Candice Breitz. We in the audience are "all those nice people" who listen to the story, perhaps only because it is retold by a celebrity. The story is retold in the sphere of the popular, and it is therefore consumable. We, the visitors, are offered the position of conditional listeners, tied to the economies of attention and affect.

Candice Breitz's motivation for the installation was to reveal the hierarchical positioning of stories, storytellers, and listeners. Her website explains: "The work deploys the hypervisibility of Moore and Baldwin to amplify stories that might otherwise fail to elicit mainstream attention or empathy. At the same time, it reflects on the callousness of a media-saturated culture in which strong identification with fictional characters and celebrity figures runs parallel to a widespread lack of interest in people facing real-world adversity." In doing so, she moves to a metarepresentational level from arts-based participatory storytelling: practice that potentially creates critical space and acts of citizenship but that sometimes fails to profoundly contest exclusion, stereotyping, and marginalization of refugees (Rovisco, 2015).

The gallery visitor becomes aware of the sphere of the popular and the dynamics of representation and attention: Alec Baldwin and Julianne Moore capture our attention no matter what they say. The aesthetic of the movie theater, the big projection, underline this. But importantly, when we do listen to what they say, that they tell the stories of refugees, we become alerted to the issue Breitz wants to underline: the experiences of suffering by real-life people.

The fast-paced montage interweaves lines from Baldwin that are cut to lines from Moore. This produces a kind of awkward dialogue where different parts of the world, different kinds of borders, different dangers, and different reasons to flee are knitted together. Contrary to Timo Wright's sound installation, these stories do not blur into a singular refugee experience or one abstract "no-place," an uncontextualized border. Breitz identifies the refugees, who describe in detail the places and the borders they have crossed. Nevertheless, to keep up with the fast pace of the installation, I had to ignore the details and return to them afterward. There was no time to pause and ask "where, why, which border, which conflict?" The focus of this part of the artwork emphasized the metarepresentational issues rather than the actual stories of refugees.

Only by passing through the space where Alec Baldwin and Julianne Moore reenact the refugee stories, in their American English, on a green-screen set can the visitor enter the second space of the installation and sit across from the six television screens with headphones where the six refugees tell their stories—also on a green-screen set—to Candice Breitz (who is off-screen but addressed in the stories). In this room, the viewer meets six very different contexts for fleeing. "My name is José Maria João. I am from Angola. I am born in the province, the village, of Damba. Damba is near Congo, 200 kilometers from Congo." João details how he managed to move in the borderlands between Namibia and Angola by pretending to be a mute man collecting wood and how he jumped over a metal fence between the countries. This detailed narrative paints an image of a specific borderland, which is different from, for example, the border crossing of another interviewee, Sarah Ezzat Mardini, who recalls how she jumped into the cold, dark Aegean Sea when the rubber dinghy's motor stopped running on the route from Turkey to Greece. She had been a competitive swimmer in Syria, so she swam and pulled the boatload of 17 people to safety.

Photo courtesy of Candice Breitz. Stills from *Love Story* (2016). Featuring Julianne Moore and Sarah Ezzat Mardini. Commissioned by the National Gallery of Victoria (Melbourne), Outset Germany (Berlin), and the Medienboard Berlin–Brandenburg.

The variety of the stories and of the places the interviewees fled from (Venezuela, Syria, Somalia, India, Angola and the Democratic Republic of Congo) produces potential for global solidarity, particularly so in the section where the visitor has time to listen to each of them. In the enacted section, the different narratives interconnect, and in the second room, the stories are told simultaneously side-by-side, creating a co-presence of narration and a potential co-presence of the experience of fleeing. However, in Breitz's work, the multidirectionality of the experiences makes it impossible to think of any generalized, abstract refugee or refugee voice. The work expresses the multiplicity of being a refugee—

there are narratives of persecution based on religion and sexual orientation, as well as war —and in doing so, potentially allows the spectator to recognize the diversity of refugees: "anyone, even me, might have to flee," the visitor might think. Moreover, the location of the installation's first exhibition in Stuttgart, Germany, in 2016 powerfully elucidated how the arrival of refugees is a global issue, not a predominantly European one. At the time, Europeans were caught up in the situation on their own continent, the so-called "European refugee crisis." The installation reminds the viewer that there are places and reasons to flee that do not receive the same attention in the European media that refugees arriving in Europe do. The installation evokes solidarity across different border zones and disrupts the Eurocentric representation of fleeing.

Conclusions

Both *The Long Journey Home* and *Love Story* (temporarily titled *Wilson Must Go*) produce multidirectional potential of solidarity by considering the references and connections to histories, identity positions, border zones, and experiences that might produce mutual understanding and invite reciprocity. In Wright's work, the actor and his steady emotional register amalgamate the memories of fleeing that happened in different time periods and at different borders into one narrative, possibly producing solidarity across different places and different temporalities. However, the work's position requires the viewer to identify with Karelian evacuees or with war children, which is more problematic than the installation and the surrounding historical exhibition admit. The kind of sociality that the museum presents as a foundation for solidarity is a sanitized and unified national community of Finns. Nevertheless, the installation also offers a critical position by inviting the viewer to include present-day refugees in the category of the national "we": The memories of fleeing from other places amalgamate into an equally important national memory of the forced displacements that took place at the Finnish border.

In Candice Breitz's work, the actors also reenact refugee testimonies, but the multivocality is more explicit than in Wright's work. The stories do not amalgamate into one; instead, their distinctiveness is highlighted in the second space of the installation. Breitz's work produces the potential for solidarity with refugees first by making the viewer think critically of the politics of attention and listening, the privileged positions of the celebrity, the artist, and the spectator, and then by inviting the visitor to sit at eye level with the refugees and listen to the stories they perform. The co-presence of the stories connects various conflicts and borders and by doing that produces a potential for global solidarity.

Moreover, Candice Breitz's protest in Melbourne exemplified how ethical listening (Dreher, 2012) in art that uses other people's stories, and, more specifically, stories told by those in vulnerable positions, extends to the situatedness of the artwork. Breitz acted in solidarity with the refugees she had interviewed for the installation when taking a position of protest against the "eyes that watched over murder, rape and child abuse in the detainment centers" watching not only over her own work, but also over the stories of the refugees with whom she had created the artwork.

Finally, the artworks elucidate the metarepresentational level by using celebrity actors who perform the storytelling of refugees. Both installations successfully direct the viewer's attention to the politics of listening, instead of focusing on the typical concern of "giving voice." This becomes explicit in the spheres of contemporary art and history museums. The popular actors attract the attention of the museum visitor. The popularity of the actors blurs the boundaries between genres and between the spheres of popular culture, contemporary "high" art and historical museums. The voice of the actor that reenacts refugee narratives produces familiarity, or "audibility," for the horrific contents of the stories. Yet at the same time the familiarity of the actor alerts the visitor to the politics of listening: "I am listening because I 'know' the one who tells." In Breitz's work this metarepresentational level is explicit.

The artworks therefore managed to produce the potential for ethical listening, which requires interrogation into the privileges of the listener. The celebrities produced a kind of sociality different from that of typical celebrity advocacy. Instead of being at the centre of attention, their celebrity presence drew critical attention to the politics of listening.

Notes

1. Tanja Dreher draws on the feminist scholarship of Bickford (1996) and Ratcliffe (2005).
2. https://vimeo.com/candicebreitz. The two interviews are not online because the people interviewed in them are still going through an asylum process. Breeitz (2018) asked each interviewee to decide whether he or she wished the interview to be available online or not.
3. See Neumann and Horsti (2017).

Disclosure statement

No potential conflict of interest was reported by the author.

Funding

This work was supported by the Academy of Finland [Remembering Migration: Memory politics of forced migration in mediated societies].

References

Andersin, M. (2017, January 18). *Personal communication*.
Belfiore, E., & Bennett, O. (2008). *The social impact of the arts: An intellectual history*. Basingstoke, UK: Palgrave.
Bickford, S. (1996). *The dissonance of democracy: Listening, conflict and citizenship*. London, UK: Cornell University Press.
Breitz, C. (2018, August 3). *Personal communication*.
Breitz, C. (2017a, December 12). *Why I'm sabotaging my own work*. Wilson Must Go. Public statement.
Breitz, C. (2017b, December 17). *Candice Breitz in conversation*. Melbourne: National Gallery of Victoria.
Chouliaraki, L. (2012). The Theatricality of humanitarianism: A critique of celebrity advocacy. *Communication and Critical/Cultural Studies*, 9(1), 1–21. doi:10.1080/14791420.2011.637055
Chouliaraki, L. (2013). *The ironic spectator: Solidarity in the age of post-humanitarianism*. London, UK: Polity Press.
Couldry, N. (2010). *Why voice matters: culture and politics after neoliberalism*. London, UK: Sage.
Dreher, T. (2009). Listening across difference: Media and multiculturalism beyond the politics of voice. *Continuum*, 23(4), 445–458. doi:10.1080/10304310903015712

Dreher, T. (2012). A partial promise of voice: Digital storytelling and the limit of listening. *Media International Australia Incorporating Culture and Policy: Quarterly Journal of Media Research and Resources, 142*, 157–166. doi:10.1177/1329878X1214200117

Driessens, O., Joye, S., & Biltereyst, D. (2012). The X-factor of charity: A critical analysis of celebrities' involvement in the 2010 Flemish and Dutch Haiti relief shows. *Media Culture Society, 34*(6), 709–725. doi:10.1177/0163443712449498

Erll, A. (2011). Travelling memory. *Parallax, 71*(4), 4–18. doi:10.1080/13534645.2011.605570

Evershed, N., Liu, R., Farrell, P., & Davidson, H. (2016, August 10). The Nauru files: The lives of asylum seekers in detention detailed in a unique database. *Guardian*. Retrieved from https://www.theguardian.com/australia-news/ng-interactive/2016/aug/10/the-nauru-files-the-lives-of-asylum-seekers-in-detention-detailed-in-a-unique-database-interactive

Fassin, D. (2012). *Humanitarian reason: A moral history of the present*. Los Angeles, CA: University of California Press.

Goodman, M., & Barnes, C. (2011). Star/poverty space: The making of the "development celebrity." *Celebrity Studies, 2*(1), 69–85. doi:10.1080/19392397.2011.544164

Horsti, K. (2013). De-ethnicized victims: Mediatized advocacy for asylum seekers. *Journalism: Theory, Practice & Criticism, 14*(1), 78–95. doi:10.1177/1464884912473895

Husband, C. (1996). The right to be understood: Conceiving the multi-ethic public sphere. *Innovation: the European Journal of Social Sciences, 9*(2), 205–215.

Laitinen, A. (2013). Solidarity. In B. Kaldis (Ed.), *Encyclopedia of philosophy and the social sciences* (pp. 948–950). London, UK: Sage.

Laitinen, A., & Pessi, A. B. (2015). *Solidarity: Theory and practice*. Lanham, MD: Lexington Books.

Landsber, A. (2004). *Prosthetic memory: The transformation of american remembrance in the age of mass culture*. New York, NY: Columbia University Press.

Musarò, P. (2017). The art of de-bordering: How the theatre of Cantieri Meticci challenges the lines between citizens and non-citizens. In L. Iannelli & P. Musarò (Eds.), *Performative citizenship public art, urban design, and political participation* (pp. 93–113). Milan: Mimesis International.

Neumann, K. (2000). *Shifting memories: The Nazi past in the new Germany*. Ann Arbor, MI: University of Michigan Press.

Neumann, K. (2016, May 10). *New lives in a new country?* National Library of Australia lecture series. Retrieved from https://www.nla.gov.au/audio/new-lives-in-a-new-country

Neumann, K., & Horsti, K. (2017, December 20). It's hard to put a lid on the world. *Inside Story*. Retrieved from http://insidestory.org.au/its-hard-to-put-a-lid-on-the-world/

Ong, J. C. (2014). "Witnessing" or "mediating" distant suffering? Ethical questions across moments of text, production and reception. *Television & New Media, 15*(3), 179–196.

Papastergiadis, N. (2010). *Spatial aesthetics, art, place, and the everyday*. Amsterdam, NL: Institute of Network Cultures.

Raninen-Siiskonen, T. (1999). Vieraana omalla maalla. Tutkimus karjalaisen siirtoväen muistelu-kerronnasta. *Suomalaisen Kirjallisuuden Seuran Toimituksia 766*. Helsinki, FI: Suomalaisen Kirjallisuuden Seura.

Ratcliffe, K. (2005). *Rhetorical listening: Identification, gender, whiteness*. Carbondale, IL: Southern Illinois University Press.

Rorty, R. (1989). *Contingency, irony, and solidarity*. Cambridge, UK: Cambridge Universtity Press.

Rothberg, M. (2009). *Multidirectional memory: Remembering the Holocaust in the age of decolonization*. Stanford, CA: Stanford University Press.

Rovisco, M. (2015). Community arts, new media and the desecuritisation of migration and asylum seeker issues in the UK. In C. Kinnvall & T. Svensson (Eds.), *Governing Borders and Security: The politics of connectivity and dispersal* (pp. 99–116). London, UK: Routledge.

Sallinen-Gimpl, P. (1994). *Siirtokarjalainen identiteetti ja kulttuurien kohtaaminen*. Kansatieteellinen arkisto 40. Helsinki, FI: Suomen Muinaismuistoyhdistys. doi:10.3168/jds.S0022-0302(94)77044-2

Scholtz, S. (2008). *Political solidarity*. Philadelphia, PA: Pennsylvania University Press.

Spivak, G. C. (1988). Can the subaltern speak? In L. Nelson & L. Grossberg (Eds.), *Marxism and the interpretation of culture* (pp. 271–313). Chicago, IL: University of Illinois Press.

Sreberny, A. (2006). 'Not only, but also': Mixedness and media. *Journal of Ethnic and Migration Studies, 31*(3), 443–459. doi:10.1080/13691830500058828

Ticktin, M. (2011). *Casualties of care: Immigration and the politics of humanitarianism in France.* Berkeley, CA: University of California Press.

Wake, C. (2009). After effects: Performing the ends of memory. *Performance Paradigm, 5*(1), 5–11.

Webb, J. (2009). Sentences from the archive. *Performance Paradigm, 5*(1), 66–81.

Wright, T. (2018, July 17). *Personal communication.*

How Can We Tell the Story of the Colombian War?: Bastardized Narratives and Citizen Celebrities

Omar Rincón and Clemencia Rodríguez

This article explores how popular culture theory can be used in postconflict situations to raise awareness about human rights violations. This case study investigates a media narrative produced by the Memory Center in Colombia, about a political assassination of a community leader. On February 12, 2009, Luis Arango was murdered in the Colombian region known as Magdalena Medio. Arango was a fisherman and a leader of local and regional fishing communities struggling to defend wetlands and natural environments from encroaching cattle and agribusiness economies. Arango was murdered to stop his leadership and environmental agendas. Arango's assassination was selected as an emblematic case that illustrates well how Colombia's armed conflict impacts community leaders trying to advance social justice agendas. This article explores how a new understanding of "the popular" was used to frame a media narrative about Arango's case.

> My whole education is based on popular culture. That which has really supported me, moved me and motivated me is popular culture . . . it is not a matter of studying, but living it. I'm always aware of how things are out there, what the singers are singing about.
> —Gabriel García Márquez (2006)

Introduction

Colombia has existed in a state of war since the mid-1950s. Between 1958 and 2012, the war cost the lives of 220,000 Colombians, 81.5% of whom were civilians (Historical Memory Group, 2013, pp. 31–32). However, despite the immense scale of the impact of war on certain communities, many Colombians do not yet know of the terrifying experiences that so many Colombian men, women, and children have endured. Nor do they understand the resilience and survival skills so many Colombians have demonstrated in the context of the war. Thousands of Colombian men, women, and children survived massacres carried out by the paramilitaries, kidnapping by guerrillas, landmines planted by both sides, torture, disappearances, and forced displacement at the hands of armed forces. Yet all these Colombians have forged new lives. They remember what they experienced, but tragedy has not defeated them. They have carved out a new place for themselves in the world, where the memories of pain and loss live side by side with humor, joy, and hope.

A central question facing the country now is how to recount the war to those who have not lived through it. Finding an answer is critical because, first, it will create an understanding between the victims of armed conflict and those who have been able to live untouched by the war. Second, it will shed light on the plight of victims of conflict and raise public awareness of both the pain and the resilience of the individuals and communities who have been victimized by the various armed groups. Third, only when the majority of citizens realize how dangerous it is to resolve social conflict at gunpoint will we be able to make sure such violence against civilian communities never happens again.

This article explores one initiative in which specific narrative strategies grounded in popular culture were designed to tell the story of the Colombian armed conflict. The text aims to propose a new understanding of "the popular," focusing on the case of Luis Arango, a community leader who was the victim of a targeted assassination in 2009, and the ways in which his murder was transformed into popular narrative.

Media narratives and armed conflict

How do media stories respond to a society at war? Wherever there is armed conflict, violence, explosions, and mangled bodies, mainstream media will respond with its default strategy: if it bleeds it leads (i.e., if it bleeds, it sells) (Ellis, 2006; Girardet, 1996; Moellner, 1999; Rodríguez, 2011). If they have a choice between covering a community of a thousand people living their everyday lives, with their own stories, or ten gunmen, we know the mainstream media's cameras and microphones will focus on the ten armed men, directing every effort to telling the stories of men with guns and constructing narratives from their perspective (Rodríguez, 2008).

Colombian media are no exception. In recent years, the most salient Colombian media have brought a series of high quality television dramas to the screen centered on the perpetrators of violence. Among the best known are *El Patrón del Mal* [Escobar: The Drug Lord] (produced by Caracol TV in 2012), a television series that chronicles, in 113 thirty-minute episodes, the life of drug lord Pablo Escobar (Franco García, 2012). With a cast of 1,300 actors shooting in more than 400 locations, *El Patrón del Mal* explores in detail the personalities, culture, lifestyle, and behavior of the main characters in the world of organized crime in Colombia during the 1980s and 1990s. Another hit series was *Los Tres Caínes* [The Three Cains] (produced by RCN/MundoFox in 2013), a Colombian/Mexican co-production about the Castaño brothers, paramilitary leaders who slaughtered hundreds of people in farming and indigenous communities. In 70 forty-fiveminute episodes, *Los Tres Caínes* explores the lives of the brothers of the Castaño family, their relationships with wives, girlfriends, and lovers, their complex relationship with their mother, and their inability to overcome the trauma of having their father kidnapped and killed by a guerrilla group. Finally, *Commando Elite* [Elite Commando] (produced by RCN/MundoFox in 2013) is a series of 91 one-hour episodes co-produced by two television companies, RCN of Colombia and MundoFox in Mexico, about an intelligence unit of the Colombian police. These series have three characteristics in common: first, high production values; second, high ratings; and third, they all tell the story of the Colombian war from the point of view of different armed groups, including paramilitary groups, guerrilla organizations, organized crime, and the Colombian armed forces.

In a column in the newspaper *El Tiempo*, television critic Omar Rincón asked why the series *Los Tres Caínes* was only narrated from the perspective of the perpetrators and never from the victims' side:

Colombia, what kind of biased angle is this on your screens? Why not tell Abel's side of the story? Why not fictionalize the experience of the victims? If you wanted to highlight the victims who resisted the paramilitaries, why are their stories excluded from the narrative? Why devote the first few weeks just to the Castaños and their thugs? Perhaps it's all about glorifying the victimizers while erasing the victims' point of view? (Rincón, 2013b)

The problem with media narratives such as *El Patrón del Mal* and *Los Tres Caínes* is that, despite their superb production quality and high ratings, audiences are not led to connect emotionally with the victims but rather with the perpetrators of violence. The question then is how to embrace the narrative conventions of popular culture and mainstream media, and tell the story from the victims' point of view? In the following pages we try to answer this question using the case of the murder of Luis Arango, a grassroots leader of fishing communities in Colombia.

The case of luis arango

Luis Arango was 50 years old when he was killed by members of a growing criminal gang known as *Los Rastrojos* on February 12, 2009. The murder of Arango needs to be understood within the context of the new forms of armed conflict in Colombia that have emerged since 2005, when the paramilitaries demobilized under the administration of Alvaro Uribe (Corporación para el Desarrollo del Oriente Compromiso, 2012). At the time, the demobilization of paramilitary groups was highly contested. It was said that the disarmament was not genuine, that the paramilitaries were only giving up one weapon out of every four, and that their intention was to persuade the country that it was the end of the paramilitary era, while the truth was that these groups were simply re-inventing themselves. Through some murky processes, more than seven thousand demobilized paramilitaries reappeared on the national stage in a new wave of criminal gangs involved in smuggling drugs, weapons, and gasoline, among other rackets.

In the late 1990s, Luis Arango, a member of the fishing community of El Llanito on the shores of one of the many wetlands in the region known as Magdalena Medio, emerged as a community leader committed to environmental activism in defense of the wetlands and marshes, and smallscale fishing as a way of life. Since the mid-20th century the marshes and wetlands (and therefore small-scale fisheries) have been threatened by oil businesses, ranching, and the agribusiness of African palm production (Jimenez Segura et al., 2012; Lasso, 2011). Arango insisted on bringing the police and the army in to monitor the marshes. It did not suit the local criminal gang, *Los Rastrojos*, to have the armed forces monitoring the area, since their illegal business used the wetlands, marshes, and creeks for drug trafficking and arms and gasoline smuggling. The *Rastrojos* murdered Arango to prevent state agencies from entering the region to monitor what was happening in the marshes and waterways.

The targeted killing of Luis Arango is emblematic of the Colombian war. In 2012, a historical memory team of researchers, working with video producers, assumed the task of documenting the life and death of Luis Arango. Based on the final report documenting the case of Luis Arango's death (Quijano Triana, Bohórquez Farfán, & Rodríguez, 2014), the video narrative (González, 2014) developed by the historical memory team tries to recount the war from the victim's perspective, using a narrative rooted in popular conventions. In the following pages we try to explain, first, how we define the concept of "the popular," and second, how the narrative of Arango's death was framed within this conception of "the popular."

Reimagining "the popular"

Diverse attempts to theorize "the popular" have emerged within the ranks of critical scholarship and post-Marxism. Gramsci (1977) states that the working classes have their own world-view, their own version of life but, unlike the "cultured" version of the ruling classes, the popular version is not documented or organized. Gramsci (1977, p. 217) reminds us that "the popular" is encoded in melodrama, a narrative form that bridges urban and rural, and can be found in a multiplicity of cultural expressions, from collective oral and theatrical practices to funeral rituals and ceremonies.

Bakhtin (1988, p. 11) defines popular culture as a "second world and a second life" for the common people; it is a secondary lived experience because the first order of business is always to survive in the realm of work while existing in a hybrid space between submission and complicity. In the symbolic order, the popular subject finds catharsis, play, provocation, humor, and emotional excess, using masks that break the identity of the face, allowing the body, and especially the lower body, free rein to engage in joy, "to commune with the life of the lower body, the belly and genitals" (Bakhtin, 1988, p. 25). In other words, popular culture cannot be accessed as spectacle, it has to be experienced to be understood.[1]

Alabarces (2012) describes authentic popular culture as inhabiting "music and folk dancing, sexuality, daily life, a sense of place, working, partying, ceremonies, religiosity, beliefs, politics, creativity, magic, conservatism, the urban and the rural worlds, violence, migration, mass culture" (p. 32). Michel de Certeau calls to re-signify "the popular" and suggests understanding popular culture as "the markings left by doing," or "ways of practicing" the "tactics" of the quotidian or "the weapons of the weak" (De Certeau, 1988). Likewise, "the popular" recovers the time in-between what is deemed important and legitimate—mainly work—and everyday pastimes, leisure, lounging about, all those instances of everyday collective being together. "The popular" shares concerns such as family values, religion, control of violence, and the cultural practices that regulate sex. In our time, popular culture inhabits multiple circuits, including high culture (art) and folk culture (traditions), media culture (the entertainment market), and the culture of connectivity (social media).

Colombian communication and cultural studies scholar Jesús Martín Barbero (1981) asserts that "the popular" is a point of view, a perspective that looks at the world "from the other side," or the experience "of what people do with"—meaning what people do with what they consume, what they do with what they find in social media, what they do with what they get from the media industries. "The popular" is, above all, a public lived experience, a performance that engages the subject in its entirety. Latin American cultural studies scholars have theorized popular culture as the culture of the public plaza, of spectacle, comedy, and gossip. Martín Barbero (1987) notes that it is in "the popular" where the battle is played for meaning because it is here that different forms of social imagination are located; however, Martín Barbero cautions that "the popular" is not pure but always intervened, co-opted, and encoded by the media industries. The political potential of "the popular," according to Martín Barbero, exists beyond the influence of the cultural industries:

> Popular cultural practices show us how to imagine a truly alternative communication... a communication that goes beyond manipulating popular culture, toward embracing its core principles; it's not about bringing communication to the masses, but detecting and empowering all the

different cultural practices that are muzzled, censored, dominated, and made impossible with the imposition of mass media culture. (Martín Barbero, 1981, p. 19)

Based on the theories of these authors, we propose understanding "the popular" as bastardized narratives, aesthetics, and moralism that exist side-by-side with the traditional rational discourse of modernity. "The popular" is bastardized because it has no recognized father, it takes from anywhere: that is the nature of "the popular." The bastardized popular assumes that communicative purity is not present among the colonized or hegemonic identities. The term "bastardization" refers to what Jesús Martín Barbero explains as "the thick mesh of interlaced practices of submission and resistance, contestations and complicities" (Martín Barbero & Muñoz, 1992, p. 23) that comprises "the popular." The bastardized popular then, consists of the playful combination of the archaic with the modern, the folk with the mainstream. The bastardized narrative is impure, unclean, and pagan, but also rich, expressive, and cathartic. It allows the subject to express him/herself without inhibitions and without seeking authenticity or originality, as a complex subject localized in a specific community.

According to Argentine cultural studies scholar Néstor García Canclini, the term "the popular" evades fixed meanings (García Canclini 1985, 1989), and this ambiguity or multiple signification of the popular has come about as the result of the many practices, processes, and experiences embraced by the term itself. In Latin American contexts and circuits, a plurality of understandings of "the popular" circulate:

1. *"The popular" as "of the people,"* is a notion evoked by any discourse that refers to the ways of life and lifestyles of subjects of lower social classes, including the working classes and their common beliefs, their ways of eating, talking, dressing, and seeking pleasure. All these cultural practices end up tangled in what is sometimes called folklore, or forms of expression located in rituals, festivals, and complex layers of identity.
2. *"The popular" as equated with the subjugated, dominated, excluded, or colonized subject.* This understanding of the popular can be found in discourses that idealize the location of *the other* as weak, subjugated, and dominated by barbarian western-white-patriarchal cultures. The popular, then, becomes the subject-other, assumed to exist in separate cultural, historical, and narrative spheres, and includes groups such as indigenous people, afro-descendants, women, and LGBTIQ (Alabarces, 2012; Adichie, 2010; Bhabha, 2002). These notions of "the popular" aggrandize the political agency that supposedly exists in the experience of the subordinate other; thus, in Latin America, "the popular" "names that which falls outside of the visible, the mentionable, the nameable" (Alabárces, 2012, p. 32). The popular is full of silences and omissions because its voices and stories have been excluded from official narratives and media public spheres, a historical injustice in itself. Adichie explains the absence of narratives about the popular in public spheres and circuits of power as "the danger of the single story," a single narrative that "shows a community as just one thing, over and over again, until the community actually becomes that." There is a lot of power in having "the ability to tell the story of another person, and put it forth as the definite story of the other person . . . the consequence of the single story is that it robs the people of their dignity and makes the recognition of our shared humanity difficult" (Adichie, 2010). The key is that the process of narrating

is strongly linked to power and politics because "wherever your symbolic referents are, that's where your senses and desires reside" (Adichie, 2010). Then, "everything changes when different and multiple stories are told." This is even more the case when the stories are about those who have been marginalized and excluded. A multiplicity of stories is key to re-instating the dignity of a people.

3. *The politicized popular* is displayed when governments co-opt popular culture as a strategy and tactic for influencing the citizenry, a strategy also known as populism (Laclau, 2005). Populism is a way of constructing identity, persuading, manipulating, and intervening symbolically in order to impose a plausible narrative that defines a new political order. The use of popular culture for political purposes becomes the new spectacle, in which politicians pose as leaders of the people or "one of us." A wide variety of this use of "the popular" grows in the Latin American political landscape; politicians of different strands use all kinds of notions of the subordinate subject or "one of us" to encode their own identities: a woman in Chile (Michelle Bachelet), a widow in Argentina (Evita Perón), a woman and ex-guerrilla–cum-union activist in Brazil (Dilma Rousseff), an ex-guerrilla in Uruguay (José Mujica), a priest in Paraguay (Fernando Lugo), a soldier in Venezuela (Hugo Chávez), an educated migrant in Ecuador (Rafael Correa), a hard-working entrepreneur in Panama (Ricardo Martinelli), a journalist in El Salvador (Mauricio Funes), and a "thug" in Colombia (Alvaro Uribe). All these political celebrities demonstrate the successful use of "the popular" in political discourse. "The popular" is used deceptively by Latin American politicians to command, repress, exclude, and legislate against, all in the name of "the people." This is another use of "the popular," as a performance for the people and on behalf of the people, using and co-opting the values, aesthetics, and practices of the people.

4. *The mainstream popular* is the use of the term "popular" as a synonym for the culture of media spectacle. This way of understanding the popular focuses on the values of mass culture, the spectacular, and media entertainment as made-in-the-United States: Hollywood, the hit parade, bestsellers, Shakira, Brad Pitt, and television series. Mainstream pop culture speaks only English, its emotional geography is limited to the United States, and its proposal is the end of cultural hierarchies as new cultural values are imposed on all. According to Martel (2011), these values center on whatever is "cool, hip, buzzing, the culture of commodities, but imbued with cultural diversity to make it look more colorful" (Martel, 2011, p. 180).

5. *The artistic popular* emerges when the creators of art use "the popular" as inspiration; they re-invent and update the popular, generating actualized meanings. This trend explains recent developments in the world of art in Latin America, such as avant-garde art centered on the Virgin of Guadalupe, or Colombia's Divine Child, or literary takes on *narco-corridos*, or Peru's "*chicha*" culture.

6. *The porn-popular* arises when academics or artists embrace and celebrate the lifestyles of the working classes of Latin America, including their popular religiosity and rituals centered around ayahuasca or peyote, which are then displayed as playthings for avantgarde artists and thinkers. This is how authentic popular practices become the code of "the bizarre," a collection of exotic and exhibitionist cultural practices appropriated by elites.

7. *The popular based on new sensibilities* is a way of understanding "the popular" that names those other forms of collective enjoyment based on "dense sensitivities," such as indigenous identities or afro-descendant culture; here, "the popular" attempts to name other ways of participating in life and understanding identity, the body, and the collective.
8. *The techno popular* includes new cultural practices that emerge with the culture of networks, internet, mobile phones, and video games. These cultural practices embody novel forms of "the popular" as contemporary expressions of what it means to be a friend, a member of virtual communities, or engage in "emotional activism." This new mode of "the popular" is founded on practices such as co-production, linkages and linking, and solidarity. This is "the popular" of likes, trending topics, and clicks.

Our proposal is a notion of "the popular" as a bastardized mixture of all the above; "the popular" is authentic, resistant, submissive, complicit, always full of innovation and aberration, and fused together like typical Latin American food: Colombia's *sancocho*, Brazil's *moqueca*, Argentina's *puchero*, or Ecuador's *fanesca*. In all of these dishes, everything goes into the same pot, multiplicity and togetherness, all stirred to obtain delicious flavors; it is a cuisine founded on simultaneity, catharsis, submissions, and re-inventions. The bastardized popular, then, plays with the mainstream culture that thrives on English, made-in-the-United States, and the tyranny of "the cool" (Martel, 2011), but at the same time it takes from and enjoys the music and soap-operas of Brazil, Colombia, Mexico, and Korea.

The bastardized popular leads us to propose the notion of "citizen celebrity," understood as the Latin American notion of "to be somebody" in the media, seeking higher levels of individual self-esteem, recognition, and fame in one's own community. "Citizen celebrity" is a bastardized phenomenon that links "popular political" notions of citizenship as political agency with the "mainstream popular" as spectacle, as favored by the attention of the media. "Citizen celebrity" is about the subject-other gaining any type of visibility in public spheres—visibility in the media, digital visibility, visibility in carnivals and festivals, or visibility in the streets of one's community. These processes of "citizen celebrity" use every available path to the public sphere and do not discriminate between colonized practices or practices of resistance. Instead, they reinvent resistance, using the cultural imaginaries of the colonized pop cultures as well as the popular that has resisted domination.

Drawing from Chantal Mouffe's notion of citizenship as processes of acquiring political agency and power in everyday life, and understanding power as the effort to increase the social and symbolic wellbeing of one's community (Rodríguez, 2001), we propose the notion of "citizen celebrity" (Rincón, 2010) to name the process by which the subjugated subject, the marginalized, and the working classes push their own narratives into the circuits from which they have been excluded—media industries, digital cultures, the public spheres—and do so in the registers of "the popular": the codes of spectacle and pleasure rooted in popular culture, one's own cultural roots, one's own aesthetics, and one's own voice. Citizen celebrity is collective action, a cultural expression of being-with-others; it is asserting one's identity or finding a place in the world to be a celebrity on your own screen, and on your own terms.

Clearly, this notion of citizen celebrity is closely related to Rodríguez's theory of citizens' media (Rodríguez, 2001). Based on Mouffe's (1993, 1994) notion of citizenship, Rodríguez (2001) defined "citizens' media" as alternative, community, or radical media that facilitate, trigger, and maintain processes of citizenship-building, in Mouffe's sense of the term. Rodríguez' citizens' media are those media that promote symbolic processes that allow people to name the world and speak the world on their own terms. Rodríguez connects Mouffe's notions of radical democracy, citizenship, and political action with Jesús Martín Barbero's theories of identity, language, and political power (Martín Barbero, 2002). According to Martín Barbero, the power of communities to name the world on their own terms is directly linked with their power to enact political actions. In Spanish, Martín Barbero plays with a linguistic pun on the terms *"contar"* (to narrate) and *"contar"* (to have a strong presence, to count) and explains that only those who can *"contar"* (narrate) will *"contar,"* only those with the ability to narrate their own identities and name the world on their own terms will have a strong presence as political subjects.

A manifesto for narrating the war

Thus, looking at "the popular" from the perspective of "the bastardized popular," "citizen celebrity," and "citizens' media," we propose the following manifesto, anchored in the registers of the people, for designing strategies to intervene in the social and political arenas:

1. Breaking away from narrative forms that name the *subject-other* as content. Rather than narratives *about* indigenous communities or victims of armed conflict, we propose to narrate *from* the aesthetic and narrative sensibilities of these communities.
2. Realizing that narrative is an area of political struggle, a struggle to become visible, to be recognized not only as a victim or oppressed subject but also as a subject capable of pleasure and joy, a subject capable of narrating the surrounding world.
3. Intervening in communication technologies, transforming them into new tools in the service of popular magic and paganism, tools with the potential to make anyone an author, a communicating subject.
4. Questioning the notion of the authentic popular, in order to recognize that the very nature of popular culture is the non-genuine; it is porous, made of intersections and cross-pollination. We must acknowledge that it is precisely in the contamination of the mainstream popular, the populist popular, and the subaltern popular that aesthetic possibilities and cultural codes emerge to narrate the stories of the other.
5. Innovating beyond technology and spectacle. Innovation should be understood as an exploration of the narrative codes used by the people, seeking and finding the aesthetic styles, narratives, and stories that exist and circulate in popular communities, and bringing these forms to both mainstream media and citizens' media. We need to go beyond merely displaying the cultures of the people as anthropological spectacle and start *using* popular culture to develop media narratives.
6. Valuing what popular communities have to say, their creativity and story-telling, as tactics for social change in grassroots communities.
7. Believing that each community can and must decide how and why it wants to intervene in the public sphere, how and why it wants to communicate, and choose its own perspective, codes, and narrative strategies. Each community should decide how to enact its visibility in the public sphere.

In this context, how can Communication for Social Change (CCS) contribute to postconflict reconstruction and peacebuilding in a society at war? The answer is twofold: first, we need to highjack narratives from the realm of the dead, reinstating story-telling in the world of the living. Second, we need to transform every survivor of the war into a celebrity, a subject overflowing with dignity. The role of communication in post-conflict contexts is to push forward narratives about the lived experience of war, narratives that can disrupt and break through the comfortable silence of the powerful and the unaware. Postconflict communication has to go beyond narratives of death, terror, and violence, and push into narratives of survival and resilience. Narratives need to zero-in on life, and although the role of memory is unquestionable, memory needs to embrace the future. A country such as Colombia needs to produce narratives of "activist memory," focused on multiple horizons that can delineate alternative futures, desires, and hopes. On this foundation, transforming war survivors into citizen celebrities and narrating the war from their experiences means:

1. Avoiding the glorification of the survivor as victim, and learning to narrate the survivor as a subject full of dignity and hope, and possessing a future;
2. Giving up narratives that assume that historical memory should be an end in itself and committing to narratives that explore the lived experience of specific subjects, express historical memory as lived experience, and remain open to future possibilities and hope;
3. Avoiding static notions of historical memory marked by rigid notions of truth, reconciliation, and justice, and embracing more fluid narratives in which memory is open to the possibility of a future;
4. Avoiding narratives focused solely on the tragedy of war and exploring narratives that recount in epic terms the stories of those men and women who survived the war and the life-worlds they have since built; and
5. Letting go of memory as solemn and dry and embracing a different type of memory, lived as bastardized and playful.

Applying the manifesto to luis arango's case

The production team challenged themselves to find a strategy for developing an emotionally engaging media narrative to recount the case of Luis Arango. The narrative they proposed is rooted conceptually in the notion of experience (Baricco, 2008), in-between spaces (Bhabha, 2002), the theory of mediation (Martín Barbero, 1987), hybrid cultures (García Canclini, 1989), radical media (Downing, 2001), citizens' media (Rodríguez, 2001, 2008), and media narratives (Rincón, 2005).The production team responsible for narrating the case of Luis Arango applied the concepts of bastardized popular culture (Rincón, 2010) and citizen celebrity (Rincón, 2010) to developing an audio-visual narrative about the murder case. The team developed a narrative strategy that utilizes all available aesthetic registers and expressive codes without regard to their origins.

What is seductive about the notion of the bastardized popular is its potential to promote narratives tightly connected to life, joy, and pleasure, allowing the grassroots subject a symbolic existence. In the case of Lucho Arango, the team responsible for producing a video narrative about his assassination chose a bastardized perspective. For example, when selecting the soundtrack for the video, *vallenato* music was privileged over the musical genre known as *tambora*. While *tambora* is a traditional musical genre associated with the fishing communities of Arango's hometown in the Middle Magdalena region, it is more of an ascribed identity than a real identity. While folklore experts and anthropological documentaries generally portray the fishing communities of the Middle Magdalena as *tambora* communities, the actual people of these communities opt for more commercialized *vallenato* music. During our fieldwork, it became clear that Arango's family, friends, and fishing buddies identified much more with the bastardized *vallenato* than the pure *tambora*. Thus, the video about the murder of Arango rejected an anthropological perspective about this fishing community and instead privileged the bastardized perspective with which the community identifies. The production team decided to narrate in the codes of the grassroot subject, instead of the elite, highly educated subject. Bastardized narratives can be appreciated as practices of expressive activism because they assert:

> the "right" to signify from the periphery (. . .) as spaces [that] provide the terrain for elaborating strategies of selfhood—singular or communal—that initiate new signs of identity, and innovative sites of collaboration, and contestation, in the act of defining the idea of society itself. (Bhabha, 2002, p. 18)

The concept of citizen celebrity (Rincón, 2010) points to a narrative that transforms people into stars of public life. Citizen celebrity occurs in the realm of the experience of the people; for example, during an indigenous audiovisual festival in the Wayuu[2] territory of northern Colombia, it was found that for this indigenous audience, the most salient element of the festival was the enjoyment of seeing themselves and their daily lives on the screen. Laughing at themselves, they enjoyed being the stars; in words of a Wayuu participant, "we appreciate genuine laughter from those who identify with what they see on the screen, their own language, and their own culture" (Villanueva, 2012). Here, communication loses its value as content, and gains meaning as a tactic to see and recognize one's own self, exercise the right to one's own image, and be entertained in terms encoded in one's own culture.

The videos about Luis Arango were produced using this same approach, as drawings done by Arango's relatives and fishing buddies were incorporated into the narrative. Using animation techniques, the drawings in which Arango's community expressed who they were and how they perceive their everyday life, local landscape, and cultural practices became the stars of the narrative. The canoes, the marshes and wetlands, fishing, nets, Luis, and Luis's mother appear in the videos as perceived, remembered, and imagined by the members of Arango's community.

Likewise, Arango as a community leader was shown in the video in all his genuine complexity. Luis did not have a problem embodying contradictions: on one hand, he was absolutely committed to the environmental struggle, the protection of the marshes and wetlands, and the defense of the artisan fishing economy; on the other hand, he was a man who never interrogated patriarchal ideologies. In one scene of the video, Maris, his life partner, remembers him telling her: "My love, I don't like my female children." She continues: "And I said, 'God will punish you; you'll see He will give you only granddaughters' . . . and that was the case" (as cited in González, 2014).

The key to narrating historical memory and justice in postconflict contexts and incorporating into national and regional media those narratives that audiences do not necessarily want to see, lays in constructing narratives that draw from different aesthetic codes, formats, and media registers, including ways of understanding citizenship that do not negate that we are bastard children of the mainstream (Martel, 2011) and at the same time children of diverse local cultures that bind us to territory, aesthetics, stories, and local expression.

In the 21st century, communication has become all about screens on which two apparently contradictory registers intersect. We aspire to practices of citizenship and participation in the public sphere (Arendt, 1955, 1958; Mouffe, 1993, 1994) while simultaneously each feeling entitled to becoming a celebrity. Jesús Martín Barbero explains this apparent contradiction by theorizing communication as processes of emotional energy and cultural recognition rather than as transmission of content (Martín Barbero, 1987). In Martín Barbero's work, the popular relates to catharsis, pleasure, and seduction and positions itself in opposition to all that is virtuous, pure, and original. More than in the realm of arts and high culture, the popular finds its preferred modes of expression in carnival, fiestas, play, laughter, and spectacle. The popular is about the corporeal, lived experience transformed into narrative and story-telling, the ways in which ordinary people speak, and their everyday life rituals. Martín Barbero (1987) understands the popular as a "matter of re-cognitions" rather than knowledge (cognition); the popular is "memory of lived experience that rejects discourse and is only accessible via recounting (as in story-telling)" (Martín Barbero, 1992, p. 23).

Popular narrative forms exist in the space between hegemonic aesthetics and one's own desires and expressions. They are bastardized because they are neither pure domination nor the sole expressions of resistance. In the case of the narrative of Luis Arango's assassination, the video assumes that the murder had a tremendous negative impact on the family and the community, but this is assumed as a starting point, not as an end point. For example, the video includes Arango's son remembering how his father led an active social life and was a popular guy frequently surrounded by friends. He loved to organized huge *sancochos* (a form of Colombian stew), cooking the entire dish by himself under the shade of his favorite tree. The video incorporates moments of laughter and humor, as relatives and friends remember Arango. In the video, Luis Arango appears as a political leader, but also as a guy who sought joy, a partier who took pleasure in everyday socializing. One of Arango's sons recounts: "We sat around for hours to talk about my mom, my grandmother, and the wetlands, the three creatures he loved the most" (son of Arango as cited in González, 2014). The video combines the political (the struggle of the fishing community) with the humorous (enjoying his friends), progressive ideologies (the environmental agenda) with conservative hegemonies (patriarchal ideologies); traditional codes and icons, such as their fishing canoes and fishing nets, and mainstream modernity, as in the soundtrack in *vallenato* style.

In the Colombian post-conflict context, the act of narrating the war is key in processes of peacebuilding. Narrating the historical memory of armed conflict and war in ways accessible to all audiences is critical in constructing a collective memory. The political assassination of Lucho Arango presented a challenge in terms of narrative style. The historical memory production team assumed this challenge as a way to experiment with a narrative style framed by notions of the bastardized popular and "citizen celebrity." Told in registers that belong to the popular, the resulting video about Lucho Arango does not get caught up in the seduction of media spectacle, and also refuses to commit to the notion of a pure other engaged in anti-colonial struggles.

Notes

1. In Barranquilla, Colombia, where the most important carnival in the country is held every February, common sayings capture this idea: "Quien lo vive es quien lo goza" or "Whoever lives it, enjoys it," or "Qué pobre es quien no sabe bailar" or "He who cannot dance is extremely poor."
2. The Wayuu indigenous community is one among 89 indigenous ethnic groups that inhabit different regions of the Colombian territory. The Wayuu's territory is located in northern Colombia, a region known as La Guajira (Rodríguez y El Gazi, 2007).

Acknowledgment

This article was translated by Nick Robinson, PGCE CELTA, November 2014.

References

Adichie, C. (2010). El peligro de una sola historia. *Arcadia*, 56(May–June), 24–25. Retrieved from https://www.youtube.com/watch?v 4gH5oB1CMYM

Alabárces, P. (2012, June). *Transculturas pospopulares. El retorno de las culturas populares en las ciencias sociales latinoamericanas*. Paper presented at the Seminario Cultura y Representaciones Sociales, en el Instituto de Invetigaciones Sociales de la UNAM, México City, México.

Arendt, H. (1955). *Los orígenes del totalitarismo*. Madrid, Spain: Taurus. Arendt, H. (1958). *La condición humana*. Barcelona, Spain: Paidós.

Bakhtin, M. (1988). *La cultura popular en la edad media y en el renacimiento*. Madrid, Spain: Alianza Editorial. Baricco, A. (2008). *Los bárbaros. Ensayos sobre la mutación*. Barcelona, Spain: Anagrama.

Bhabha, H. K. (2002). *El lugar de la cultura*. Buenos Aires, Argentina: Manantial.

Corporación para el Desarrollo del Oriente Compromiso. (2012). *El hilo del laberinto. Conflicto armado y desarme, desmovilización y reintegración–DDRde grupos armados ilegales en Santander*. Bucaramanga, Colombia: Corporación para el Desarrollo del Oriente Compromiso.

De Certeau, M. (1988). *The practice of everyday life*. Berkeley, CA: University of California Press.

Downing, J. (2001). *Radical media: Rebellious communication and social movements*. London, England: Sage.

Ellis, D. G. (2006). *Transforming conflict: Communication and ethnopolitical conflict*. New York, NY: Rowman and Littlefield.

Franco García, D. (2012, May 26). Asesino en serie. *El Espectador*. Retrieved from http://www.elespectador.com/ noticias/temadeldia/asesino-serie-articulo-349050

García Canclini, N. (1985, September). *Gramsci y las culturas populares en América Latina*. Seminario "Le transformazioni politiche dell'America Latina: La presenza di Gramsci nella cultura latinoamericana," Instituto Gramsci, Ferrara, Italy.

García Canclini, N. (1989). *Culturashí bridas*. México: Grijalbo.

García Márquez, Gabriel. (2006) *La escritura embrujada*. Madrid, Spain: Ediciones Fuentetaja.

Girardet, E. R. (1996). Reporting humanitarianism: Are the new electronic media making a difference? In R. Rotberg & T. Weiss (Eds.), *From massacres to genocide: The media, public policy, and humanitarian crises* (pp. 45–67). Washington, DC: World Peace Foundation.

González, A. (2014). *Quién es Lucho Arango?* Belén de los Andaquíes, Caquetá, Colombia: Escuela Audiovisual Infantil [Video]. Retrieved from http://vimeo.com/77862639

Gramsci, A. (1977). *Cultura y literatura*. Barcelona, Spain: Península.

Grupo de Memoria Histórica. (2013). *Basta ya! Colombia: Memorias de guerra y dignidad*. Bogotá, Colombia: Centro de Memoria Histórica. Retrieved from http://www.centrodememoriahistorica.gov.co/micrositios/informeGeneral/ descargas.html

Jiménez-Segura, L. F., Granado-Lorencio, C., Gulfo A., Carvajal, J. D., Martínez, A., Márquez, V., . . . Palacio, J. (2012). *Uso tradicional de los recursos naturales pesqueros y conservación de la biodiversidad en regiones tropicales en desarrollo: Hacia un modelo de ecología de la reconciliación*. Report. Bogotá, Colombia: Universidad de Antioquia, Universidad de Sevilla, Agencia Española de Cooperación Internacional para el Desarrollo, Cormagdalena.

Laclau, E. (2005). *La razón populista*. Buenos Aires, Argentina: Fondo de Cultura Económica.

Lasso, C. A. (2011). *Pesquerías continentales de Colombia: Cuencas del Magdalena-Cauca, Sinú, Canalete, Atrato, Orinoco, Amazonas y Vertiente Pacífico*. Bogotá, Colombia: Instituto Humboldt.

Martel, F. (2011). *Cultura mainstream: Cómo nacen los fenómenos de masas*. Barcelona, Spain: Taurus.

Martín Barbero, J. (1981). Prácticas de comunicación en la cultura popular: Mercados, plazas, cementerios y espacios de ocio. In M. Simpson (Ed.), *Comunicación alternativa y cambio social*. México City, México: UNAM. Retrieved from http://www.scribd.com/doc/6334231/Practicas-de-comunicacion-en-la-cultura-popular-mercados- plazas-cementerios-y-espacios-de-ocio

Martín Barbero, J. (1987). *De los medios a las mediaciones*. Barcelona, Spain: Gustavo Gili.

Martín Barbero, J. (2002). Identities: Traditions and new communities. *Media Culture and Society*, 24(5), 621–641. Martín Barbero, J., & Muñoz, S. (1992). *Televisión y melodrama*. Bogotá, Colombia: Tercer Mundo.

Moller, S D. (1999). *Compassion fatigue: How the media sell disease, famine, war, and death*. New York, NY: Routledge Mouffe, C. (1993). *El retorno de lo político: Comunidad, ciudadanía, pluralismo, democracia radical*. Barcelona, Spain: Paidós.

Mouffe, C. (1994). La democracia radical. ¿Moderna o posmoderna? *Revista Foro*, 24, 13–23.

Quijano Triana, M., Bohórquez Farfán, L., & Rodríguez, C. (2014). *Lucho Arango: El Defensor de la Pesca Artesanal. Memoria Histórica desde Las Regiones*. Bogotá, Colombia: Centro Nacional de Memoria Histórica.

Rincón, O. (2005). Comunicar entre lo techno y lo retro: Activismo y estéticas en experimento. *Revista Signo y Pensamiento*, 47(24), 41–53.

Rincón, O. (2010). Estos/medios/apropiados: Cuentos indígenas de la paciencia, la identidad y la política. *Revista Folios*, 21–22, 181–196.

Rincón, O. (2013a). Las identidades y las sensibilidades como innovación mediática y narrativas colabor-activas. *Revista Dixit*, 19, 4–15.

Rincón, O. (2013b, March 17). El mito de RCN/El otrolado. *El Tiempo*. Retrieved from http://www.eltiempo.com/ archivo/documento/CMS-12696942

Rodríguez, C. (2001). *Fissures in the mediascape. An international study of citizens' media*. Cresskill, NJ: Hampton Press.

Rodríguez, C. (2008). *Lo que le vamos quitando a la guerra. Medios ciudadanos en contextos de conflicto armado en Colombia*. Bogotá, Colombia: C3 Fundación Friedrich Ebert. Retrieved from http://www.c3fes.net/docs/ quitandoalaguerra.pdf

Rodríguez, C. (2011). *Citizens' media against armed conflict. Disrupting violence in Colombia*. Minneapolis, MN: University of Minnesota Press.

Rodríguez, C., & El-Gazi, J. (2007). The poetics of indigenous radio in Colombia. *Media, Culture, and Society*, 29(3), 449–468.

Villanueva, R. (2012, November). *Pütchieiyatüluakuaipaa [Imágenes y palabras para contar y construir]*. Presentation at the Indigenous Audiovisual Festival DAUPARA 2012 -Territorio WayuuLa Guajira.

Transcendental meditation's tipping point: the allure of celebrity on the American spiritual marketplace

Corrina Laughlin

ABSTRACT
Since 2005, the film director David Lynch has been the most visible and vocal proponent for the spread of Transcendental Meditation (TM), a practice brought to the United States by Maharishi Mahesh Yogi in the late 1950s. This paper analyzes the public-facing operations: website, books, and celebrity benefit concerts, through which the David Lynch Foundation interacts with its American audience and charts two moves that the David Lynch Foundation has made in order to market TM. First, I assert that they have positioned TM as a technique rather than a spiritual practice and I understand this through Foucault's theory of techné. Second, I argue that they have leveraged the auracular quality of celebrity as a modality through which to brand TM for the spiritual consumer. Ultimately, I made claims on how these moves represent a shift in how American spiritual seekers are understood and marketed to in popular culture.

Introduction

Carnegie Hall is filled with people, but apart from individuals shuffling slightly in their seats, and the occasional cough, the packed house is silent. Attendees today have paid up to $650 dollars per ticket to see Jerry Seinfeld, Sting, Katy Perry, and other famous performers but to start the evening off, we have been asked to close our eyes and meditate. This scene comes from the "Change Begins Within" benefit concert put on by the David Lynch Foundation for Consciousness-based Education and World Peace in 2015. At this benefit, performers were introduced not only by their celebrity bona fides, but also by the amount of time that they had been doing Transcendental Meditation, referred to as TM. We learn that Jerry Seinfeld has been practicing TM for 43 years, George Stephanopoulos 4 years, Katy Perry, 5 years. When Jerry Seinfeld leaves the stage after performing a ten minute set, George Stephanopoulos, the night's emcee, tells the cheering audience "A lot of evidence there for how great TM is, right?"

Since the death of Maharishi Mahesh Yogi, the founder of the practice, in 2008, the enigmatic, eccentric film director David Lynch has become the most vocal and visible proponent for Transcendental Meditation. David Lynch began meditating in 1977, and claims never to have missed a meditation session since. In 2005 he established the David Lynch Foundation for Consciousness-based education and World Peace (typically referred to as The David Lynch Foundation) a nonprofit (510 (C) (3)) organization whose initial goal was to raise seven billion dollars to fund Transcendental Meditation programs in schools. Since 2005, however, because of its success, it has expanded its mission to prisons, homeless shelters, women's groups, military academies and hospitals, Indian reservations, and refugee camps in Africa. In fact, the foundation's executive director, Bob Roth, told me in an interview that because of the foundation, Transcendental Meditation is now at what he calls a "tipping point" by which he means that the organization can no longer supply enough certified TM instructors to meet demand. Transcendental Meditation has been successful at attracting adherents as Roth's comments suggest, and it has also been successful as a fundraising organization, the "Change Begins Within" concert I attended in November of 2015 cleared over a million dollars for the foundation in no small part because the A-list celebrities who performed, including Sting, Katy Perry and Jerry Seinfeld, did so completely free of charge.

This paper explores the ways Lynch and his foundation market TM as a product geared toward an American audience. I employ textual and visual analysis of the David Lynch Foundation's website, its sister sites, Lynch's 2006 book *Catching the Big Fish: Meditation, Consciousness and Creativity*, as well as evidence gathered from from attendance at a foundation-sponsored benefit concert in 2015. This paper investigates how spiritual practices are marketed by celebrities and what this means for the American spiritual marketplace and its related imaginaries of religious practice. I argue that Lynch and his foundation have refined TM into a product that can be effectively pitched to appeal to contemporary American spiritual sensibilities. To this end, the foundation has made two significant moves. First, it has re-positioned TM as a technique rather than as a religion or spirituality. And second, it has mobilized the auracular quality of celebrity as a modality through which to market this technique to the American spiritual seeker.

Ultimately I make claims on how this shift in marketing points to how notions of celebrity inherited from popular culture are intertwined with American understandings of creativity, personal power, individualism, and wealth creation. Celebrities stand in for these things that sit at the aspirational apex of popular culture. And thus, the spiritual marketplace of American religious consumers rewards those like the David Lynch Foundation, who are able to attract celebrity adherents and to position their practices within these frameworks.

TM as a technique on the spiritual marketplace

The spiritual marketplace

Transcendental Meditation was developed in India by Maharishi Mahesh Yogi, born Mahesh Prasad Varma.[1] Mahesh received his education at Allahabad University in Physics and Math, but left directly after graduating to pursue enlightenment under the tutelage of the famous Swami Brahmanand Sarawati, or Guru Dev, a spiritual leader in the tradition of Advaitic Hinduism. During his hermitage in the Himalayas, Mahesh developed a novel meditation practice that would eventually evolve into Transcendental Meditation. Mahesh based his philosophy on the premise that ordinary people, those who were not trained in esoteric spiritual practice, could experience and benefit from the discipline of twice-daily directed meditation. He believed that all people "experience a divided consciousness, a conflict between the illusory experience of the physical world and the unchanging Reality of the Absolute" (Cowan & Bromley, 2008, p. 65). To connect with this absolute reality, which proponents also call "the Unified Field," practitioners of TM engage in two twenty-minute meditation sessions per day, once in the morning and once in the evening. During these sessions, meditators sit with their eyes closed, and silently repeat a mantra given to them by their TM instructor.

In 1957, Mahesh embarked on a world tour with the hopes of spreading his meditation practice across the globe. He believed that if enough people practiced TM, the positive energy that they would generate would bring about world peace. He called this quest the "Spiritual Regeneration Movement." His tour began in Southern India, but from the beginning, his purpose was to bring meditation to the United States. He felt that TM was ideally suited for an American populace because, as Mahesh said "the country is most advanced because the people of that country would try something new very readily" (Mahesh as quoted in Mason, 1994, p. 33). Here Mahesh voices a deft understanding of the spiritual marketplace characteristic of American religious belonging in that he sees Americans as a populace particularly primed to try new religious and spiritual practices.

In the 1980s and 90s, sociologists of religion began to track historical fluctuations in religious affiliation in the United States as a means to counter the overly-blunt model of secularization inherited from earlier sociological paradigms – that is, the idea that religion would decline in significance as Western societies became more and more modernized (see Berger, 1967; Luckmann, 1967; Parsons, 1966, 1967). These scholars found that around mid-century, religious attitudes began to change, though the changes they pinpointed did not bolster theories of secularization. Hammond (1992) traces this change to the 1960s, when what he calls the "third disestablishment of American religion" took place and individual choice began to take precedence over traditional collective religious affiliation. Wuthnow (1998) looks back to the 1950s as the decade when religious belief shifted in the United States from a "spirituality of dwelling" to a "spirituality of seeking." The scholarly consensus found that at some point in the middle of the twentieth century, a declining trust in institutional religion led vast swaths of the American population to move towards seeker-oriented, spiritual belief (see Ellingson, 2007; Roof, 1993; Roof & McKinney, 1987). "Seekers" valued the experience of their own personal spiritual journey (see Heelaas & Woodhead, 2005; Lynch, 2007; Roof, 1993). They were more likely than previous generations to try New Age religious practices like Transcendental Meditation, yoga, or Zen Buddhism, a shift that, for some scholars, indicated that spirituality had actually surpassed religiosity in the United States (see Heelaas & Woodhead, 2005). Furthermore, seekers tended to pick and choose among diverse traditions, which many noted made American spirituality a kind of mix and match exercise (see Wuthnow, 1998; Cimino & Lattin, 1998).

What Wade Clark Roof (1999) dubbed "the spiritual marketplace" constituted seekers and those spiritual producers who competed for their influence. Because this marketplace has often proven lucrative, strategic religious players, such as the "affluence gurus" studied by Carrette and King (2005) stand to make money by popularizing and spreading their practices. Savvy branding techniques can produce significant monetary returns (see Lau, 2015), and because of this, as Banet-Weiser (2012) notes, religious leaders, especially the evangelical Christian preachers touting prosperity gospels and those believers shepherding New Age Eastern-inspired movements like TM, have become adept at branding their movements. They must, after all, sell their products to Americans who are inundated with branding in every other aspect of their lives. Banet-Weiser points out that "Branding religion is an integral part of advanced capitalism, not simply a reaction to it" (2012, p. 170). Some proponents of Eastern spiritual practices have proved successful market players by emphasizing the idea that their "brand" is compatible with modern science (Campbell, 2007; Harrington & Zajonc, 2003) others have emphasized their connection to an Orientalized, exoticized vision of a purer form of spirituality (Campbell, 2007; Prashad, 2000). Eastern-based beliefs and practices that fit under the umbrella of "the New Age" also tend to highlight a therapeutic relationship to the self (Tucker, 2002).

In this vein, the David Lynch Foundation markets TM primarily as a "technique." In fact, "technique" is the word most associated with TM on the foundation's official website, and it was repeated again and again at the foundation's benefit concert I attended in New York City. At the benefit concert, one performer, Angelique Kiddo asserted about TM: "It's not a religion, it's not a cult, it's just good for you." In this framework, TM is seen as a hygienic practice rather than a spiritual one and this rhetoric shifts TM's position from an Eastern, religious-based ritual to a Westernized "technology of the self" (Foucault, 1984/1986, 1988). Michel Foucault first explored the various systematized daily habits meant to engender a better self – or techné – in *The Care of the Self* (1984/1986). Since antiquity, techné or technologies of the self have been formulated and practiced in a framework of medical reflexivity (Foucault, 1984/1986, p. 10). One goes to the gym daily as a means to attain a healthier body and mind, and in so doing, one takes responsibility for one's own medical care. When conceived as a technology of the self, TM is just like going to the gym – a daily hygienic activity that is a means to a better body and a better self.

Techné and American spirituality

The strategic labeling of TM as technique of self-care, then, also reflects the Foundation's canny understanding of American spirituality. Scholars have asserted that American belief is characterized by its emphasis on "the instrumentality of faith and spirituality" (Roof, 1999, p. 83). American spiritual seekers look for spiritual practices that will have a discrete positive, often quantifiable impacts on their lives. Because TM has no stated cosmology associated with it (at least not as presented by the David Lynch Foundation's literature) it is characterized as a free-floating techné that may augment any religious lifestyle and is thus also suited to the patch-work nature characteristic of American spiritual seeking (see Wuthnow, 1998).

The Lynch foundation emphasizes that TM is a practice that engenders positive change in the individuals who adhere to it and, furthermore, that this change can be scientifically measured. Of course, the attainable results promised by implementing this techné depends on the self that one begins with. Where Foucault notes that in ancient times only the privileged few were expected to actively care for themselves (Foucault, 1984/1986, p. 43), the David Lynch Foundation posits that TM is a productive technique for all people. Closing out the "Change Begins Within" benefit, Lynch said, on a video "Transcendental meditation is life-transforming for the good. It works if you are a human being. Every human being has a treasury within and Transcendental Meditation gets you there easier and effortlessly and it changes life for the good."

For children, the foundation asserts that TM helps with stress relief, for Native Americans, they say that TM can help with alcoholism, for soldiers with Post Traumatic Stress Disorder (PTSD), it can cure PTSD. On the foundation's website, each of these claims is supported by evidence in the form of lists of studies published in academic and medical journals. This approach emphasizes scientific research as a means to prove that TM is an effective technique. The foundation places all of their claims about their technique in a scientific framework. In an interview,1 Bob Roth told me that proof of this kind was crucial to understanding TM. He told me,

> I'm a firm believer in any form of meditation that has scientific research, repeated scien-tific research to show that it works. You can't just say all medicines are good for you, or all food is good for you or all meditation is good for you. We now know that that's not the case ... Transcendental Meditation is highly effective for reducing the physiological impact of stress and trauma so use it for that. So I'm in favor of anything that has solid research. (B. Roth, personal communication, June, 2015).

Similarly, at the benefit, the pop superstar Katy Perry professed that, "when I meditate there's something physical that actually happens. Something medical, scientific. Where I feel like the neuro pathways in my brain open up like they've had cobwebs on them for days or weeks and I feel my most sharp" (Perry, 2015). Perry describes her feelings about meditation in a scientific manner, referencing "neuro pathways." It is clear that she is not claiming to understand exactly what happens to her brain when she meditates, but the fact that she places her understanding in this framework follows from the foundation's branding.

The foundation's site visually and textually embeds TM in a medical framework, in an attempt to sever the practice from religious complications and instead inscribe TM as techné – a means to a better self. The ideal self, the current high priest of the movement is no longer, however, an "exotic" guru. Instead, its primary spokesman is another transcendent figure: David Lynch.

Rebranding TM: from orientalism to celebrity

There are scant references to Maharishi Mahesh Yogi on the David Lynch Foundation's website, and his image has virtually disappeared from the literature that the site presents. Instead, Ellen Degeneres, Paul McCartney, Jerry Seinfeld, Soledad O'Brien, Russell Simmons (who is also on the board of advisors for the foundation) and, of course, the man himself, David Lynch, all testify to the impact that TM has had on their lives and creative visions. With celebrity, the referent each of these figures point to is one characterized by wealth, power, and creativity. It is no accident that the Foundation holds benefits at places like Carnegie Hall, prestigious institutions that appeal to a certain class of people that consider themselves elite. And this strategy is especially evident in regard to the way the foundation uses Lynch to brand TM as the preferred practice of the cultural and artistic elite; trading in on the allure of this strange Midwestern art-house director who makes enigmatic, dark movies. But, as I argue below, it was the Maharishi who was the original spokesperson for the practice and the shift from this persona to that of Lynch is significant in understanding how the David Lynch Foundation brands TM in order to make it appealing to the contemporary American spiritual seeker.

Orientalism in the early marketing of transcendental meditation

In the 60s, devotees of the Maharishi were struck by his exoticism. One follower describes seeing him for the first time, noticing, "A small man with long, dark hair and beard just beginning to turn gray, wearing traditional white silk robes, the Maharishi moved and spoke with an extraordinary combination of gentleness and strength" (Forem, 1973, p. 2). Mahesh's biographer Paul Mason similarly recalls,

> A figure of slight stature draped simply in a pure white robe with long, wayward, wavy black hair tumbling about his shoulders. He was a sunny, amiable countenance, with large glistening chestnut-brown eyes, broad flattened nose and cheeks both generous and shining, partially obscured by a flourishing growth of beard. On espying the carpet role he clutched, any child might have fancied him to be an Arabian fakir come drifting in upon a magic spell. (Mason, 1994, p. 3).

It was the Maharishi's separateness that granted him an aura of otherness, and, by extension, holiness. That Mason conflates the Indian guru with an Arabian fakir is a clear indicator of the discourse of Orientalism that initially pervaded the TM movement. Edward Said (1978/2003) defined Orientalism as a tendency in Western culture to see the Orient as an exotic place, marked wholly and often in the manner of caricature by its difference from the West. Following from this, Richard King writes about the ways Western culture has characterized the "mystic East" (1999) and Vijay Prashad (2000) has noted that a Western understanding of Indian spirituality based in racialized exoticism has led to the creation of "God Men" like Deepak Chopra and, of course, the Maharishi. Similarly, for Sarah Banet-Weiser, New Age spirituality is the product of "a racist ideology of Orientalism and Asian 'mystique'" (2012). With the Maharishi, many Westerners were willing to follow a guru who supposedly had an ethnic claim to a purer form of spirituality. His connection to India, and the fact that he constantly wore robes and flowers made him appear "cosmic" – a term that John Lennon used to describe him that connects his reception in the West to discourses of Orientalism and otherness (as quoted in Mason, 1994, p. 139).

The Beatles met the Maharishi in 1967 through Ravi Shankar. In 1968, the band, along with their wives and girlfriends, stayed in the Maharishi's ashram, where they were trained in TM. This was a defining moment for the TM movement. The Beatles' sojourn with Mahesh was widely documented in the Western media and images of the Maharishi, often enshrouded in imagery borrowed from the psychedelic aesthetic,[2] graced the cover of multiple American pop culture magazines in late 60s. This publicity changed the tenor of the "Spiritual Regeneration Movement" because, as Mahesh's biographer Paul Mason notes, "With the endorsement of his teachings by pop 'royalty', the Maharishi found it particularly easy to woo the youth of America" (1994, p. 125). With celebrities implicitly endorsing the Maharishi, his profile and mystique grew and celebrity endorsement became a central tool in TM's spread. Celebrities both explicitly and implicitly claimed that their creative power, and also their wealth, was a direct result of their practice of TM. For example, Mike Love of the Beach Boys was quoted as saying that practicing TM "shot our record sales up to about five million last year from about two and a half million" (*Chicago Tribune, 1968*).

The David Lynch Foundation has kept the strategy of celebrity endorsement but they have changed the figurehead of the movement. No one at the foundation wears robes, and it is rare to hear the continent of India mentioned at all. In an article published in *the New York Observer* one journalist described the executive director of the Lynch Foundation, Bob Roth as "Silvered, well-spoken and handsome, with a nice selection of trim suits, he is the opposite of a robe-wearing swami" (Widdicombe, 2014). It is clearly a strategic move on the foundation's part to emphasize their difference from the historical roots of TM. Instead, David Lynch, has replaced the Maharishi as the dominant figure of the TM movement, at least as publicized by the foundation. Though the website has since undergone a redesign, initially, upon opening the home page for The David Lynch Foundation, a video immediately started to play. In black letters, the name "David Lynch" appeared on a brown background. Next to the video player we saw a faded image of Lynch, his shock of white hair characteristically swooping. This still image framed all of the video testimonials on the site. As abused women, soldiers, prisoners, and students tearily recalled how TM had changed their life, Lynch's faded image watched them, smiling.

As one reporter who visited the foundation relays "one thing that is abundantly clear inside the foundation's office is that the Lynch brand of Transcendental Meditation is vibrant and uncomplicated and unburdened by TM's more controversial past." And significantly, in her account: "Maharishi's visage was nowhere to be seen" (Hoffman, 2013). Similarly, at the benefit concert the Maharishi was only discussed in one video clip, in passing, by Howard Stern. Why has the foundation filed away the image of TM's founder, a man that Lynch and others nearly worship?[3] Again, this speaks to their understanding of the contemporary American public and how to effectively market to them.

The aura of celebrity on the spiritual marketplace

The nature of celebrity is difficult to pin down. Celebrities are individuals, but they also have a transcendent power in media-saturated cultures. Since at least Horton and Wohl's (1956) pathbreaking work on the "parasocial" – that is the intimate, one-sided relationship viewers have with television personalities – scholars in Media Studies have been preoccupied with defining what is meant by celebrity. Celebrity is a function of media – and the media in which a celebrity traffics may influence the kind and quantity of power and appeal the celebrity has. For example, David Giles argues that our understanding of celebrity is fundamentally changed by a contemporary digital culture in which convergent media allow for new audiences and new relationships with celebrities to form (2018). The literature in celebrity studies parses the notion of celebrity in various ways. Fan studies, the creation of publics that surround particularly charismatic figures has been a particularly fertile site for research on celebrity influence (see especially Booth, 2010; Jenkins, 1992, 2006). This literature relates in some ways to what is happening with the David Lynch Foundation, but it would be overly simplistic to call those drawn to TM as a spiritual practice simply fans.

Nor, would it be particularly apt to use Max Weber's (1968) notion of charismatic authority as a defining heuristic for how the David Lynch Foundation deploys Lynch and other celebrities. Weber defines charismatic authority as functioning via "devotion to the exceptional sanctity, heroism or exemplary character of an individual person, and of the normative patterns or order revealed or ordained by him" (Weber, 1968, p. 215). And though in some ways Lynch might fit this mold, he also diverges from it in many ways. Erik Hendriks (2017) rightly problematizes the line typically drawn between celebrities and charismatic authorities. For Hendricks, the logics Weber's charismatic leaders to not neatly fit onto contemporary mediated celebrity culture and, he argues, are in fact contradictory types of power.

For my purposes, this understanding of the auracular power of celebrity is central to understanding how Lynch and others want to present TM on the spiritual marketplace. Daniel Herwitz writes of the celebrities that particularly capture the public's imagination, such as Jacqueline Onassis that "the media seems to levitate around her. And since the public's only real way of knowing her is through this levitation, an absolutely peculiar aura is formed" (2008, p. 133). Here Herwitz borrows Walter Benjamin's (2010) notion of the "aura" to indicate the way that celebrities are able to retain their authenticity within mediated mass culture. Herwitz writes that as popular culture becomes more and more inundated with images of celebrities – especially those focused on using their celebrity to market to the public there is a deadening effect on the aura of celebrity. Within the logic of consumer capitalism, then, stars proliferate and become homogenous and therefore those celebrities that retain their aura become even more valuable as brands, as marketing tools.

Many alternative spiritual movements, like TM, also profit from high-profile spokespeople. Celebrity believers are often strategically publicized by religious players; as has been the case with A-list actors' affiliation with Scientology (s ee Wright, 2013) and in Madonna's promotion of Kabballah (see Einstein, 2008). Mara Einstein argues that in its connection with Hollywood and deployment of celebrities such as Madonna, "the Kabbalah Centre has turned 'Kabbalah' into a household name – a brand. The Centre has repackaged and simplified this practice to be sold to the masses, Jew and non-Jew alike" (Einstein, 2008, p. 147). Thus celebrities like Madonna lend their aura to the spiritual practices that they endorse or participate in. Kathryn Lofton writes that "because of the way late 20th-century tabloid culture penetrates and specifies, nothing about the celebrity – from their choice of dog leash to their choice of denominational home – is insignificant to the culture in which they appear (2011b, p. 349).

David Lynch is a mysterious and incongruent figure as David Foster Wallace captured in his 1996 profile for *Premiere*. Wallace's subtitle is illustrative: "In which novelist David Foster Wallace visits the set of David Lynch's new movie and finds the director both grandly admirable and sort of nuts" (1996, p. 91). Chris Rodley (1997), who edited a book of Lynch's interviews, explains that with Lynch, "we are left with the apparent contradiction of the 'regular guy' who makes 'deviant' cinema: the humorous, charming, 'folksy' director from Missoula, Montana, who keeps looking under the rock to expose darkness and decay" (p. xii). Lynch's personality presents contradictions, and this makes him an intriguing figure who rises above the run of the mill celebrity – and retains his uniqueness, that auratic quality that makes him such a potent figure. By offering Lynch as an icon of creative power, the David Lynch Foundation uses him to sell TM. Lynch, himself, is a recognizable brand. Consider the adjective: "Lynchian" – His style is seen as so unique as to merit a new word that refers only to its particular quality.

Lynch is a style icon and an elite auteur and the allure of his celebrity aura is a clue to why the site and its sister site, DLF.TV (David Lynch Foundation TV), only enhances Lynch's mysterious aura while simultaneously purporting its ability to be accessed. DLF.TV has a section called "The Daily David" that offers short clips – most are less than one minute long – of Lynch discussing topics such as love, education, and films. The aim of "the Daily David" is to provide a space "where David speaks candidly about anything and everything ranging from filmmaking to consciousness" (David Lynch Foundation Television, 2013). The Daily David claims to be a place where hard-core Lynch fans and young filmmakers can go to peruse short clips from Lynch's press tours and interviews, but the videos only offer epigrammatic fragments. In one 44-second long video labeled "Tesla, Marconi and Fishy ideas," for example, Lynch discusses the inventors, Tesla and Marconi, and extemporizes a theory of how ideas function in the collective unconscious: "like they release a whole bunch of little fish and they kind of disperse and over here on this bank Sam catches one and over here they catch the same kind. And it's that kind of thing, I think" (David Lynch Foundation Television, 2013). These videos do little to clear up the questions surrounding Lynch's identity. Rather than pinning him down, they only enhance his mystery, his aura. But it is not a mystery based on Orientalism, rather it is one that taps into the American fascination with celebrity. Thus Lynch and his foundation proffer his aura as an example of TM's main benefit, enhancing creativity and, by extension, gaining wealth.

Celebrity, creativity, wealth

In her study on the spiritual influence of another celebrity phenomenon, Oprah Winfrey, Kathryn Lofton argues that Winfrey is able to garner devotion in American popular culture because, "Every product of Winfrey's empire combines spiritual counsel with practical encouragement, inner awakening with capitalist pragmatism" (2011a, p. 24). In *O Magazine*, Winfrey's calendar provides her readers with aspirational daily goals and as Lofton (2011b) explains, "Winfrey's voice pervades throughout these instructions, modeling her suggestions through the order of her singular life. It is her face peering fro the corner of every Web page, from the cover of every magazine, and from the center of every television screen" (p. 25). In this way, *O Magazine* offers readers a way in to the technique that might make them as spiritually and materially fulfilled as Oprah just as The David Lynch Foundation offers TM as the quotidian practice that will bring them the creativity they need to succeed both spiritually and in the marketplace.

Lynch's 2006 book *Catching the Big Fish: Meditating, Consciousness and Creativity* provided Lynch and the foundation another outlet with which to market TM through the prism of Lynch's peculiar and fascinating persona. All of the proceeds of the book went to the foundation. The review of the book from the foundation's site states that it "provides a rare window into his methods as an artist and his personal working style. In *Catching the Big Fish*, Lynch writes candidly about the tremendous creative benefits he has gained from his thirty-two-year commitment to practicing Transcendental Meditation" (David Lynch Foundation, 2012b). This review promises that the book will help fans know Lynch's process and gain the keys to his creativity, and even calls it "a revelation to the legion of fans who have longed to better understand Lynch's deeply personal vision" (David Lynch Foundation, 2012b). However, like "The Daily David," the book offers only pieces of the puzzle that is Lynch. Some of the chapters in the book are only a sentence long. The book cannot reveal a ten-step process to becoming David Lynch. If it did so, it would in fact be the technique by which seekers might access their own creative power. The fact that Lynch's mysteriousness is only enhanced by the book is no accident, rather it is a way to sell the technique of TM as "the keys to his creativity." Lynch must remain inscrutable for the technique to be appealing. TM as techné becomes a decoding mechanism meant to allow practitioners entry into the velvet-roped arena of Lynch's aura. And by extension the practice offers a skeleton key into the world of power and money that Lynch occupies.

If there is a dominant narrative in *Catching the Big Fish* it is that TM is a means to greater creativity – which is, in Lynch's view, a means to greater wealth. TM will not make you David Lynch, or Paul McCartney, but it will release your own, inner creative genius because "It is a Field of pure bliss consciousness, absolute intelligence, and infinite creativity" (Lynch, 2006, p. 180). The celebrities who performed at the "Change Begins Within Benefit" also proffered this idea. Katy Perry asserted that she meditated before she wrote her songs, for example. These testimonials point out that creativity is a virtue of personal power. Similarly for American seekers, as Wade Clark Roof (1999) has noted, "an emphasis placed upon personal *power* – a fascination with finding a key to unlocking one's life" (p. 82, emphasis in the original). The foundation's rhetoric is sensitive to this attitude. Lynch (though in a tongue and cheek manner characteristic of his strangely ironic attitude) proffers the personal power gained from practicing TM as techné when he invokes his readers to:

> experience that Self, that pure consciousness. It's really helped me. I think it would help any filmmaker. So start diving within, enlivening that bliss consciousness. Grow in happiness and intuition. Experience the joy of doing. And you'll glow in this peaceful way. Your friends will be very, very happy with you. Everyone will want to sit next to you. And people will give you money! (Lynch, 2006, p. 159)

Though this selection cannot be taken completely seriously as it is written in Lynch's characteristic tounge-in-cheek manner, it is indicative of a theme in Lynch's book. Lynch asserts that practicing TM will garner for the subject a variety of rewards: it will increase the practitioner's social capital, it will increase the practitioner's cultural capital, and it will increase the practitioner's monetary capital.

The metaphor of "catching the big fish" refers to generating ideas by accessing the "Unified Field" during meditation. Lynch explains that "there are all kinds of fish swimming down there. There are fish for business, fish for sports. There are fish for everything" (2006, p. 1). Lynch's rhetoric implies that the creativity gained through the practice of TM can be applied to any career. Again, TM becomes the means to access the personal creative power that is valued in the American economy. Lynch's creativity, however is not only a resonant theme with artistic strivers, rather creativity as a commodity is valued in the business world as well. Banet-Weiser notes that in the American context the concept of creativity has been commoditized to the point that "Creativity itself (rather than the tangible products of creativity) thus becomes a means to accumulate profit" (Banet-Weiser, 2012, p. 111). This discourse may connect especially well with the American business elite and their wannabes. Claire Hoffman's *New York Times* report on the David Lynch Foundation reveals this in her discussion of one TM practitioner and businessperson who decided to learn the practice simply because there were so many successful, famous people, who he calls "masters of the universe" that did it (Kevin Law as quoted in Hoffman, 2013).

Creativity is an elusive, unquantifiable quantity. We only know a person has it after the fact, when we can see the fruits of their creative labor. This is why powerful people, celebrities, and especially Lynch are so crucial to the foundation's marketing plan. They make carnate that indefinable commodity that is so valuable and seemingly scarce – creativity. Thus, embodying the mysterious and powerful aura of celebrity, high-profile practitioners of TM symbolizes a central value of the economic marketplace that can be accessed by learning and practicing a spiritual technique and in this way, celebrity endorsements and Lynch's peculiar charm justify the practice of TM as techné.

Conclusion: celebrity and the changing marketplace for American spirituality

Lynch and his foundation continue the Maharishi Mahesh Yogi's vision to spread TM as a means of ushering in an era of World Peace. However the David Lynch Foundation is updating this vision, once so appealing to the American counterculture, so that it attracts a contemporary American audience. The foundation strategically positions TM by presenting it as a technique that can be incorporated into a medically-reflexive, healthy lifestyle. And The David Lynch Foundation's rebranding of TM from a practice rooted in Orientalitsm to one endorsed by the elites of the pop culture media ecosystem suggests that current American spiritual seekers may be more interested in practices endorsed by celebrities, than in practices that can claim Eastern roots. Instead of the Maharishi, celebrities, most notably Lynch himself, are proffered as symbols of the benefits of practicing TM. Celebrities represent creativity as a commodity – something that is valued highly in American popular and business culture.

The spiritual marketplace is a fluid concept, one that changes in tandem with American cultural norms. That TM has reached a "tipping point" indicates that the marketing strategized the David Lynch Foundation have used have been successful. By mobilizing celebrities, the foundation communicates the utility of TM; its use value as a creativity-enchancing, wealth-generating technique. Where the Maharishi once emphasized his exoticism, his connection to Eastern traditions, the David Lynch Foundation flips the script and positions TM as a useful practice that will yield personal rewards for those spiritual seekers who subscribe to it. From this case, I argue, we can see that the celebrity aura is a particularly powerful modality through which spiritual and religious institutions and actors communicate the worth and importance of their practices and techniques. And furthermore, this reveals an imaginary of spiritual practice as a means to an end––in this case, to becoming a broker of creativity and wealth.

Lynch transcends other, simpler definitions of celebrity. He is not a star. He does not fit neatly into the accepted categories of celebrity. He is not an actor, or singer. He is an artist, but does not traffic in the celebrity of the so-called "art world." He is singular. And like others who occupy this rarefied air of authenticity, he has found a way to use it to market to the American consumer – in this case to the spiritual consumer.

Notes

1. For a detailed account of Mahesh's life and travels see Mason (1994).
2. See Iwamura, 2011, pp. 63–110 for her analysis of how the Western media covered Mahesh and his movement through an Orientalist lens.
3. See Hoffman (2016) for a first-person account of growing up in the Maharishi Vedic City in Iowa.

Disclosure statement

No potential conflict of interest was reported by the author.

References

Banet-Weiser, S. (2012). *Authentic TM: The politics of ambivalence in brand culture*. New York: New York University Press.
Benjamin, W. (2010). The work of art in the age of its technological reproducibility [First Version]. *Grey Room*, 39, 11–37. doi:10.1162/grey.2010.1.39.11

Berger, P. (1967). *The sacred canopy: Elements of a sociological theory of religion.* Garden City, NY: Doubleday.
Booth, P. (2010). *Digital Fandom: New media studies.* New York, NY: Lang.
Campbell, C. (2007). *The Easternization of the West: A thematic account of cultural change in the modern era.* Boulder, CO: Paradigm.
Carrette, J., & King, R. (2005). *Selling spirituality: The silent takeover of religion.* New York, NY: Routledge.
Cimino, R., & Lattin, D. (1998). *Shopping for Faith: American religion in the new millennium.* San Francisco, CA: Jossey-Bass.
Cowan, D. E., & Bromley, D. G. (2008). Transcendental meditation: The question of science and therapy. In D. E. Cowan & D. G. Bromley (Eds.), *Cults and new religions: A brief history,* 48-71. Malden, MA: Blackwell Publishing.
David Lynch Foundation. (2012b). *Catching the big fish: Meditation, consciousness, and creativity.* Retrieved from http://www.davidlynchfoundation.org/catching-the-big-fish-meditation-consciousness-and-creativity.html
David Lynch Foundation Television. (2013, May 3). *Tesla, Marconi & fishy ideas.* Retrieved from http://dlf.tv/2009/music-marrying-film/
Einstein, M. (2008). *Brands of faith: Marketing religion in a commercial age.* New York, NY: Routledge.
Ellingson, S. (2007). *The Megachurch and the Mainline: Remaking religious tradition in the twenty-first century.* Chicago: University of Chicago Press.
Forem, J. (1973). *Trancendental meditation: Maharishi Mahesh Yogi and the science of creative intelligence.* New York: Bantam Books.
Foucault, M. (1984/1986). *The care of the self: Volume three of the history of sexuality.* New York, NY: Pantheon Books.
Foucault, M. (1988). Technologies of the self. In L. H. Martin, H. Gutman, & P. H. Hutton (Eds.), *Technologies of the self: A seminar with Michel Foucault* (pp. 16–49). London, UK: Tavistock.
Giles, D. (2018). *Twenty-first century celebrity: Fame in digital culture.* Bingley, UK: Emerald Publishing.
Hammond, P. (1992). *Religion and personal autonomy: The third disestablishment in America.* Columbia: University of South Carolina Press.
Harrington, A., & Zajonc, A. (eds). (2003). *The Dalai Lama at MIT.* Cambridge, MA: Harvard University Press.
Heelaas, P., & Woodhead, L. (2005). *The spiritual revolution: Why religion is giving way to spirituality.* Malden, MA: Blackwell Publishing.
Hendriks, E. C. (2017). Breaking away from Charisma? The celebrity industry's contradictory connection to charismatic authority. *Communication Theory (1050-3293), 27*(4), 347–366. doi:10.1111/comt.2017.27.issue-4
Herwitz, D. A. (2008). *The star as icon : Celebrity in the age of mass consumption.* New York, NY: Columbia University Press.
Hoffman, C. (2013). David Lynch is back ... as a guru of transcendental meditation. The New York Times Magazine.
Hoffman, C. (2016). *Greetings from Utopia Park: Surviving a transcendent childhood.* New York, NY: HarperCollins.
Horton, D., & Wohl, R. R. (1956). Mass communication and para-social interaction; observations on intimacy at a distance. *Psychiatry, 19*(3), 215–229. doi:10.1080/00332747.1956.11023049
Iwamura, J. N. (2011). *Virtual orientalism : Asian religions and American popular culture.* New York, NY: Oxford University Press.
Jenkins, H. (1992). *Textual Poachers: Television fans and participatory culture.* New York, NY: Routledge.
Jenkins, H. (2006). *Convergence culture: Where old and new media collide.* New York: New York University Press.
King, R. (1999). *Orientalism and religion: Postcolonial theory, India and 'The Mystic East'.* New York, NY: Routledge.
Lau, K. (2015). *New age capitalism. Making money east of Eden.* Philadelphia,PA: University of Pennsylvania Press.

Lofton, K. (2011a). *Oprah: The gospel of an icon.* Berkeley, CA: University of California Press.
Lofton, K. (2011b). Religion and the American celebrity. *Social Compass, 58*(3), 346–352. doi:10.1177/0037768611412143
Luckmann, T. (1967). *The invisible religion.* New York, NY: MacMillan.
Lynch, D. (2006). *Catching the Big Fish: Meditation, consciousness and creativity.* New York, NY: Penguin.
Lynch, G. (2007). *The new spirituality: An introduction to progressive belief in the twenty-first century.* New York, NY: I.B. Tauris.
Mason, P. (1994). *The Maharishi: The biography of the man who gave Transcendental meditation to the West.* Rockport, MA: Element.
Parsons, T. (1966). Religion in a modern pluralistic society. *Journal of Religious Research, 7*(3), 125–146. doi:10.2307/3509920
Parsons, T. (1967). *Sociological theory and modern society.* New York, NY: Free Press.
Perry, K. (2015). Stage performance. In *Change begins within.* New York, NY.
Prashad, V. (2000). *The karma of brown folk.* Minneapolis: University of Minnesota Press.
Rodley,C. (1997). *Lynch on lynch.* Boston: Faber and Faber.
Roof, W. C. (1993). *A generation of seekers: The spiritual journeys of the baby boom generation.* New York, NY: HarperSanFrancisco.
Roof, W. C. (1999). *Spiritual marketplace: Baby boomers and the remaking of American religion.* Princeton, NJ: Princeton University Press.
Roof, W. C., & McKinney, W. (1987). *American Mainline Religion: Its changing shape and future.* New Brunswick, NJ: Rutgers University Press.
Said, E. W. (1978/2003). *Orientalism.* New York, NY: Penguin Books.
The beach boys and their guru. (1968, May 13). *Chicago Tribune (1963-Current File).* Retrieved from http://search.proquest.com/docview/175755812?accountid=14707
Tucker, J. (2002). New age religion and the cult of the self. *Society, 39*(2), 46–51. doi:10.1007/BF02717528
Wallace, D. (1996). David Lynch keeps his head. *Premiere, 10*(1), 90.
Weber, M. (1968). *Economy and Society.* Berkeley: University of California Press.
Widdicombe, B. (2014, August 6). For some of New York's most successful, Transcendental meditation. *The New York Observer.* Retrieved from: http://observer.com/2014/08/for-some-of-new-yorks-most-successful-transcendental-meditation/
Wright, L. (2013). *Going clear: Scientology,Hollywood and the prison of belief.* New York, NY: Knopf.
Wuthnow, R. (1998). *After heaven: Spirituality in American since the 1950s.* Berkeley, CA: University of California Press.

Index

Note: Page numbers followed by "n" denote endnotes.

Abidin, C. 16, 79
activism 3, 17, 37, 38, 40, 43, 46
activist celebrities 38, 44
actors 4, 5, 68–70, 72, 73, 105, 106, 112, 119, 121, 122, 148
aesthetic approaches 94–96
aesthetics 95, 102, 110, 129–131, 135
agency 3, 6, 8, 11–14, 17, 23, 53, 59
Alabárces, P. 128
Albers, S. 61
A-list celanthropists 39
A-list celebrities 79, 139
American spirituality 140, 141, 148
American spiritual marketplace 138–148
Andersin, M. 116, 117
Andrejevic, M. 67, 73
anti-welfare common sense 31
armed conflict 3, 125–127, 132, 135
Aroncyzk, M. 67
Asperger's syndrome 37, 40, 41
asylum seekers 110, 115, 116
attention economy 9–12
audiences 10, 22, 29–31, 38, 56, 74, 79–82, 84–88, 117, 119
austerity 22, 23, 25–27, 31
authenticity 3, 4, 54, 98, 99, 101–105, 145, 148
automated connectivity 96

Bakhtin, M. 128
Baldwin, A. 120
Baldwin, J. 54
Banerjee, M. 53
Banet-Weiser, S. 17n2, 140, 141
Benjamin, W. 95, 145
Beta, A. 84, 85
Bhutto 72
Bickford, S. 122n1
biopolitics 56
Bolin, G. 67
Bolsanaro, J. 45
Bramall, R. 22, 32

Breeitz 122n2
Breitz, C. 113, 117–121
Brockington, D. 37
Brunei 79–89
Brunwasser, M. 94

campaign 30, 38, 50–54, 56–59
Carrette, J. 140
celebration selfies 100, 101, 104, 105
celebrification 80, 83, 87–89, 102–105; process 78, 80, 83, 87–89
celebrity culture 2, 8, 9, 12, 13, 16, 79, 80, 82, 83, 87–89
celebrity diplomacy 65–68, 71
celebrity endorsements 38, 43, 71, 143, 147
celebrity exemplars 52, 53, 58–61
celebrity humanitarianism 38
celebrity migrants 50
celebrity power 39, 53, 54
celebrity selfies 4, 94, 95, 104, 105
charity 22, 23, 28, 29, 31
Chouliaraki, L. 38
citizen celebrity 3, 125, 131–135
civic movements 26
Claessens, N. 25
climate change 37, 40–42, 44–46
collective entity 7
Colombia 125–127, 130, 131, 133
Colombian War 125–127
commodified celebrity-self 7–17
commodified identity 12
commodities 3, 10–12, 16, 38, 87, 130, 147, 148
common sense explanations 23
communication 2, 38, 57, 58, 68, 95, 128, 133–135
communicative capitalism 95
consciousness 80, 81, 83, 85–87, 138, 139, 145–147
conspiracy theory 45
consumer citizen approach 37
contemporary attention economy 7–17
contemporary culture 8, 10–12, 14, 16
Cooper, A. F. 67

INDEX

corporate capitalism 37
corporeal schema 53
corporeal sociability 98, 100, 101
cosmopolitan monolingualism 52, 61
Couldry, N. 6, 10, 11, 88
Craig, G. 38
creativity 128, 132, 139, 142, 146–148
cultural/culture 8–11, 14–17, 66, 83, 86, 88, 128, 130, 134; envoys 65, 69, 72, 74; practices 2, 128–131, 134; transformation 13, 17

David Lynch Foundation 138, 139, 141–148
Dean, J. 95
democratic values 55
dialectical approach 96
digital narratives 97
digital news 93–107
digital self-representation 93, 95, 97–99, 106
dignity 129, 130, 133
discursive intertextual chains 37
diversity 52, 61, 62, 79, 121
dramatization 25
Dreher, T. 111, 122n1
Driessens, O. 11, 87
dualist ontology 96

eccentricity 29
eco-celebrity 36–39, 46
economic crisis 24, 26–28
economic elite 32
economic individualism 17
eco-politics 37
empathetic curiosity 101
environmentalism 37, 38, 44
everyday racism 54, 56, 60

financial crisis 21, 23
Finland 113–116
Football Leaks 21, 22, 24, 26, 27, 30
Franck, G. 8
Fraser, N. 24
Frosh, P. 98
Fuqua, J. V. 103

García Canclini, N. 129
Germany 50–57, 59–61, 113, 117
Gibson, J. 68
Gillespie, M. 94
Girard, R. 24
global celebrities 4, 6, 65, 69, 71, 82, 86
global media 40
global stardom 69–71
global trade 68
global visibility 98
Goldhaber 8, 9
Goodman, M. 46

Gramling, D. 51, 52
Gramsci, A. 128

Hammond, P. 140
hate discourse 101
Hearn, A. 89
Hendriks, E. C. 144
Herwitz, Daniel 144
hijabi micro-celebrities 80, 83–85
hijab practices 83, 84
Horton, D. 144
Howard, C. 86
humanitarianism 25, 38, 103, 111

immigrants 27, 30–32, 50, 51, 53, 55–57, 81
impartial spectatorship 97–99, 102
impression management 43
Indonesia 79, 80, 83, 85, 89
industrialized agency (IA) 2, 7, 8, 14–17
inequality 24, 26, 29–32, 54, 59
Inglis, F. 7
innocent Germans 54
instrumentalization 68, 71, 73; celebrities 66, 71–73
integration 6, 8, 50–53, 56–58, 60, 61; campaign 5, 51; classes 59; discourse 51, 52, 56, 57; failure 51
intellectual deficits 56

Kaneva, N. 67
King, R. 140
Kiyak, M. 59

language 14, 42, 51, 52, 56–59, 61, 132, 134; deficits 56; politics 52
Lilti, A. 8
linguistic pluralism 52
Littler, J. 46
Lofton, K. 146
Love Story 113, 117, 118, 120, 121
Luis Arango, case 125–127, 133–135

Malaysia 79–81, 83, 84, 89
Malaysian celebrities 80, 87
malfeasance 24, 26, 31
Marshall, P. D. 67, 85
Martel, F. 130
Martín Barbero, J. 128–129, 132, 135
Maxwell, R. 45
media 2, 3, 5, 9, 10, 24, 37, 38, 67, 106, 125, 131–133, 144; narratives 39, 126, 127, 132, 133; portrayals 22, 28, 30; representation 37; scandals 25
Meister, M. 37
memories 95, 113–116, 125, 133, 135
Mendes, Jorge 30
Miazhevich, G. 67
micro-celebrities 78–89; practices 78–89
migrant-related selfies 3, 93, 94, 96–99, 106

INDEX

migrants 4, 5, 50, 93, 94, 97–106; celebrities 50; selfies 3, 4, 93, 94, 98–100, 102
Miller, T. 45
misrecognition 101, 102
monolingualism 59
Moore, Julianne 120
Mouffe, C. 131
Mukherjee, R. 17n2
multiculturalism 50
multidirectional memory 114
Muslim-majority states 78–89

narratives 3, 4, 61, 62, 96–99, 105, 115, 126, 129, 132–134
narrativization 25
nation branding 65–68, 71, 73, 74
negative stereotypes 54
neoliberal forms 73
neoliberalism 22, 24, 28, 31
neoliberal times 21–32
Nisa, E. F. 84, 85

offshoring practice 21–32
online culture 9, 14, 16
online micro-celebrities 17
orientalism 142, 143, 146

persona 8, 14–17, 105, 142, 146
political economy 2, 66, 68, 69, 95
the popular 3, 125–132
popular actors 5, 70, 112, 122
popular culture 3, 5, 8, 105, 122, 125–128, 130–132, 139
populism 130
Portugal 21, 22, 24, 26, 28, 29
power 8, 13, 16, 17, 38, 39, 46, 54, 82, 96, 107, 129, 130, 132, 144; dynamics 3, 66, 68, 111
Prashad, V. 143
privatization 73
privlic culture 17
promotional hypocrisies 37
prosthetic memory 114
pseudo micro-celebrities 80, 85, 86
public identity 8, 9, 12, 16, 17
public sphere 8, 23–25, 44, 54, 56, 129, 131, 132, 135

racial discrimination 55
racism 54–56, 60, 61, 81
Ratcliffe, K. 122n1
recognition 3, 14, 36, 102, 106, 107, 129, 131
Redmond, S. 85
refugees 3, 4, 93, 101, 104, 106, 110–112, 116–121; testimonies 110, 113
remediation 4, 94, 96–103, 105, 106
representational politics 36–46
representational power 38, 40, 44
respectability politics 55

Rodley, C. 145
Rodríguez, C. 131
Rojek, C. 53, 86
Ronaldo, Cristiano 21–32
Roof, W. C. 140, 147
Rothberg, M. 114

Said, E. W. 143
scandal 22, 24–31
Schoenhoff, S. 89
Schudson, M. 103
Schwarzenegger, Arnold 41
self-disclosure 78, 79, 88, 89
selfie-as-news 99
selfies 4, 93–106
selfie-taking photographs 94, 100
self-promotion 70, 86, 88
self-representation 4, 93–107
self-selectivity processes 88
smartphones 94, 101
Smith, Adam 97
Smith, M. 55
social cohesion 58
social conflict 126
social deficits 50
social exclusion 55, 57, 60
social imagination 128
social media 8–10, 40, 78, 79, 83, 84, 88, 89, 94, 95, 98, 99, 128; platforms 8, 10, 15, 16, 79, 81, 95, 101
socio-cultural relations 66
sociotechnical approaches 94
sociotechnical process 95
soft power 65–73
solidarity 4, 94, 98, 102, 103, 110–114, 116, 118, 121; selfies 94, 102–105
Southeast Asia 78–89
sovereign power 107
Spain 5, 21, 22, 24, 26, 27, 30–32, 70
Spanish judiciary system 30
spectatorship 96, 97, 99
spiritual marketplace 2, 138–140, 144, 148
spiritual movements 145
spiritual practices 2, 139–141, 144, 145, 148
storytelling 3, 25, 111, 112
symbolic bordering 93, 96, 106, 107
symbolic capital 4, 102, 104
symbolic performance 58
sympathetic spectatorship 98, 99, 102

tax: avoidance 5, 22, 27, 31; evasion 21–32; havens 22, 23, 27; justice discourses 23, 27
techné 141–142, 146, 147
techno-institutional relationships 99
technological embeddedness 94
techno popular 131
Thunberg, Greta 36–46
Tiger, R. 25

transcendental meditation 2, 138–142, 144, 146; tipping point 138–148
transgressions 24, 25
transnationalism 24
transnationalization 66, 68
Turkey 65–74, 94, 99; celebrity diplomats 69; TV celebrities 65–74
Turner, G. 39, 44

unfairness 29–30
ungrateful immigrants 5, 54, 55
Urry, J. 22

values 2–4, 8–11, 13, 14, 16, 17, 23, 24, 103, 130
Van den Bulck, H. 25
Van Dijk 96
Van Krieken, R. 7, 89
Vaughan-Williams, N. 107
ventrilocation 105
Vierikko, Vesa 113

visual narrativity 99
Vitrinel, E. 72, 74
Volcic, Z. 67, 73

Watts, J. 42
wealth 10, 21, 22, 27, 28, 31, 46, 142, 143, 146, 148
Weber, M. 144
Western media 93, 94, 97, 99, 106, 143
Western values 51, 61, 62
Wheeler, M. 67
white Christian Germanness 50
Wittgenstein, L. 100
Wohl, R. R. 144
women empowerment 83–85
Woodall, A. 24
Wright, T. 112
Wuthnow, R. 140

youth-centered climate movement 36, 46